Whispers OF LOVE

Spirit's Messages from Heartbreak to Hope

Whispers OF LOVE

SPIRIT'S MESSAGES FROM
HEARTBREAK TO HOPE

Gina Simone

Featured on Gwyneth Paltrow's **goop**

outskirts
press

Whispers of Love
Spirit's Messages from Heartbreak to Hope
All Rights Reserved.
Copyright © 2020 Gina Simone
v3.0

The opinions expressed in this manuscript are solely the opinions of the author and do not represent the opinions or thoughts of the publisher. The author has represented and warranted full ownership and/or legal right to publish all the materials in this book.

This book may not be reproduced, transmitted, or stored in whole or in part by any means, including graphic, electronic, or mechanical without the express written consent of the publisher except in the case of brief quotations embodied in critical articles and reviews.

Outskirts Press, Inc.
http://www.outskirtspress.com

ISBN: 978-1-9772-1625-0

Cover Photo © 2020 www.gettyimages.com. All rights reserved - used with permission.

Outskirts Press and the "OP" logo are trademarks belonging to Outskirts Press, Inc.

PRINTED IN THE UNITED STATES OF AMERICA

Table of Contents

Endorsements i
In Loving Memory v
Dedication ix
Acknowledgments.. x
Foreword... xvi
Introduction xix

Part One
Let the Roller-Coaster Ride Begin 1

Chapter One: Arguing with Destiny: Early Years with Spirit and
"Hating to be Different" 4
Chapter Two: Listen to Husbands, Children, or Invisible Forces?
Married Years with Spirit: Still…Nothing "Normal" 20
Chapter Three: Finding the Elixir: Mixing Spirit with Daily Life
Current Years and the "New Normal" 45

Part Two
Knowledge and Knowingness Equal Enlightenment
The Tool for Anchoring Your Life Voyage 67

Chapter Four: Psychic or Medium? Wait, There's a Difference? 76
Chapter Five: Mediumship You Can Trust: Certifying
the Messenger who Bridges Life and Death 98

Part Three
Grief
After the Wind Is Knocked from Your Sails …
Dealing with Unspeakable Tragedy and Pain 115

Chapter Six: Why Did They Leave Me and Where Are They Now?. 126

Chapter Seven: Visible and Invisible Ever-Present Signs:
              Learning the New Language of Love 138
Chapter Eight: Grief Is Exactly Like Fear... 150
Chapter Nine: Smooth Sailing Is Not Life: Practical Steps for
              Surviving Another Day 172

Part Four
Spirit: The Compass in the Storm
How to Learn, Listen and Allow Your Self (Soul) to be Guided   187
Chapter Ten: Trust Means Overcoming Fear 193
Chapter Eleven: H-e-l-l-o Karma: Dreams, Visitations,
              Soul Contracts, and More!......................................210
Chapter Twelve: Law of Attraction:
              We Are Our Own Worst Enemies 235
Chapter Thirteen: Spirit on Board:
              Steering Your Life with Spirit in Charge 247

Conclusion 271
Bibliography...277
Notes 282

Endorsements

Whispers of Love is much more than just another spiritual book. With a very down-to-earth approach, author and medium, Gina Simone shares her personal journey of tragedy and triumph by reaching across dimensions and bringing us on a magical journey of spiritual awakening through unconditional love.

With complete honesty and candid details, Gina shares valuable life lessons learned after living with the greatest loss of all—the death of her son Anthony. Together with his presence and her powerful Spirit Guides and Angels, she teaches others to shift their life perceptions from limitation and fear to faith, love and never-ending miracles. It is a must read for all ages. Bravo to Gina Simone and her Spirit Team.

—**Kim Russo**, Psychic Medium, Author of *The Happy Medium* and *Your Soul Purpose: Learn How to Access the Light Within*, Host of A&E Network's TV show 'Celebrity Ghost Stories,' and featured on *The Dr. Oz Show*, *Today*, and *Good Day New York*

Packed with wisdom, truth and insight, this book is the perfect travel companion for anyone on a spiritual journey. Through sharing her own story, Gina teaches us that we are never alone, and that hope and love will always carry us home. A comforting and enlightening read.

—**Laura Lynne Jackson**, Psychic Medium, NY Times Bestselling author of *Signs: The Secret Language of the Universe* and *The Light Between Us*, and featured on *The Dr. Oz Show*, *Today*, and *Good Day New York*

I cried, I laughed out loud, I hugged everyone I knew after reading *Whispers of Love* and wish it had been available when my 44-year-old brother-in-law died suddenly. I've seen many psychics through the years and Gina is hands down the most authentic and gifted medium. For 7 years I've treated myself to an annual reading with her and she is spot on every time, both with the direction my life is taking and with communicating messages from beyond.

Reading about her childhood was such a beautiful reminder to trust that things happen to teach us the lessons we are here to learn. This was a big one for me and completely shifted my thinking. Now I look for the lessons! I've personally been struggling with trust; trusting that the universe and spirits are guiding me; trusting that when a path resists there is a reason, so it truly helped restore an unexplained deeper faith in me, which feels empowering. I also loved learning about our soul's contracts and what we sign up for before we come into this world.

Sharing words about her son that were so vulnerable, raw, and beautiful, gave me a deep sense of peace as I think of all my loved ones in heaven in their joy. Ever since reading this I've been looking for their signs. I will be buying this book for everyone in my life who suffers from loss and grief. This is a *must* read not only because of the coping tools provided but the spiritual knowledge that helps you begin to make sense of tragedy and death and trust that our path is unfolding exactly as it should be.

—**Kim Weiler**, Founder and CEO of The Love Group, TEDx Speaker and Author of *Ps—It's All About Love: How A Painful Journey With Psoriasis Became A Life Devoted To Healing Others*

Through *Whispers of Love*, Gina takes us by the hand through the highest and lowest of human emotions. The bliss of sharing a precious moment with a loved one, the unspeakable pain of losing a child, the comfort of those we've loved who never truly leave us, along with a practical understanding around how the Universe is always conspiring in our favor. Gina masterfully shares powerful stories with honesty, bravery and humor; giving comfort and hope to anyone struggling to make sense out of life's biggest questions and challenges."

—**Dr. Debi Silber**, Author of *The Unshakable Woman: Four Steps to Rebuilding Your Body, Mind and Life After a Life Crisis*, President of The Silber Center for Personal Growth and Healing and Founder of The PBT (Post Betrayal Transformation) Institute

In Loving Memory

In Loving Memory of Our Son Anthony
(10/23/91 - 1/4/2019)

"Hello in there. It's me, Daddy. Everything is going to be fine, and I can't wait to meet you!"

I never imagined that I would be writing a few paragraphs to be included in a book, and certainly not about my son Anthony. I held your hand until the very last moment on this Earth and I hope these few words resonate as you shine your light down from heaven. Know how honored I am you chose me to share your way-too-short journey of life with.

Whether we like it or not, parenting is about planning. The problem is that it's not always that picture-perfect life we dream of. Just when we think we know what the future will hold for us, have tried our best to plan things out in our lives and are feeling secure, there is always a surprise, an unseen "bigger plan" in the works.

Having Anthony, only a year after being a twenty-one-year-old newlywed, was certainly part of that "bigger plan," but at the time it seemed too soon to start a family. Looking back at how the past twenty-seven years have unfolded, it was exactly the *right* time. I just didn't know it then. During his mom's pregnancy, we had a medical scare and I would talk to her belly every day and say, "Hello in there. It's me, Daddy. Everything is going to be fine, and I can't wait to meet you!" Fortunately, everything did end up fine, and that experience taught me just how important it is to stay positive and never give up, no matter the odds.

I still remember bringing Anthony home from the hospital. You need to have a car seat, are given diapers, formula, and that's it! I thought to myself, *They are actually letting us take him home? Where are the instructions?* Like any father, I helped teach him to walk, talk, etc. As he grew older, I taught him to play video games, bowl, play baseball, and as Anthony liked to call it, "have a catch." We tossed around footballs and always made a game of something. I taught him to love the Pittsburgh Steelers, and he rekindled my love for the NY Yankees, my childhood team. He treated me once to a Pittsburgh Penguins Stanley Cup game, and I was hooked. You see, sports was our thing and helped us bond on an even deeper level. We cheered together, got frustrated together, and were fortunate enough to share in quite a few championships.

Every moment and stage as he grew was a new initiation and a stronger bond formed for us. You can't describe the incredible love a father is able to feel for his child. The joy, the pain, the laughter, and even the tears all combine and create an unconditional and inexplicable feeling that defies all human words.

When I taught Anthony how to drive, I still remember him pulling out of the driveway, only to hit the telephone pole in front of the house, seconds later. I even got to share with him what he said was his "first beer," but his skills at playing beer pong later in life made me think he might have already tasted quite a few on his own! We created everlasting memories that I am even more grateful for now that he's no longer here.

With all the things I taught him, all the life skills shared, and all the lessons I tried to impart to him for what life would be like as an adult and father, the "bigger plan" had him heading in a direction that one just prays they *never* have to head in. Unfortunately, he didn't win his fight; for that there are no words.

Despite the pain and shock I still feel, the truth is that my son taught me so much more than I ever taught him. I watched him bravely fight and beat cancer twice and be the definition of strength. One of the toughest things I ever had to do in my life was look him in the eyes when he was only sixteen years old and break the news to him that he had cancer. Just like I had done before he was born, I told him, "Everything is going to be fine." Not that I had any proof, except for the hope and belief that it was going to be so. Fortunately, we were blessed, and after three years of treatment, Anthony's cancer was in remission. He tried to resume as normal a life as possible, went away to college, and didn't come home with a degree, but with our first grandson, Austin. Years passed as Anthony progressed further down the road of remission only to have it snatched away right before his twenty-sixth birthday. Once again, a "bigger plan" was in the works and we questioned *why*. Anthony ended up needing a bone marrow transplant, but not before he made sure he was at the birth of his second son, Christian. Unfortunately, years of chemo, radiation, and medical procedures took their toll, and Anthony would end up passing from complications.

I miss my son beyond words and am so very thankful that the "bigger plan" blessed me with my two grandsons. A piece of Anthony will forever be in those boys. Just as before my son was born, and I talked to him every day, I still do; it's just done in a different way. I know he hears me and is always around. He sends me signs on a daily basis. I am so very grateful for every single one of them.

The twenty-seven years I was blessed to spend with my son certainly had their share of adventures and challenges. In a strange way, I am thankful for all of them, both good and bad. It made Anthony who he was and made me who I am today. It created a bond between the two of us that will never be broken but simply continues on in a different way. Love is eternal and never dies. I don't know when the "bigger plan" will have me meet my son again, but when I do, I know he will be waiting for me with his glove, so we can "have a catch" like old times, maybe even share a beer–or two–or three, and I can play for him again Led Zeppelin's "Thank You":

"If the sun refused to shine, I would still be loving you,
When mountains crumble to the sea, there will still be you and me."

Your first and last breath are mine to remember forever.

Love, Daddy

Dedication

Thank you to Spirit's infinite and unending love and guidance in my life, even when I was unaware of your helping hand. I am forever grateful to your loving and sometimes forceful hands navigating and escorting me through this process of Life. This has been a journey I could not have imagined or created for myself, which is exactly *why* I know there was a force behind me, always allowing mistakes to be made, and then learning to come forth from those experiences. I'm sorry I fought with you, didn't believe you were there for me, and yes, even yelled at you at times when things did not go "my way," especially these last few years from the end of 2017 all the way to the start of 2019. I know there were times when you bowed in frustration. I know there were times you bowed seeing my hurt. I even know there were times you brought in light and joy and crazy laughter in the midst of this pain to help mend my broken heart.

Thank you for not giving up on me, for guiding me, and most of all for unconditionally loving me with all my human faults. I am eternally grateful for your love and all those you continue to send my way, whom I promise to cherish and care for with all my might and all my heart.

Acknowledgments

To my incredible life partner Anthony, whom I trust and believe in more than anyone in my life. Thank you for your endless encouragement in continually believing the best of me was always there, even when I could not see it myself. Your support and love have brought me through many painful moments in life. Our relationship has taught me about true love, not only its many beautiful moments, but also its ugly and complicated sides. Who would have known, all those years ago, that we would both glide and trudge through life's maze of experiences of joy and heartache? I am grateful that Spirit spun its magic to bring us together. You were, and continue to be, the guiding light in the darkness, and the glue that puts me back together when I can't even find the pieces. Our souls are forever bound, and I wouldn't want anyone else by my side. Love you, my sexy-pants!

In loving memory of my son Anthony: It is because of you that this book has been birthed. You are the breath behind my words. There isn't a minute that goes by that you're not on my mind, that my arms don't ache to hold you, my ears to hear you, and my eyes to see that smile. Though my heart will always have a hole that can be filled only by you, I know you are at peace, sitting front row at every sports game imaginable. And, although I didn't give birth to you, thank you for allowing me to be your second mom in this life, and to see you grow into such an amazing man. You taught me about strength and resiliency during your cancer battles, and I want you to know how proud I am of you! Thank God we are blessed to have your love, spirit and light that is captured in the hearts and souls of your two sons, Austin and Christian. Rest with the angels my son – my love for you extends through time - until we meet again soon. I love you Dude.

To my son Matthew: My first born and the one who taught me all my "firsts" in being a parent. I'm sorry if I didn't always get things right! You are a treasure from above, and I am so proud of the man you have become and the beautiful changes you are making in your life. Your drive and determination will always be your strength. I am honored to be your mom and you are loved today, tomorrow, and always!

To my daughter Christina: There are not enough words to express my gratitude for your unconditional love. You are my cheerleader in life! I remember you arriving into the world and knowing you were a very special soul, here for big things. You have given me more love in this world than I could ever imagine, and you are truly my heart and soul. I am blessed to be your mama. I love you Teen-Beans.

To my daughter Christina: I may not have given birth to you, but you have been such a beautiful soul since the day I met you. How do we even begin to thank you for your selfless act of giving a second chance of life to your brother? That is the strength and determination deep within you that inspires me every day. Thank you for being my daughter and for teaching me about owning your power and striving to be the best you can be. Nothing will stop you. I love you Cutie.

To my mother Elide: Thank you for giving me life and having the courage to start a new life in a foreign land. You helped bring my soul to its purpose, and even though you didn't understand all of this in the beginning, you have supported this path since. I am grateful for your unending love and support. Mama, I love you always.

To my sister Mimi: Thank you for being the one true love of my life growing up. We are bound to each other through blood, heart, and spirit. I could not imagine my life without you in it, and your sense of love, commitment, and support takes my breath away. You are truly selfless and always care for others before yourself. I would give you the world if I could, and your support and love mean everything. I could not have done this life thing without you. Ti voglio tanto bene Principessa.

To my brother Angelo: Thank you for being there for me and my family throughout our lives. We were always there for each other growing up and continue to do so now. You are not only my brother, but my friend that I love so much.

To my friend Laura Southwick: I could not have endured the primary years of divorced life if it were not for you—your love, support, and laughter. God absolutely placed you in my life to blow breath and healing into my being. I cannot thank you enough for your unending support and love in adding laughter and friendship to my life at a time when it was most needed.

To my soul sister Bobbi Allison: It all started with you and the magical way you naturally bring people together to connect their threads of light on Earth. You are selfless, caring, and would fight a lion to protect those you love and care for. I thank you for your constant love and unending friendship, and always cheering others on to be the best version of themselves they can. You are truly a Light Worker and I am blessed to have you in my life.

To my friend Paul Saladino: Thank you for believing in me, pushing me, and laughing with me. Even though we don't always see eye to eye, we manage to laugh and get through some of life's crazy moments. You are always there to help others, whether it's a friend, or someone down and out on their luck, and you were there through every step of Anthony's illness. God placed you here for a big purpose, and I thank you for your friendship and support.

To my Spirit Soul Sister group: I am thankful for each of your hearts and personalities in my life. One of the greatest rewards in doing this work is the beautiful circle we have created, with different minds and qualities, but a similar purpose of bringing healing to others. You have brought a bond of light, love, and friendship into my soul, and we can thank Bobbi again for bringing our hearts together. We will continue to spread Light into the world!

To my dad, Vincenzo. You were my biggest lesson in life. Thank you for showing and teaching me through the pain and suffering. I didn't understand then, but I understand now, the many lessons we agreed on from the other side to learn from each other. Thank you for teaching me the lesson of strength of character through the pain. May you continue to find peace on the other side.

To my brother-in-law and sister-in-law Anthony and Andrea: I could not have asked for better complements to our family than you. You both love my siblings so much, and I am grateful to you for making them happy. Thank you for your kindness, love, and support throughout the decades. I am so happy to call you *familigia*.

To my nephews AJ, Nicholas, and Michael: You are the light of my soul, and I love how you each look at life so differently. You were my first "bellos" and I will always remember our holidays with chicken cutlets, our backyard parties in the pool and remember "lock the top lock." You are all so grounded and loving, and I am so excited to see the amazing lives you will each create. Remember to always believe in yourselves, and Zia loves you.

To my Intuitive Development and mediumship students: Thank you for trusting me to be your teacher, but as I've always told you, I believe when the student is ready the teacher appears. Thank you for allowing me to be one beacon of light along the path of your journey and for the many gifts you have each given me as a student of life.

To my clients and friends Suzie Fonseca and Laurie Katz: Thank you for allowing me to share the stories of your children to validate Spirit's unending love for us. I understand your pain all too well, but you are the voices and angels to carry on your children's memory. We continue to hold them close and love them with all our might, for they are no longer physically here, but remain bonded in our hearts. Thank you for showing me the resiliency of a mother's strength and love.

To my *bella angela della scrittura* (my beautiful writing angel): Thank you for taking all of my thoughts, beliefs, ideas, and multitude of scrambled concepts in my head, and helping to formulate cohesive messages shared in this book. Thank you for the constant advice, suggestions, and guidance you have shown over the course of this project. Now maybe you understand what my Spirit guides endure on a daily basis! Your gentle nudging during this difficult time in my life kept us both on course. Thank you, Universe, for bringing me this lovely soul that helped navigate the ideas and concepts held by Spirit, into a testimony of love and healing. I am forever grateful to our synchronistic connection.

To my grandsons Austin and Christian: You wouldn't both be here if it wasn't for Anthony, but unfortunately you will grow up without him. You are forever a thread in the tapestry of his soul. Your eyes, your smiles, your giggles, will be our permanent reminder of him. My heart is so full knowing that you have a special angel watching and guiding you every day of your life, and I love you, my peanut and my little man.

To Bob and Phran Ginsberg of Forever Family Foundation: I am blessed to be a part of this amazing organization, alongside other very gifted mediums, all working toward the goal of showing that consciousness of life does continue after death. I am humbled to share in this work with you and to be a part of this beautiful family.

To the mediums before me: I am so appreciative and grateful for the mediums that have paved the way before me and worked so hard to show we are bonded in the Light of serving and healing. To the very well-known names that have television shows and have brought the concept of mediumship to people's homes all over the world, thank you. But also a huge gratitude to the hard-working mediums I have learned so much from, and respect because of the amount of time they have put into their gift, as well as the huge hearts they have to serve with: Bobbi Allison, Kim Russo, Laura Lynne Jackson, and Paul Saladino. You have all been doing this work for decades and have had to stumble over obstacles far greater than I have. You have all taught me about the perseverance of continuing with this gift, even when sometimes it can be a bit overwhelming. It is because of your hard work and paving roads through the decades, when mediumship was unheard-of, that has made my path easier. Thank you for being pioneers here on Long Island, and now all over the world. Thank you for your service, and friendship. But most of all, thank you for seeing the light and healing that needs to be brought to humanity. It has not always been easy, but we continue with the work nevertheless. I am humbled to have this gift, and to be working alongside each of you. I am honored, like you, to have heeded the call of Spirit.

Foreword

There are no coincidences. As it goes, even I was not exempt from the pain of life. One month after starting this book and working with my *bella angela della scrittura* (my beautiful writing angel), our son tragically relapsed from two courageous leukemia battles and what we believed to be a successful bone marrow transplant. Unfortunately, with a final relapse, and a sick body, he ended up in the ICU for six weeks and could no longer sustain the disease. He went into cardiac arrest but due to heavy sedation, thankfully, felt no pain. He died on January 4, 2019 at the tender age of twenty-seven with a full life ahead of him, leaving all of us heartbroken, confused and scrambling to make sense out of another one of life's flames blown out too soon.

You can perhaps start to imagine how writing these words and going through the motions, as difficult as they are, are now for him. And, as you will later read, there are even words and signs directly *from* him. Thankfully, you, Anthony, are a very strong Spirit on the other side, and the signs you send on a daily basis are blowing our minds. Who knew you would be the impetus and the direction this book would take? (Well, yes, Spirit knew.) Know back, that we love you and miss you *every* second of *every* day.

As I share and make it through the tumultuousness of the grieving process, I need the readers to know that ultimately, this book is dedicated to you, the learners … lifers-in-training, because I want to offer you hope and share that you are *not* destined to live a life simply in the material. Loss, pain, suffering, desperation, etc. are not part of the divine plan. It is my mission to help others through grief, become aware of the lessons being presented to us, and find a higher meaning for everything we're going through – even though we may not understand it in the moment. There is an immense world out there of love, compassion, growth, empathy, and healing, and there is a higher reason for why we are here, and especially why we are here *now*. I hope to be your compass in the storm until you find your way to Spirit and healing, or at least a better understanding of the purpose of pain. I will show you how to navigate through the difficulties, and I will point you in the direction to learn about the possibility of healing with the power of faith, positivity, and the laws of the Universe.

Now, as this compass, as this guide, make no mistake that I am not claiming to be an expert in helping *everyone* out of their storms. That is a job for Spirit! (God!) But what I am trying my best to do is show you via example, with over a half century of experiences, and continued hope, that each individual reader can take a part or the whole of this book and apply it to your own lives. Making some sense out of what feels like needless pain and knowing our loved ones are still around us after death can change so many of our beliefs, and at times even shorten the grieving process.

Making a little more sense of our physical world and feeling the strength to contact myself or other gifted mediums that help you connect to your loved ones is a gift we all owe ourselves. Contact with Spirit is not evil. It should not be denied or frowned upon. It is an inherent gift we are all given—some of us have just been smacked with it from a younger age!

No matter what pain, confusion, or even "bad media" about mediums might suggest, I want you to devour, then digest, this book and know there is something much greater for you. There is a purpose, a reason, a calling, and I'm here to help you explore it. Freedom from this suffering and grief is within your reach, and it does not have to be as difficult as you have been led to believe. If you have no place or person to turn to, then trust me to guide you to the way, just as I trust that Anthony, in Spirit, along with Spirit, is guiding and showing us the way now.

Introduction

*The spiritual journey is the unlearning of
fear and the acceptance of love.*

—Marianne Williamson

If you have picked up this book, you are looking for the answer to something; you are searching for something, perhaps missing something. You might be on the start of your spiritual journey or you might have been at this for decades but have hit a bump in the road and don't feel you can pull yourself out quite yet on your own.

Are you aching for a change, something new and better to happen in your life or simply to stop grieving the losses and hurts that add up over time for all of us? Are you perhaps in a place in your life where you feel alone or lost? Have you started to see life from a different perspective but don't really yet have those friends to share your thoughts with? Have you been told by a loved one "If you don't change, we're through"? Or have you slowly started to awaken yourself and are now drawn to all books that share the mysteries of life above us and around us that we can't see but know are guiding us?

Whatever the reason, we know you are here because you want change to happen in your life and are ready for it now. What that change is, you may be very unclear about. You may not even be sure it can happen. I know that is why I seek knowledge, or I seek guidance from others at different points in my life. It's because I have hit what feels like an impasse—okay, a brick wall—and I'm ready to go in a new direction. You can't be an authority on all things at all times.

But do you want to know a secret?

I know someone who can: Spirit.

Amazingly, a true authority on all things at all times exists out there, but do you have the nerve to be willing to change, to ask for help?

This word "Spirit," for some who are new on the spiritual journey, feels like it is something way outside and beyond themselves, but imagine if it were much closer, like right inside of you just waiting to answer every question you have ever had. What if you could simply close your eyes and hear the message or open your eyes and see a sign? Wouldn't life be easier? Wouldn't you be less afraid to dive into that new territory and try change more willingly? So, the word "Spirit" will be used to describe the Universal Oneness of all that is: angels, guides, Holy Spirit, God, and loved ones on the other side. Everyone and everything works together, as One source. So when I'm saying "Spirit," I am talking about the whole picture and the energies of the Universe combined which is why at times I refer to the plural and say they.

I know it is an emotionally confused and very harsh environment we live in today. The world seems to be floating energetically from one extreme to another as we accept and take on more stress and more duties, as we try to do it *all*. We are finding life is completely overwhelming, some, or even most days. No wonder we are all feeling a little fragmented, a little exhausted, and more than just a little burnt out. Then pile on a death of a loved one and tell me— how are we supposed to cope?

I'm here to tell you, it's not supposed to be this hard. We are not supposed to be suffering as we are. We are not supposed to be helpless or feel stranded or feel alone. The universe is not a malevolent one. It truly is not. Underneath all of the mess there is the most loving, most kind, most accepting and universally unconditionally loving source that awaits us to access it, to watch it, to create with it. But will we even try?

It turns out that many of us still don't want to learn more about how the universe wants to help us. With all our distractions, we have forgotten the most important pieces to who we really are. We've forgotten to even ask the right questions. We are spirits in body and not bodies in spirit. We are spiritual souls having a human experience, but this is something we are not often taught to believe. It is time for us to flip our thinking and come to the real truth behind who we are and what our purpose on Earth is.

In reality, our body is a vessel, like a ship, that is placed in numerous crazy storms. We are knocked and rocked and shaken and shocked until some days we don't even know if we can take another moment. We wonder why we even bother to venture out and try to dip our toes in those crazy waters—why we even bother to leave the safety of the shore. As we age, we seem to lose more and more parts of ourselves, and some days we don't even remember why we are here, to say nothing of knowing who we are or want to be.

That is the reason why it is imperative we start to reconnect with our true selves, with the universe and nature around us, and with all that lies *beyond* what we can physically see in front of us. Imagine if in the midst of our storms, even before and even after, there are signs, clues that something much bigger has been there the entire time to guide you? Would you be as scared to venture out? Would you be more willing to venture into uncharted waters? Would you be willing to suspend your fear for one second longer and try to see that behind your ventures is an unconditional love silently pushing you, hoping to move you forward and into peace, despite what the tidal waves may be telling you?

In many ways, our life is like that of a sailor commandeering the wind to get to their destination. An experienced navigator knows the signs of sailing safely come from nothing other than the wind. Can we see it? Not directly, but we can see its effects on the waters, the waves, the leaves. But no matter our profession or where we are in life, if we dare to step outside and pay attention, amazingly, we too *can* feel the wind. But just because we *feel* it doesn't mean that all of us will *listen* to its calling.

So, who creates the winds? Spirit. Who speaks through the winds? Spirit. Who nudges you when you don't feel like moving? The breadth of Spirit does. Some call it God, some call it Source, some call it Universe, some call it Soul, but no matter the name, it is something that exists and moves through you unseen to the physical eye.

Even for a baby – they are simply a vessel until the breath of life through Spirit brings on their first glorious cry. Yes, I know they are probably truly screaming, "What in God's name was I thinking? Put me back in that nice warm-water womb!" I know that's what I'm thinking some days! But the fact is, the breath of Spirit comes into the body and we are born. The breath of Spirit leaves the body and we die. That can no longer be disputed.

It's fascinating, because similes that refer to Spirit like the *wind* have been used through various civilizations and centuries. You are "filled" with the breath of God or Spirit. In a sense, it's something that takes over control of an activity or belief in your life, in a good way. Your body is the vessel, but it is directed silently by the wind or Spirit. Just like the wind can fill the sails and blow a sailboat across a lake, with listening to Spirit you can be blown toward peace. By ignoring Spirit, you can hit those choppy waters and remain in turmoil.

The lesson here is that there is much to be learned, clued in about, on how to handle the stormy weather and the vessels we live in, and even on how to overcome our fears by reading the signs. One place to look that provides us a multitude of lessons, if we are willing to observe, is nature. It works in perfect harmony to balance itself. Think about it. There are storms and there is the calm before the storm. There are the ones you see coming and are warned about and the ones that appear to hit out of nowhere. There are the tsunamis that result from an earthquake on another part of the Earth. There is the snow that melts into water and can cure a drought or cause a flood. In life, like in nature, there is the constant bi-polarity of male/female, yin/yang, spirit/body, life/death, happiness/sadness, victory/defeat, love/hate, fear/peace, acceptance/rejection, lightness/darkness and the list goes on and on. All of this exists to find harmony and balance; that is, if we allow it to!

The question becomes: How are we ever to make any sense of all the options and choices and decisions thrown at us on an hourly basis? How can we remain positive and believe—or even better, *trust*, that if we can make it through all of these storms and losses in life there will be (and already have been) the most beautiful moments, seconds of pure love and light and a feeling of oneness all beyond our wildest imagination?

If you are grieving right this second, you may not be able to believe there is light beyond. But, with Spirit, I am here to tell you there is a wondrousness, so good in fact, that if you were asked to trade it in and accept the pain in this world, you would choose the suffering to get to the gift. You would choose to see another day, because you, like all of us, are waiting for the *one* thing you can count on: the sun to rise, the pain to leave.

That is the story of life. There are the invisible forces that cause us to change direction at certain points in our life and things that no matter how well we are prepared, we can't control. One of those is death: our own, our loved ones, our pets. No matter who we are, how old we are, how many we have experienced or when death hits, our worlds, our lives and those of loved ones are turned upside down.

Then, ironically, often simultaneously, there is that birth, that reward, that gift, that incredible news that keeps us wanting more. This *is* choppy water.

People who choose to believe they can prepare and then control all of the elements are in for a rough ride. Those who "go with the flow" but are *armed* with knowledge, and accept the power of Spirit, have found an answer, a way, a miracle of sorts that keeps them grounded and happy and grateful in even the worst of times.

Unfortunately, no matter who comes to their aid, some people stay upside down. Their vessel controls them, and the elements are too strong to conquer. Why? Because they are missing one very simple fact, that Spirit is here to get us upright—to sit us back up again—no matter how deep the pain has been, how long we've lived with it, or how quickly we've been shocked by it.

These are some images I want you to keep in your head as you read this book, because this book is here to help encourage you to find peace. I want you to think that even if your vessel is completely upside down with no oxygen or help in sight that what sails above us in Spirit is here to set us straight, to guide us, to whisper to us, to comfort us, to love us, and to prove to us that we are not meant to do this all alone. I am here, this book is here, to speak to you in a way that you—or your soul—may never have heard before and to help you move through the deepest grief, confusion, and frustration you have ever felt in your life.

If your life were perfect now, you most likely would not have picked up this book. If you were content and happy and understood the workings of the universe, you would not have picked up this book. If you understood how the law of attraction works, what Spirit does, and you could do all of this for yourself with *no* fear, pain, or resentment, you would not have picked up this book.

But you have. Something has driven or guided you here. There are hundreds of books on the market now with absolutely incredible psychics and mediums who, thanks to the evolution of thinking, and with the nudging of God or Spirit, more and more people are looking to for guidance, for their answers from above or beyond. People are no longer simply dismissing us psychics and mediums as charlatans.

Oh, I know—many of you still don't have an ounce of belief and even when you get hit over the head with signs from Spirit or loved ones you still choose not to connect the dots. And, there are plenty of charlatans still out there – therefore, do beware and do your homework, because all sorts of sordid people are willing to take money and make false promises, and shockingly, many still get away with it. But that is not me, and it is not the psychics and mediums that I have such great respect for. We all strive to do the best, from the really famous ones such as the Caputos and Edwards and Van Praags to the not as famous ones, yet, just as talented, we are all here to serve a purpose. We are here to share our gift and our calling to help *you* heal.

I had great reservations about writing this book, because my biggest concern was that with all these incredible psychics and mediums and authors, how could I possibly add one more book to the mix that would add value, and what could I possibly say that hasn't already been said?

Well, Spirit pushed back, as they always do, and pushed me into the path of validations and timing that proved my story, my experiences, and my message could be heard in a new or different way; just enough to grab certain people and souls that might not yet have vibrated with someone else's message. We all reverberate at a different place and time, and if this works for you now and you move on to another medium or author later, that is all good.

This book has a spin and deals with issues of resolving grief, death, illness, and answers some questions that may appear to be a little unpopular—more than some mediums have been sharing publicly. But I want to go there so that we can all grow and move forward. I want to push any boundaries I can to help you move out of that fear mode and into embracing that love waiting to guide you from above.

One of the most important points I am here to share is the bottom line: If you are consulting me, or other reputable mediums and psychics now, that is wonderful—but you need to know that *you too can do this*. We each have intuition, *the gift*, we may just not choose to exercise it, and without exercise it won't grow any stronger. I am here to share some ways to help you connect with your own true gift.

We are in a life of constant change. And, for the most part, collectively, we work on change for the *better* despite what we may see in front of us. After all, and without getting too religious—faith is believing in the unseen. That being the case, why don't we embrace the unseen and think of faith as that something guiding us from above, whispering to us, and sending us messages of love? It's time to smile at the heavens, thank them for their devotion to us, and become stronger and more united with them as we make use of our imagination and solidify and accept how valued we are to them. After all, imagination is the first step to allowing ourselves to grow.

And, if you are feeling different, so *very* different from the rest of the people on this planet, I assure you I *can* relate. I share my story and keep the emotions raw, unfiltered, because I want you to know that we all have hurts and obstacles and betrayals and mountains to climb and impasses and times when no matter what we've tried, we just don't think we can do another day. But in the end, if you choose to pay attention, if you choose to forearm yourself with a little knowledge, you will find your life was not as uncharted as it may have felt. Yes, you have free will, but you are also guided from above. You are nudged and sometimes even hit over the head in more ways than you can ever, ever believe until you start to put the pieces together to uncover and reveal the picture they really make.

So, please, hang on tight with me. The ride may get bumpy, but trust me when I say that what whispers to us and loves us from beyond the veil is the greatest gift we could ever have been given. Don't be afraid to dip your feet into the waters of life, and don't ever stop yourself from the beauty of love and the challenges of life, because the "work" and growth that come from the nurturance of Spirit, if we tune in, can be heart-altering, life-changing. Believe me when I say that there is something beyond us. There is a benevolent universe out there that the naked eye can't see, but the heart can most definitely feel. If you pay close enough attention, you too will see the signs, hear the whispers of love, in everything you do, with everyone you touch.

The most important lesson is that we must learn to let go of our fears and be willing to jump in. We can't fight the storms. We can't let fear keep us stuck in one reality, in one place. If we do, then fear or even grief has won. We have to find a way to move through these human emotions and discover the zillions of beauties and wonders beyond all the pain. There really is a wonderful world out there to be explored and many, many people to share it with. I would be honored if you will allow me to be one more put in your path to nudge you!

This book is my way of sharing everything from the pain of my childhood, the many, many ways I tried to fight my gift so I could be "normal," the tragedies and losses that made me have to face grieving, and the tools I have found helpful along the way. My heart is aching now, but it will all feel complete, all serve a purpose if I can persuade even one of you to let go of fear, dive in, and accept that your spiritual journey truly is the greatest gift of love you will ever know and it's right there, above you, just waiting to make itself known.

In Love & Light,

Gina

Part One

LET THE ROLLER-COASTER RIDE BEGIN

The most beautiful people we have known are those that have known defeat, known suffering, known struggle, known loss, and have found their way out of the depths. These persons have an appreciation, a sensitivity, and an understanding of life that fills them with compassion, gentleness, and a deep loving concern. Beautiful people do not just happen.

—Elisabeth Kübler-Ross

Deep in my heart, when I think of some of the most valuable lessons I've learned in life and how they have shaped me as a woman, wife, mother, medium, I can say that accepting where we are at now, embracing who and what we have now while letting go of pain, fear, and regrets tends to stay at the top of my list. This is not easy, it did not come naturally, and no, I didn't have a "normal" childhood. I can't even say I have a normal life now, but I can say that in all the strange paths I've gone down, being a medium is not the one I knew I was going to land on when my life's journey began. As a matter of fact, I've taken many detours. Let me repeat that! I've taken many, many, many detours. That's part of being human. Some were by choice, some were through the worst tragedies one can imagine, and some were "intent," finally understanding that my life actually has a purpose beyond the roller-coaster ride of the day. I'm here to tell you my story, but even beyond this to provide guidance, a direction, and most importantly hope that you can overcome the deepest pain to find your calling and become a beacon of light to those around you.

Some of my stories are raw and harsh, and so I am warning you ahead of time, but pain is raw and harsh, and we can never understand it in the moment. Unlike many other books written in the world, I am going to leave the raw parts in and let you sift through what you can relate to and discard the rest. As you will have also learned from the introduction, the writing of this book has transpired during the final relapse and death of our son and, therefore, I am not in a mindset to make less of the true emotional loss and grieving that I am experiencing. However, this is not a book of doom and gloom. This is a book of hope and one that will help move you through to a level of love, understanding, connection to the other side—a level that you may never have believed even you can access.

This book is written with the love and guidance of Spirit. It exists to help you find true comfort in this lifetime, no matter the circumstances. It is here to guide you to peace amidst the worst storms and unimaginable tragedies. It is here to give you hope. It is here to prove that you, too, can overcome.

Chapter One
ARGUING WITH DESTINY

EARLY YEARS WITH SPIRIT AND "HATING TO BE DIFFERENT"

A person often meets his destiny on the road he took to avoid it.

—Jean de La Fontaine

Let me begin by sharing that my family immigrated to Long Island, NY from Italy in 1966, when I was three years old and my brother Angelo was only nine months old. I obviously don't remember much about those early years, but I do remember, around the age of six, standing in the New York City Naturalization department, overhearing seventy adults say the "Pledge of Allegiance" and taking their oaths as new citizens of the United States. I can still remember everyone reciting in unison and being in awe at the power of those words, even though I had no understanding of what they meant. I was now a citizen as well.

Life with parents as immigrants was not always easy. We came to Long Island, NY because that's where my parents' family friends had moved when they arrived from Italy, and the Italians go where the Italians already are. My parents always spoke, and to this day, still do speak, broken English. They never really learned how to read or write but learned just enough to get by in understanding a bill or a letter that came in the mail. They had friends in town who had already lived here for some years; consequently they knew the same Italian lawyer, doctor, accountant, travel agent, and dentist. Everyone would go to the same professionals who spoke Italian and would help with the day-to-day issues and concerns of life.

As children, we were always translating for them, or helping them write notes or checks as needed. Starting out this way, turned out to be just the beginning of feeling different from all the other kids at school or people I'd later encounter in life. As a result, being different became an uncomfortable norm for me.

My mother was a self-taught seamstress and later would do housecleaning work; my father a welder down at the local marina working on barges. We grew up our entire childhood in Port Washington, not knowing what an affluent town it would later turn into. My sister Mimi arrived one year after we landed in New York. My mother always tells the story of having given birth in the hospital in Mineola, NY and wanting to call my father on the phone, not knowing how to do that. As she picked up the receiver, she would cry. The operator on the other end asked her questions in English, and she would just cry because she couldn't speak the language. How difficult that must have been for her. I give my parents a tremendous amount of respect for picking up their lives and going to a country where they didn't know the language or customs, to create a new life. As strong as I think I am at times, I don't know if I would have the balls to make a move like that.

We lived in a small one-bedroom apartment with a tiny kitchen. With three small children, every night had a bedtime ritual. My sister, being the baby, slept in the crib by my parents' bed, my brother Angelo would sleep on the couch in the living room, and because I was the oldest (I was five years old by then), they would roll out a cot into the living room, make it with sheets, blanket, and pillows and lean it beside the sofa so Angelo could not roll out overnight. I still remember that routine.

We lived upstairs from Nicolina and Lorenzo, family friends of my parents from their old hometown in Italy. We always had to be quiet, and not run around in the apartment, for fear we would disturb the landlords downstairs. The apartment had a small pull-down staircase in the ceiling that went up to an unfinished attic space. At the top of that pull-down staircase was a window. I spent a lot of time up there alone, either drawing by the window, writing or playing with the "imaginary" people speaking to me in my mind. Many, many times my mother would hear me talking and in Italian would always say, "*Con chi stai parlando?*" ("Who are you talking with?") and I would just say, "To myself."

My mother hated that I answered her in English. I was trying to be American: act American, speak American, dress American, and she would always make me answer her in Italian. I'd respond in English each time, and she would say in Italian, "Gina ... answer in Italian, please."

At one point, I remember responding, "If I have to speak to you in Italian, then I won't speak at all." Yeah, defiance started early with me.

Our "yard" was a small patch of cement in the front of the house, where we played hopscotch, jump rope, and had a tiny plastic four-foot-round pool—the blue pool with painted fishies that we all grew up with. I thought we were filthy rich when we got that pool. Cold or hot water temperature didn't bother me; we had a pool and it was my way of getting out of that house!

My best friend, Patty, lived three houses down from us. She came from a family with seven siblings. My goodness, *seven* siblings, how awesome was that, I'd say to myself! In the summer I would run down every day after breakfast and spend the whole day at her house. One day, I was extremely eager to get out of my home, I shoveled breakfast down my throat, put my coat on, and ran down to her house. When I arrived, I took off my coat and realized I had never put a shirt on and was just wearing my pajama undershirt. All the siblings were laughing at me. Their mom Pauline was exceedingly gracious and kind. She just gave me a shirt from the folded laundry and made me a snack. Again, weird, different…always different.

The back of their house butted up to our town cemetery. I was always curious about that space, and because the backyard fence was worn down and rotted, we were able to crawl through the hole and go to the other side. I never really wanted to because I always felt weird there. Like someone was trying to get my attention, but I didn't even know that was the feeling then. It just registered that feeling, *weird*.

After a few years of living in that apartment, my parents had saved enough to buy their own home. Plus my father was tired of other people's rules, and wanted his own place. We stayed in Port Washington but just moved a few blocks away, closer to the train station, where my mom still lives today, in that same yellow house. There's a lot I don't remember about my childhood from 7-14 years of age. There was a lot of dysfunction happening in that home.

My father was an alcoholic, and very abusive; therefore I tried as a child to block out many of the memories. In many ways, I think Spirit helped with that, because they[1] allowed me an opportunity to escape the sadness of those years, which helped me cope – as best I could. Even today when one of my siblings says "Remember when…?" I honestly don't have any recollection of that memory. That saddens me.

My father was always angry, always pissed at something or someone. We had to tiptoe, like walking on eggshells so as not to disturb the angry bear. Nothing worked. He was always angry, always throwing something at us, always pissed at life, always taking it out on us. My mom did the best she could to tame the angry bear, but she wasn't always successful, and I think over time, it just pissed him even more when she tried her best to contain him. He'd get even wilder because he wanted to be mean.

As a child, I thought, *He doesn't love us; he is taking out his anger on all of us because he hates us.* How I could understand this at five or six years old, I'll never know. What I do know is there was this out of body understanding I had with him, as well as an overwhelming fear. He was here to hurt us; I knew that as a child.

I remember at nine years old, getting in and out of the car when we'd travel as a family. There were two adults sitting in the front of the car, and three kids in the back. At some point, when we got out of the car, all *four* doors were going to open and close as everyone had to get out of the vehicle. I can still remember my father yelling and cursing at us because he'd count and get annoyed that he'd hear the sound of four doors closing. *What?* I don't know why it pissed him off that he had to hear doors slamming shut four times. I guess he wanted all three of us to only get out of one door in the back so he wouldn't have to hear doors slamming. *Unbelievable.*

As we entered elementary school and onward, it became increasingly clear we were so different than the other kids. When other children brought peanut butter and jelly sandwiches for lunch, we brought smelly salami sandwiches. Kids would laugh and make fun of me for it. *Different, you're different* is what I'd hear in my head. Friends would come over to play after school; my mother spoke broken English and the kids never understood her and I'd have to translate for her. *Different, you're different* is what I'd hear again in my head.

My father hunted every fall and would bring the deer home and hang them upside down in the garage and leave the garage door open for everyone to see. We lived at a major intersection in town, with stop signs on each corner, so, of course, traffic would stop and everyone would look, watch, and linger. *Different, you're very different* I would hear in my head, and cringe.

My parents thought they still lived on a farm, so they'd keep chickens and roosters in the backyard, crowing at 5 a.m. and the local police came to warn my father this was against "code" and the roosters must be removed. My father got *so* angry. Who were *they* to tell him what he could or could not do on *his* property? Again, I heard in my head *Different, you're so different*. And then one day, our parents allowed us to get this pretty, little beige tabby cat. (Spoiler alert: Warning to animal lovers and empaths, this story does not end well.) She was extremely cute and little. Since they didn't want animals in the house, she stayed in the garage, but every chance we got, we stayed with her, played with her—oh, she was so precious to us. We'd fight over who could hold her. She was developing some sort of skin rash and started losing her hair. My father told us to stop picking her up, as all the cuddling and holding we were doing was making her lose her hair. But we couldn't stop because we loved her more than anything else in the world!

Our father would warn us, over and over again, "She's losing her hair because you're holding her too much." Did he ever think it might be the quality of her food or lack of vitamins? Maybe she just had some sort of allergy? Nope, as far as he was concerned, her losing hair was only because we were playing with her too much. Then, one day he called all three of us out to the garage, again yelled at us for holding her when he specifically told us not to. He had had it and since we weren't listening to him, we wouldn't be allowed to have her anymore.

Oh, how I had wished what he meant was he was going to give her away to another family. I wish that was his way of fixing the problem, but it wasn't. He picked up that beautiful, innocent kitten with his huge hand, raised her into the air and slammed her down onto the cement garage floor. She didn't die, so he picked her up again and slammed her down, again. All the while forcing us to watch. We cried and screamed in agony and pain for our little pet. I saw her take her last breath; it was just too much to bear. Same message I heard in my head, as I walked away in agony and pain, *You're different, you don't belong here with these people.* Was this me saying this to myself, or someone else giving me the message?

I dreamed about that kitten for weeks. I didn't know back then, those were visitations. She was letting me know, "I'm okay, happy and playing with the other animals here." Visitations became a theme for me. A family friend or relative would pass, and I would get dreams or visitations of them for several nights. I never understood why and certainly would never tell my parents, for fear of not being accepted, or being different in some way. It had felt like my entire life I had been living in a bizarro world—how could I tell the parents I was supposed to feel protected by, that somehow their daughter was even stranger than the weird experiences and life she was currently a part of? It was too much for a small girl of seven or eight to handle.

In this new home, I was about nine years old and shared a room with my sister. I never felt safe in that house. It was an old home, over 100 years old, and even as a child I felt like the rooms and walls had eyes. Even when no one was home, or no one was moving around, the floor boards creaked. Weird. Everyone thought that was weird when I'd joke about it or say something off the cuff. Most of the time, I just said nothing and dealt with it in my own silence.

Around the age of twelve, my bedroom was moved to the attic, third floor, and that's when all activity and hell broke loose with Spirit really amping up. There was a very narrow staircase that led to the attic. Once I was inside my room, I felt relatively safe, but any time I had to go into that hallway, to either go downstairs to the bathroom or go back upstairs to my room, I hated it. There seemed to be "energy," as best I could describe it—or maybe the word is ghosts I felt around me? I don't know, all I can remember is racing either up or down those stairs, as fast as I could, because I just felt weird in that space. It got so bad over the years, that I would hold my breath, and run as fast as I could, up or down, to the point I would sometimes stumble with my feet and fall. I didn't understand *what* I was feeling; I just knew it didn't feel right to me.

One evening, sitting on my bed in my bedroom doing homework, as I had done many times before, I suddenly noticed right beside me, the bed being depressed, as if someone sat right down next to me. I saw it with my own eyes, and as I looked at that depression in the bed, I immediately screamed, threw my school books in the air, and ran screaming down the stairs.

My parents were frightened as to what had happened. "*Che cosa? Che successo?*" they yelled. ("*What is it? What happened?*") I explained what I saw in detail, and the look of disbelief and anger in my parents' eyes was baffling to me. I'm explaining the fear and horror of what I just witnessed, and all they could do was yell at me, to let me know they were sick and tired of hearing about these "stories" and I had either better stop, or they were taking me to the priest. I was confused. *What are they talking about?* I understand their lack of understanding, and their worry over whether their daughter was mentally ill. I get that, but instead of receiving any type of understanding or support, I was basically told for the last time, *"Basta, non voglio sentirlo più!"* ("*Enough! I don't want to hear this anymore.*")

To make matters worse, I remember in that moment my father threatening if I ever said I saw anything in the house again, he would burn it down. *W-h-a-t?* That was extremely frightening for any twelve-year-old to hear, especially from an abusive, dysfunctional parent, who had already shown he was capable of creating pain. As a twelve-year-old, hearing your home would be burnt to the ground, and it resting all on my shoulders, was more responsibility than any child should hold at that age. I quickly learned…*you can't trust those you thought you could, so just stop talking about it.*

Whenever I was in my room, I got visitations from Spirit, especially at night. In my room studying, it felt like there were eyes on me. Since I had no one to turn to, I figured another way around it. I would play music really loud in the room, hoping to drown them out…most of them loved the noise. Go figure. But the music made them stop "staring" at me, if that makes any sense. They were still in the room, I could sense them, but somehow the music made me feel less awkward, as if there was other energy in the room with me that was helping to make me feel less afraid. Well, we now know that music is energy, and able to change our emotions from sadness, to fear, to extreme happiness. With the limited amount of knowledge I had at the time, I tried anything I could to help balance my thoughts. Dancing, music, word games, puzzles, whatever I could do to get them out of my head. But they always visited.

At night when the lights were out, I was left "feeling" them around me. I hated darkness. I couldn't see Spirit, but I always felt like something was right there in the room with me. I was petrified of waking up in the middle of the night, opening my eyes and "seeing" something, so I always slept with my bed sheet over my head. Silly, and it makes no sense today, but as a child that sheet was like a protective barrier, helping me stay safe should my eyes just suddenly open to see someone inches from my face, staring right back at me! To this day, when I am reading for a client, and I can sense their child is also gifted, Spirit shows me the same scene: the child placing the bed sheet over their head. When I'm able to confirm their child does this and the parent with wide eyes says, "Yes," it now all makes sense to me. I had to go through that in my past, so Spirit could recollect the memory that would one day be pulled as a validation for others going through the same thing.

There's a lot of that medium "symbol" system that I'll explain in further detail later, but for now suffice to say that each memory, experience, situation a medium is involved in throughout their life goes into a special "file" which is later pulled by Spirit when we're in a reading session—more on Spirit communication later in the book. People are always fascinated to learn that Spirit doesn't speak in the same way they did on Earth, and they actually pull and use the memories and symbols in a medium's mind, body, and feelings in order to communicate.

Opposite my bedroom in the attic, across the small hall, was another bedroom. There was a spare bed in that room, and some dressers and small furniture, but no one ever used it. There was always this strange feeling of it being "haunted." That was the best way I could explain it. Every time I'd bring it up to my family, they would say I was crazy. My mother would actually get pissed that I would bring it up.

While I lived in my parents' home, I was never interested, nor had the knowledge or yearning to even want to figure out "what" the energy was. I just stayed clear of that room. I wouldn't dare open that door. All I could discern was that someone or something weird was in that space. Through the decades, as I learned to hone this gift, and once I was in a place of understanding, I knew nothing could hurt me, and energy was energy. I would occasionally stop in and visit that bedroom when visiting my mom. Even to this day, there is still the weird energy when you walk into that space, but I now understand it's a stuck energy of a young male adult, perhaps someone with disabilities of some sort. Certainly nothing to be afraid of. But it all makes sense how as a young teenager, this must have been one of the souls always trying to visit me in my room, across the hall, wanting to spend time with me. Even though I still get an uneasy feeling around that energy, at least I understand why, as a child, I wasn't able to discern if it was something evil or good.

For the record, "smudging" or cleansing a house with sage can help remove any negativity and even help stuck souls move along. I do cleanse and sage my own home, because of the number of clients I see in my home office. To this day, my mother scoffs at my even wanting to visit that bedroom in the attic to see what's there. Since she's kind of freaked out about all of this, certainly smudging the space in her home is too far out for her. Burn something and the smoke clears it away? That's too "frou-frou"! She says leave it alone. So, since it's not my house, I respect that.

School and friendships were always a source of uneasiness for me. I had become exceptionally good at faking who I was, partly because of my dysfunctional home life, and wanting desperately to be like everyone else and be accepted—probably what a lot of children feel growing up. No one wants to be seen as different. But I came from such different stock; it was very difficult running away from that foundation. To assimilate, I became what everyone needed me to be: a great chameleon. The good, academic student. The child that put my heart and soul into my schoolwork so I would be praised by teachers, so I could prove to my parents, specifically my father, that I was worthy. Much of my childhood was being whatever everyone wanted and needed me to be.

My friendships were based on who my friends needed me to be, not who I was. As I began to make friends, I was always careful not to share any information about what I felt or saw around me. The school halls were not only filled with students and teachers walking about, they also had other energy that whispered in my ear or made me feel uneasy. It felt strange and weird at the same time. A few times I tried sharing this with my "closer" friends. Such a mistake to unburden myself to kids who couldn't and didn't understand.

Rumors would start to spread, and back in the early '70s, the only word we had for this gift was "witch." As I moved through junior high school, to be labeled as a witch was more than any child could bear. My parents were weird, my family life was weird, my gift was weird, and now kids at school called me a witch? Trust me, I shut that shit down right away (pardon my language, but there is no other way to put this!) and played it off as a joke. A big, funny joke. The more I could poke fun at myself to keep the focus off of me or whatever rumors were running around, the better I was. I also learned, as I had at home, *I could trust no one*. Talk about feeling completely alone. No one to trust at home, no one to trust at school. I was operating on autopilot, learning how to be everything to everyone. At least I felt accepted for who they *thought* I was.

If I got a 94 on a test, my father's response was "It wasn't a 100." Nothing was ever good enough for him. Only he was perfect. Only he did great things that others could praise. No one else. I remember in art school one year, around the age of fourteen, we were making cut-out flowers from painted burlap and pipe cleaners. The pipe cleaners were first shaped in a petal format, then glued to the burlap, then you carefully cut away the excess material. You were left with floral petals that were twisted together and shaped like a flower. I remember taking my time with each leaf, shaping it carefully, making sure each petal was exactly the same measurement as the other petals. I remember cutting the excess material so there were no uneven cut lines; everything was smooth, clean and perfect. As I worked on this project, I could hear in my head, "Use the colored pipe cleaners…match the brown burlap with the green pipe cleaners…twist the flowers to the right…shape the petals larger." I was being guided, by what, I have no idea, but as I listened to this inner voice, I began feeling comfortable and the project took on a life of its own.

I was exceedingly proud of the flowers I had created from those petals, the way I was guided to. My art teacher gave me a 100 on this project and was especially proud of the work I had created. I was overjoyed. When I came home to show my parents, I remember my father inspecting the flowers and his response was clear and short, "You didn't make this. An adult must have made this, because it's too perfect." When I explained how I made each petal and showed him the process, and told him that I got a 100 on the project, his response was, "You didn't make this, you're a liar. *Bugiarda*," and he walked out.

I was shattered and broken. Something I took such pride in, which had been recognized by teachers, was completely dismissed by my parent. My father's insecurity, anger, and childishness superseded his ability to parent. He was a broken person, because *only* a broken soul would degrade his own children, in order not to feel insecure himself. I was being parented by a broken man, because it was one of my soul lessons to learn in this life. I address more about the psychology of the people we attract and the lessons we jointly learn later in this book, but suffice it to say, this was not a healthy start to life. This was not a role model or parent you would think you would choose to enter this world to.

That moment was huge as I realized I was not good enough and never would be, at anything. Certainly this was a theme in my life that turned out to be a huge repetitive learning lesson to overcome. But it didn't make sense. It wasn't me that made the petals. I was listening to something else—outside of me perhaps? My inside voice? I didn't understand where the messages were coming from.

Each time I even spoke a word about feeling "stuff" in the house, and my parents' response was to completely wig out, it became increasingly impossible to share any information with them. I couldn't go to my parents, certainly couldn't go to any of my friends, and teachers would never understand, or if they did, they would involve my mother and that would be a huge mistake. This sensation, this energy, this gift – whatever you want to call it had to be kept secret.

It wasn't until that fateful day when I ran down the stairs screaming something was in my room sitting on the bed beside me, that my parents responded, "If you speak of this one more time, we're taking you to the priest." That was it. There was *no* way I was going to go to the priest to explain what was happening to me. Funny thing was just the year before, in 1973, the movie *The Exorcist* had come out. Of course I was too young to see it, but everyone knew of it. If you remember, it was about a young girl acting "odd" and a worried mother taking her child to a local priest, who then performs an exorcism on the girl. I hadn't seen the movie, but trust me, I had heard a lot of terrifying stuff about it.

Everyone at school was talking about it. Did I understand as a child that the story was just a movie? Nope. I was frightened and when they said "priest," my ears opened wide. I would never tell them again of what I would see. I would share only if I "felt" weird stuff, but once I would get that look shot across at me, I would pull back and remember them saying "priest" and would stop talking.

As I turned the corner into the teenage years, I found that working kept me out of the house, and busy. With keeping busy and hormones coursing through my body, I was able to shut down the voices a bit more. They didn't bother me as much, except at night in my bedroom again; the bed sheet covering my head was how I got through each night, in that home. I would still get dreams about those that died, I still felt the presence of that "energy" across the hall that would come into my room, but now I was totally into boys, making friends, and trying to be normal. I still tripped running up and down those stairs. Nothing had really changed; I just stopped wanting to talk about it. No one cared anyway.

As I entered a local college, I began having way too much fun partying. I could care less about studying. I had wanted to be a doctor, and had taken an aptitude test in high school, that showed I not only had the interest in but also the capacity for medicine. I wanted to help people. I wanted to serve in some way, and I thought medicine was the way to go. I had also studied Latin in junior high school and high school, to prepare for med school, so I was completely psyched and ready. When I shared that with my parents, they said, "Forget it, you will bankrupt us with financial loans. Just go study accounting, and when you get married you can have a part-time job as a bookkeeper as you raise your children."

Hmm, I'm so happy they apparently had my life figured out at seventeen! Thanks, Mom and Dad; don't support me, just tell me what to do. So, not having a second game plan, I did exactly what they told me to do. I started St. John's University, and after my first year, with all the partying and skipping classes, my grades had fallen and I was expelled. That was a tough blow, but being able to get into my car and drive off each morning, and not having my parents ask where I was going, or when I was coming home, was more freedom than this seventeen-year-old could handle. As a result, I abused that college opportunity and just hung out and never went to class. Oh, I drove to school each day, but I hung out with my friends. I didn't care. After being expelled, I had to get myself together and figured my next move was to go into Manhattan to get a full-time job. My first job was as a secretary for a vice president at a small bank. Boy, did I hate that job. Didn't feed my soul or my purpose at all, but it was great money for an eighteen-year-old, and again, it got me out of the house.

I had survived my childhood years, morphed myself from being different to shuffling everything under the carpet, denying myself my true being, shutting up when I needed to talk, becoming a chameleon to match whatever everyone else needed, and I had not stood true to myself. I learned that I could not trust. I learned I was weird, and if I spoke out, I might end up forced to see a priest. I learned there was no safe place, and little by little I was forcing the "voices" out of my head, and, as a result, tightening the noose to my true destiny.

I can say with certainty now, and having learned the hard way (and next you will read about my marriage and children) that when you fight with your destiny, your calling, you will inevitably lose! I am the living, breathing, proof that "A person often meets his destiny on the road he took to avoid it."

Chapter Two
LISTEN TO HUSBANDS, CHILDREN, OR INVISIBLE FORCES?

MARRIED YEARS WITH SPIRIT: STILL...NOTHING "NORMAL"

Letting go means to come to the realization that some people are a part of your history, but not a part of your destiny.

—Steve Maraboli

In the early formative years of childhood, especially from birth to age seven, if children can't form a healthy and trusting bond with their parents, their lives become predisposed to so many emotional obstacles and so much baggage that it is hard for them to find anyone to trust or anyone to allow *in*. The child starts to feel that they are all alone

Listen to Husbands, Children, or Invisible Forces?

and they adapt themselves to tell other people what they want to hear and not what the child really feels. They even create "fake" personas to make others happy. That was me. I had become that chameleon and I knew I couldn't tell people what was really going on in my life with Spirit.

As a result of unhealthy parenting, these children feel abandoned, alone, and resentful, always wanting what others have and never feeling good enough. They bring these fears of lack, fears that people will always disappoint and abandon them, and they become hypervigilant in everything they do. They are constantly hearing from their own inner critic. These are just some of the ways we become our own worst enemies and let those negative voices in our head rule. The worst part is that unless we break these cycles, these insecurities come along with us to all new relationships, all new endeavors, and all new careers or walks of life. They are constantly taunting us, and not in a good way.

Any psychologist will tell you that early broken attachment with parents or caregivers can lead to serious neurosis and sometimes even pathologies. Until one learns to address their issues and work through their insecurities and the injustices of their childhood, whether with a therapist, gaining knowledge by reading or classes, or simply talking with a true friend, the roller-coaster of emotions and drama continues to drive the ego and the person's decisions. They are not working for their better good. They don't even get that there is a *higher* good.

Although these were all issues I was faced with, the great news is somewhere in me there remained a strength to fight, even rebel at times, and thanks to the push from Spirit, whether or not I wanted it, my experiences made me all the more committed to finding emotional and spiritual health and not repeating the "sins" of my parents. I can't say that I played every card perfectly, but I can say that each step I took, I never stopped looking and trying, and I never will! So, if you've experienced similar rejections early on, I'm here to tell you there is hope! Actually, even more than that, I'm going to show you there is even help—perhaps unseen at first, but it is there. Spirit is that guide.

So, to continue my story, I was in New York City, working full-time, eighteen years old and relieved to be out of the house. It wasn't a job I loved or felt any satisfaction from, but it was great money and it gave me some freedoms. It was here that I met my first husband, Phil. He was tremendously sweet and very cute. He wasn't Italian like we were, but came from a very loving, close family that were Albanian and Greek.

He lived on Long Island, like I did, and on one of our first dates, he forgot something at his house. We decided to stop by so he could get whatever he needed. We drove into Brookville, a very affluent neighborhood on Long Island. We drove up this huge driveway that felt like it went on for miles, and up to this huge mansion. The whole time I was nervously saying, "This isn't your home," and he would say, "Yes, it is."

Then he didn't have a key to get into the front door. I was afraid someone would come out with a shotgun. We walked around to the garage.

"Don't you have a garage door opener?" I asked.

"No," he said, "my parents have it in their car."

Hmm, this was getting weirder by the minute. We walked to the back of the house, and there was a note taped to the kitchen chandelier, but who could read it because it was turned around facing away from us. There was no way, I thought, that this guy, who was very humble, and kind, came from this kind of background.

Listen to Husbands, Children, or Invisible Forces?

But I was wrong. That was his house, and he did come from an affluent family. That's not why I fell in love. I cared for him because he never took himself seriously. He was kind and sweet, and I had never really had a decent boyfriend. It was refreshing to be made to feel special. He taught me that college and an education were very important to a more comfortable life and future. That was how he was raised. My family came from work your fingers to the bone, and just try and make it through life. His family was about taking opportunities and making your future as bright as possible. It's because of him that I decided to go back to college, at night, while I worked full-time during the day, to finish my four-year degree.

He taught me the importance of working toward a future. I'm especially grateful he came into my life to help me understand that. We dated for seven years, and the whole time I was waiting for a ring. My friends, cousins, everyone around me was getting engaged. We were dating for seven years and no ring? Even though I understood about needing to finish school, there was the part of me that was conditioned to be a wife and mother. That's what I was taught every woman needs to do.

Remember, I was conditioned. Going back to school was to help me get a better job, until I could stay home with children to raise them. I waited every year for a ring, and he never got the hint. A year after I finally graduated with a bachelor's degree in finance, that was when he proposed. This was supposed to make me happy. And, for a split second, it did. But deep inside I wasn't happy. Something was "off." I figured maybe this was just butterfly nerves of it finally happening after all this time.

I threw myself into the planning of the wedding. His family was incredibly good to us. Anything we wanted for our special day was granted. His family was large, loud, fun, and very close—everything I had wanted for myself and my future. They felt so normal compared to mine. They spoke to one another when things weren't going right. I felt like I had been given a gift. Yet, something inside didn't feel right. Having gone through my entire life of feeling odd or different, it was very normal to me to be feeling "off" at every stage in my life.

My future in-laws and family were very religious; his parents, uncles, and aunts were all on the church board, and they were instrumental in helping the priest run the Orthodox Church they belonged to. I felt that sharing my special gift and the things I was still experiencing would be too foreign for them to understand. Just as when I was younger, I wanted to be accepted, and again, I became what I thought they needed me to be, so I would fit in. Not even my fiancé knew about my childhood, the energy in my room, the things I saw or felt at school, none of it. The last thing I wanted was to be looked at like I was weird.

We were blessed to have a family friend, Father Nicholas, officiate our wedding in the Orthodox church. He was the bishop, and it was a high honor for him to marry us. As we got closer to our wedding date, and going for pre-wedding couples preparation, he informed us he would not allow the "Here Comes The Bride" song to be played as the bride walks down the aisle. His belief was that it originated as an old German beer-drinking song and did not have merit in an Orthodox ceremony. I was distraught. My entire life of playing "bride," wearing a towel draped over my head like a veil as I practiced walking down an imaginary aisle to this song in my head, and now was my *one* moment to hear this song play, and the bishop was saying no. I was beyond heartbroken. There was never a backup plan. I was lost. I remember crying my eyes out, and thinking, *What am I going to do?* There was no internet in 1990, no one location you could research wedding songs. I remember getting very quiet and just saying to the voices within me that were always there, *Show me a way around this.*

Several weeks later, I took my car to the mechanic for routine maintenance. I picked up the car several days later, and as I drove off the mechanic's lot, and began to head home, I saw on the console of the car by the floor a cassette tape. It was called "classical music." How strange, and who did this belong to? This was not the type of music I ever listened to, and had no idea how it got into my car, but I thought, *Okay, why is this here?*

I popped the tape into the car cassette player, listened, and then finally the song "Jesu, Joy of Man's Desiring" by Bach, which was a very regal song being played by both violins and trumpets and I thought, *This is the song!* It was a strong trumpet march, and even though it wasn't the original song I had always dreamed of walking down the aisle to as a little girl, it was the song I would be happy to use. The song from the cassette . . . that came out of nowhere.

I didn't realize I was being guided from above. I knew there was *no* coincidence. I was asking for assistance and within weeks this cassette that belonged to no one appears in my car. I just didn't understand how much I was being heard and steered. That's the perfection of the energy all around us in the Universe. It's always listening, even when we feel completely devastated and alone. There is a force trying to guide us. It's not the voice of God as heard by Moses at the burning bush in the Ten Commandments. It's a quiet nudge, a feeling in our gut, a gentle whisper, a friend suddenly stepping up to assist when least expected, or a cassette appearing out of nowhere. That's the infinite love and direction from above, helping us see past the obstacle and giving us another way around our problems. My life would begin to have millions of these synchronicities, both when I would ask for assistance, and when I wasn't even aware or conscious of the connection to above.

After being married for a few months, we finally moved into our marital home in East Northport—a home my husband and father-in-law owned that had been badly ransacked and destroyed by previous rental tenants. They never took care of the in-ground pool in the back yard, which had turned into a black pool of water. As we began our life there, and began renovating the home, there was this little girl spirit who used to come visit me. She was about five years old, and she told me her name was Maria. I would see her, as if seeing a hologram standing before me, all the time. I just assumed she belonged to this house, because I had never seen her before in my parents' home. She was joyful, sweet, and so different than the heavier energy that would visit me in the attic in my parents' home. Around this time, I had started to learn how to meditate. I had heard many wonderful things about meditating, and every time I'd close my eyes and ground myself, she would appear. I loved having her around.

A huge pivotal point in my life happened in 1994, when our first-born Matthew was two and a half years old. One day, gardening and watering the plants around the pool and in the back yard, I had to go to the front, to get something out of the garage. We had been in the back yard gardening, and Matthew was helping me water the flowers using his little yellow bucket that he would fill with water and help pour on the bushes and plants; it was such a gorgeous summer day. I remember telling him, "Matt, come follow Mommy; we have to go to the front of the house to get something." I wasn't paying attention to him, just assumed he was following me around the house to the front, because I saw him move toward me a few feet. When I got to the front of the house, and turned around expecting to see him there, he was nowhere to be found. I heard in my head, *"Go to him quickly."* As I began to walk back around to the back yard, I kept expecting to see him just a few feet away, but he wasn't there. The voice within me said, *"Move faster."* As I got to the back of the house, I saw him bobbing up and down in the middle of the in-ground pool, calling out "Mom," as he got swallowed back down under the water, then coming back up again and saying "Mom." I didn't realize then, but he was holding the yellow bucket in his hand he had been using to help me water the plants.

The bucket kept pulling him back down as he bobbed up for air. I froze for a split-second, which in the moment felt like eternity, then ran and dove into the water, clothes, sneakers and all, pushing him to the side of the pool. My heart was pounding out of my chest, reverberating loudly in my ears. There was no time for thinking. I could only react. As I pushed him to the side of the pool, and we both came up for air, he was shocked, coughing and spitting up water. I cleared the water from my eyes, and around the perimeter of this 16x32 in-ground pool, I suddenly "saw" several hundred white cloaked beings, hologram type of angels surrounding us. I heard them speak simultaneously in my head, *"We saved his life, you can't ignore us any longer. We need you to go help others in grief and despair."*

Was the shock of this experience causing this mental breakdown and vision? Was this really happening? How could this be happening? All I could think of was getting my baby out of the water and into the house. I put all my thinking and effort into taking care of him, pushing aside what I just *saw* and *felt* deep within my soul. Taking off his wet clothes, wrapping him in a beach towel from one of the lounge chairs by the pool, and getting him upstairs into bed was all I could focus on. I had no time to think, only react.

The whole time I kept saying to Matt over and over again, "I'm so sorry, honey…I'm so sorry for this…Mommy is so sorry, Matthew, please forgive me." A few hours later, when I had more time to process and think of the situation, it suddenly hit me. Another 30 seconds and our son would have been gone. Any more time lingering in that garage, without looking to see if Matt was with me, and this situation would have had a horrific ending. The wave of terror, fear and devastating horror finally hit me, and I began sobbing uncontrollably. We could have lost our child, and it would have been *all* my fault.

The heaviness of that possible outcome was too much to bear. As the days passed, the heaviness in my chest started to alleviate a little each day, and I began to remember the voice I heard warning me—the one letting me know I needed to go to him, and to move faster. There was someone, something looking out for me. There was an energy I wasn't even aware of, guiding me. I listened. What would have happened if I decided not to listen?

It took me weeks to process what happened, and I continued to dream about those spirits, angels, holograms I remembered seeing encircling the pool. They wouldn't go away. They would show up in my dreams, not saying anything, but when I'd awake, I'd remember the words they shared that day in the pool…that I had to go help others grieve. What did that mean?

I didn't share these dreams, or what I had heard or witnessed around the pool that day, with my husband or his family. How was I going to explain to my in-laws that I was seeing and hearing voices? I did share it with my mother and explained that although she thought I had stopped seeing spirits around me as a child, it never stopped. I just stopped talking about it, but something or someone showed up that day and told me I couldn't ignore them any longer. Our son was alive because of them, and I had to figure out what this meant for me now and what I was supposed to do with this.

Listen to Husbands, Children, or Invisible Forces?

Psychics and mediums were not on every corner back then. There were no TV shows or books on the subject readily available. Back in the early 1990s no one really understood who they were, and I certainly had *no* idea what I was supposed to do to make sense of all this. Honestly, looking back, I don't even think my mother understood what I was talking about, and we never brought it up again.

The heaviness of that experience never left me. There would be moments, just washing the dishes, or folding laundry, when I'd remember that moment of Matthew in the pool, and begin heaving and crying uncontrollably. I saw life differently; it felt like I was floating through my own life, watching myself from above. There was this "presence" beside me all the time, almost like when you're sitting in a chair and you turn around because you feel someone standing behind you, yet no one is there. Life *always* felt like that now.

Since that significant day, life was never the same. I was never again alone and didn't know or understand what it was, or how to explain it to anyone, so I kept silent. Certainly, there was no need to start bringing up the energies and voices I was hearing again. It didn't go well during my childhood, and certainly it was not going to go over well with my husband and in-laws. I tried to be as normal as possible, even though nothing about me felt normal.

As a little girl, I always felt different because of the type of family I came from, because of the dysfunction within the home that no one outside knew about, and because I heard and felt things that no one understood. I felt alone all the time. Ever since the accident with Matthew, I never felt the same again. I tried to live my life as normal as possible: family, friends, fun, making memories, yet no one else felt, heard, or saw the things I was experiencing. It was me living life again in a weird way. *Here we go again...* I would think. The *you're different* feeling from childhood came back. I didn't realize then that I was being guided, watched, prepped, for something far greater down the line. I could not have known then or comprehended the change of direction my life would later take, or the incredible experiences I would be given the opportunity to be part of. For now, I was living life with *something* right beside me, always.

A year later, our amazing daughter, Christina was born. After she was born, they took her away to clean up and check over. The next time they rolled her into my hospital room, I remember saying with a huge smile, "There she is," as if we were again being reunited after not seeing one another for lifetimes. Christina is a very old soul. She was always very sweet, sensitive, and picked up on everyone's emotions around her. She is a true empath.

Empaths are people who have the ability to pick up the emotions of other individuals. Have you ever been around a co-worker or friend and just *felt* their sadness? Or walked into a room after two people had an argument several hours before, but you could just pick up the heaviness in the room? That's an empath. Being an empath is difficult, because unless you know how to protect yourself, by meditation and grounding, you are walking into open mine fields wherever you go. That was Christina. Whether with friends, family, or at school, she was always picking up everyone's energy. One moment she was feeling just fine, and in another moment she was somewhere becoming very sad or crying uncontrollably. It was a lot to handle, and since I certainly didn't have a handle on my own empath experiences, there was no way I could help her, so we completely rode the wave of emotions together.

Places and situations that have a large number of people are usually places where empaths can't control the anxiety welling up within them. To this day, I still want to rip my skin off when I visit a mall, sports

Listen to Husbands, Children, or Invisible Forces?

complex, theater, or concert. There is way too much energy surrounding me. I usually end up feeling very anxious beforehand and can't wait to get out as soon as I'm there. To date, I have never stayed for a full music concert or stayed for an entire Broadway show till the last song was played. I can't wait to get out of there.

When I'm in a theater, I usually have my pocketbook and coat ready to go while everyone is clapping at the end of the program. I get very edgy and want to run and get out of that madhouse as soon as possible. The idea of being corralled side-by-side with a large number of people as we inch out of a location makes me tense just thinking about it. Most empaths feel the anxiety in that moment. Anxiety over new experiences, or being in crowds, or even of being enclosed in something like an elevator are usually good indicators of some empath ability. You might be getting nervous about being in certain situations that make no sense to you, but your body is actually picking up energy from those around. That's exactly what empathic energy is—picking up the energy of others around you, and that is what Christina and I have.

As time went on, the marriage began to change, as I began to change. As the Universe began to guide me toward mentors, teachers, or other people with some "ability," I began to take classes to learn more. Meditation classes, workshops on energy, learning about angels, guides, and other beings that surround us always, helping us muddle through this expansive Life experience. I did not know this, but I was being guided by some other force that was helping and assisting all the time. People from all different backgrounds were suddenly falling into my path, and I was taking the next step forward, even though it didn't feel like that at the time. To me, it was just one weird coincidence after another.

I was slowly beginning to change and see life differently. Because of that change, I was gradually becoming another person, and the marriage was now becoming a part of who I "used" to be. Yes, being a mom to two wonderful children was fantastic, but suddenly being a homemaker felt very uninspiring. There was more out there, and I wanted to soak up every bit of learning that I could.

My poor husband was seeing me change right before his eyes, becoming someone different, and couldn't do anything about it. Our relationship began to change, and we began to slowly drift apart. I was looking for something different, that challenged me, made me grow, and he was okay with keeping things as they were, and as we had created our life originally to be. Can't blame him. Sometimes as people change through life, the relationship can either sustain the changes and transform along with them, or the wedge becomes so wide, there is no recovering. For us, it became more of the latter.

I originally was looking for a partner that could provide safety and normalcy, after a lifetime of dysfunction and abuse. He provided that, but there was always this nagging "something" at the back of my head letting me know there was something different for me. I just didn't understand what. And it never had to do with wanting another relationship. It was an inner calling, change, or new direction that I think somewhere deep inside my soul I knew he could not understand or be a part of. I remember one conversation with him where he had a tough time understanding what I was sharing with him about my learning and classes, and he asked me if I had joined a "cult." He just didn't have the understanding of the changes I was going through at that time. There was considerable confusion wanting life to be normal, like everyone else, but knowing deep inside, my life was destined for another path, something far greater than just me.

After nine years of marriage, we separated and divorced. It was

LISTEN TO HUSBANDS, CHILDREN, OR INVISIBLE FORCES?

such a difficult time for us both. The guilt for my children was overwhelming. Not having had normalcy in my childhood, I wanted *only* that for them, and here we were divorcing, and now my children would have the stress of that change in their lives. It was such a difficult period for them to adjust, and for my husband and I to figure out how to make this work for us and for them, with all new rules that no one ever anticipated.

Looking back, because of the transformation that happened within me, I know it could not have all happened if my life had stayed on that marriage trajectory. My path had to change, so I could continue to grow and change. Had we stayed married, my life would have been all about them, my family, and my personal learning and growth could not have happened as they did.

We don't understand that in the moment of growth, we must often say goodbye to those we love. In the moment, it feels like we're being pulled, stretched out of our comfort zone, wondering when the discomfort or pain will subside. We don't realize we are being stretched into a new "us." And, sometimes, that means outgrowing the people we used to want, and outgrowing who we used to be. There is a mourning for losing the ones we love: There is mourning for losing who we used to be.

Just like pizza dough—it has to be kneaded and stretched beyond its original size and structure, so it can become what it's supposed to be: a pizza. When we are being pulled, pushed, strained through life's experiences, we don't realize that, like the pizza, we're being slowly transformed into someone else. We just want the pain to end. That was my life. One painful experience after another, all with the Universe's greater understanding of transforming into something else.

When each wave of hurt, betrayal, or pain would hit, I'd wonder what I did wrong to deserve this. I wasn't seeing the higher picture. A power greater than myself was giving me a tougher skin, was making me stronger by pulling and pushing, so down the road I would become a better version of who I was meant to be—so I would learn the lessons behind the experiences, so I would learn and grow. That is what this whole human experience is about, learning and growing out of the experiences we call to ourselves solely for the purpose of rising and emerging.

We all know the story of the caterpillar turning into the butterfly. That caterpillar has to metamorphose, grow, and develop within its safe cocoon, only to have to push and exert itself out in order to become the beautiful butterfly it's meant to be. That's the butterfly's destiny. Its *history* is to start as a caterpillar; its *destiny* is to become a butterfly. When we are being pushed, prodded, and poked by life, it's the same system of nature, moving us out of our comfortable cocoon, metamorphosing into something unrecognizable and far greater than we could have ever imagined.

Life as a divorced woman raising children on my own was not the easy choice. Oh no. This chapter of my life brought with it more stress, emotionally and financially, working full-time and taking care of the kids. The house was now all my responsibility. Yes, my ex-husband would see the kids and take them on his weekends, but the brunt of the day-to-day was all on my shoulders, as it is for many single parents raising a family. Again, I tried as hard as I could to keep the balance and make things as normal as possible, whatever normal is supposed to be.

Unfortunately, there were overwhelming emotions and triggers I had never dealt with from my dysfunctional childhood, and I could not function when sometimes the daily stresses of life would trigger and anger would well up. I had no coping mechanisms. I was making it day by day, but I sometimes couldn't breathe. The marital home became too much to bear on my own. Being around the energy of that old life made me feel worse about myself. All I kept hearing in my head was *You messed this all up, and you're still not happy; you are the problem.*

And still the voices in my head and the energies around me would let me know they were there. I had no mechanism to tap into them or understand what they wanted. I would feel them around me, but this stage of my life, I also felt more alone than ever. After my ex-husband left the house, the energy of the little spirit girl Maria was around me more and more. She loved when I meditated. She'd come sit by me and just look and watch. She felt so comforting that I enjoyed my daily meditation sessions with her.

Christina was also opening up more and more. One night, when she was about five years old, while I was putting her to bed, she said the "blue lights" were always in the room with her. I'd say, "What lights?" and she'd wiggle her fingers in the air, as if pointing to something above us, saying, "The blue twinkling lights that come at night to watch me." I asked if she was afraid when they would come to visit, and she said, "No, they just hang out and watch me."

I didn't realize then that those were spirits from the other side, watching and protecting her. Sometimes we wake up in the middle of the night and see a light flicker for a second; then it goes away. That is the energy of Spirit, whether it's a loved one on the other side, or some other angelic energy wanting to quickly let us see them, so we know we're not alone. But in our human mind, we dismiss those quick lights because they don't last long, and we can't identify them. An energy, without human form, is letting us know we're not alone.

I met my great friend Laura during this time of transition in my life. She also had a son, Robbie, and daughter, Erin, who were the exact ages of my children. Almost every weekend, we'd spend time together, and the kids bonded as well. Many weekends having barbecues by the pool, as they played, she and I would discuss our lives, and compare our single lives as parents. She was such a source of fun, laughter, and wisdom. We laughed and howled like hyenas whenever we were together! And because we shared that bond of being newly divorced women raising children, we connected on a very deep soul level. She became my best friend and helped me learn a great deal about myself. I could never thank her enough for her friendship, understanding, and encouragement during that time.

Laura also understood all the changes emotionally that I was going through and encouraged me to learn more about spirituality and what this gift was that I had. Whatever I learned, I shared with her. We were there to help support each other during this phase of our lives, and she would reassure and cheer me on with every step I took. We think that soulmates are supposed to be our relationship partners in life. Actually, a soulmate is someone that comes into our lives with huge karmic lessons to help us learn and grow—someone we have been attached to in another life that is here for more learning and growth in this one. Laura was definitely a soulmate for me. We would joke with one another that our connection was effortless; we just had the wrong body parts for each other; otherwise we would have become partners for sure! How we would laugh and howl when we'd say that to one another.

I definitely felt like I had known her in another life, and the circumstances of our paths crossing would have never allowed us to meet prior. It was only at this time of sharing single motherhood together that we were ready to help be the pillars of support that we were to one another. Because she fanned the flame of my desire to learn and grow, and cheer me on, she helped push me in that direction. She has been a true, dear friend, and even though life was tough during those years, we were there in friendship and support for one another.

During this time, the need to move out of that marital home became stronger and stronger. I just energetically could not stay there any longer. In hindsight, financially I should have stayed in that house, paid it off like I would have within ten more years, and set myself up financially in a better place for my future, but oh well, this was one of those life lessons stretching me out of my comfort zone. Something within me just kept saying, get out of this house. Plus taking care of the pool, raking the large back yard, shoveling in the winter, just became too much. The size of the home was more than I could handle working full-time, taking care of kids, and just keeping my head above water.

I found a smaller three-bedroom ranch within the same school district. It was bad enough my children were having a tougher life dealing with divorced parents; I could not take them away from the friends and stability of school as well. It was a quaint home that needed a lot of work. When I showed it to my sister and mother, before purchasing, they walked around silent throughout the house. I would be smiling, and their faces were somber. I was coming from a newly remodeled five-bedroom house with a large property and built-in pool, and going into this a home that was very old and in need of serious updating.

I distinctly remember standing at the end of the driveway, after we had taken a tour of the house, and talking about it with my mom. She had a blank look on her face. When my sister arrived a few minutes later, she said to her in Italian, "Talk to her, because she's gone crazy wanting this house."

I excitedly turned to my sister and said, "Isn't it awesome?"

And her response was, "Are you f---ing kidding me?"

It didn't matter. They didn't understand, again. This house was calling me, and I could see past all the cosmetic changes that needed to be made.

It was a lovely ranch-style home and I started by opening up the walls leading down to the basement. As that was being remodeled for the kids, my objective was to make it feel like a second floor to the house. I was knocking down the walls to give this home a very open, airy feeling. One day, after cleaning out a closet in the basement, I found a folded United States flag, in a triangle as they do to present to the family upon a veteran's passing, along with a beige toolbox that had all sorts of medals and pictures. Apparently they belonged to someone in the house. I thought, *Okay, someday soon, you have to find the little old lady you bought the house from and send this to her.* Certainly it was not a priority at that time.

After moving into that home, and starting the remodeling projects, weird things began to happen. I would hear footsteps at night on the hallway wood floors going down to the bedrooms. I would dismiss it: I must be going crazy. Some nights, I would hear a dog walking down the hallway to my bedroom, hear its nails on the wood floor and the dangling of dog tags, and I would get scared. We had no dog, but I noticed a doggie door in the original door of the house when I purchased it. Could they have had a dog?

In the process of getting to know the neighbors, especially my neighbor Joanne across the street, I'd speak to her about these occurrences as we stood at the school bus stop each morning. I'd ask questions about the house, who lived in it. She said, yes they used to have a large German Shepherd. *Hmm, strange coincidence*, I'd think. *Alright, let it go, you're going nuts.* Then at night I would hear the sound of heavy work boots running down the basement stairs. Remember, all the walls were torn down, and it was a small house. If there was noise on one side of the house, I would definitely hear it, especially the sound of work boots running down the wood stairs to the basement.

This would happen night after night. It got to the point, when it was daytime, I'd talk to myself, like *You're crazy for being afraid, what's the big deal, stop being a baby.* But as it got darker out, and I knew nighttime was coming, I would literally get overwhelmingly anxious and out of my mind with fear. It would happen night after night. I remember one night hearing the sound of these footsteps running down the stairs, and I shot out of bed, went to the top of the stairs and screamed at the top of my lungs, "Whoever you are, get the f--- out of my house!" I was shaking and terrified the kids would hear and wake up scared. Thank God, they didn't.

The worst experience in that house was one night I was sleeping in bed, and it felt like someone leaned in to lie down in bed next to me. I could see the depression in the top of the comforter. Remember my experience as a child when seeing a depression in my bed while I was doing homework? Well, this was ten times worse. I shot out of bed, screaming down the hallway, my heart beating out of my chest, the hairs at the back of my neck standing straight up. What was going on? I was panicked and out of my mind with fear. The next day, at the bus stop, I asked, "Who died in that house?" And my neighbor Joanne said the husband, Chickie, was ill and passed in the house. I asked what kind of work he did. Her response was he was in construction and was an electrician. Now the work boots sound running down the stairs made sense. It was him.

I kept thinking to myself, *Why is this happening?* and I would suddenly get a picture in my mind of that flag and toolbox of memorabilia in the basement. Wait…was the husband Chickie telling me this was his stuff and he wanted it returned to his family? That couldn't be. But the more that these events happened over and over again, and the more I asked why, I would always get the picture in my mind of the stuff left behind. Then I would hear within my head *Return my things*. It was such a clear feeling and message. The man's spirit was still there, and he wanted his items returned.

I contacted my closing attorney, told him I needed to return items to the seller of the home, and could I have her new address. I shipped that stuff out right away. Wouldn't you know it, I never again heard any noises, steps, dog walking. Nothing. It was like that spirit was letting me know he was not leaving and would make things very uncomfortable for me unless the items were returned to his wife. Whatever the reason was, I was listening. I don't think my family really understood me explaining this story. It was always received with an "Oh yeah, that's interesting" kind of feeling. Once I shipped his items out, the energy of the home changed. It felt lighter, happier, and I was making it my sanctuary.

As my life progressed, in 2000, my first nephew AJ was born. At ten days old, the doctors detected a heart murmur through ultrasound. He had all four veins of his heart pumping to the same side, so oxygen was not flowing throughout his body, as it should. At twenty-four days old, it became crucial for him to have open-heart surgery in order to save his life. Such a major operation, for such a little soul. I remember the entire family being in the waiting room, while this poor little baby was in surgery. As I sat and prayed for him, as we all were praying, I kept getting this overwhelming feeling of peace, and comfort. Spirit was already showing me little angels hovering above his operating table, watching and guiding the surgeon's hands. They appeared to be about a hundred little cherubs, all floating above in the surgery room, watching and protecting. I had no idea if any of this was actually happening,

Listen to Husbands, Children, or Invisible Forces?

if I was making it up in my head, or if AJ would even survive surgery. Our family had never been through anything like this before. But the unmistakable vision of seeing them all floating above, like cherubs of light, comforted me. Of course, I told my sister, and she smiled and I know she *wanted* to believe me, but fear was consuming her heart and mind.

That vision was the first *prophecy* of the future I had ever been shown by Spirit. I had never been given information about the future before, but in that moment, it was being made clear to me that he would survive and be okay. *OK*. It was a very weird feeling in such a tremendously terrifying moment, to feel that energy of peace, love and comfort. I just kept praying away and *trusting*. Many hours later, AJ was in recovery, and on his way to healing and becoming a healthy boy. Today, he is in college, studying medicine. All the trials and tribulations he endured during his childhood with doctor's appointments to make sure his heart was healing properly gave him an interest in and affinity for medicine. Spirit was guiding this soul and his path, right from day one, as they are always trying to guide every one of us as well.

As we look back on our own lives, we can remember those moments when the breath was knocked out of our body, wondering how we are ever going to get out of this pain. It is in those moments that the winds of energy are still flowing around us, trying to give us the peace and comfort to get through our obstacle. That energy is never far from us but allows us to go through our storms in order to learn and *trust*. Yes, I said it, *trust*! It is our job, on this human plane, to let go, accept what is, and trust.

My father was diagnosed with terminal cancer in 2003, and four months after diagnosis, the cancer had spread throughout his body and after a short hospital stay, he was placed in home hospice care.

His illness did not scare me; because of our estranged relationship, it became more about helping my mother get through this experience. Helping to communicate with doctors, filling out papers, talking to social workers, hospice care, and helping her come to grips that he was not going to get better, that these were his final days. There was no emotion for me, at all. It was all robotic actions. I turned forty, and the next day, he passed.

I remember getting the phone call telling me about my father's death when I was at work. My sister, who had gone to my mother's house that morning, called to let me know he had just passed. I remember hanging up the phone, allowing myself to cry for a few short minutes, and then collected myself to go there. When I arrived, he was in the middle of the living room, in his hospital bed, with my mother and sister around him. I remember walking over to his body, leaning over him, and whispering, "I hope you're at peace, and our karma together is over. Our lessons are done, and I release your soul." I had no idea where that came from, or even why I was saying those words. What I had learned so far, in my very limited studies of spirituality, was that our souls agree and are bound by soul contracts in heaven before we arrive. We select our parents, siblings, partners, children that we will incarnate with on this Earth. This is all orchestrated for us, by our souls and our master teacher spirits, to learn very specific lessons in life. This is part of the "learning" we go through here on Earth.

Now, the issue is, we agree on the other side to learn from one another as to what our roles and lessons will be once we incarnate on Earth. However, once we arrive here, all consciousness of those lessons is wiped away, and we focus only on the experience, the person, the hurt, the betrayal. We focus on the part we could not change, but that is not where the focus should be. It should be on the *lesson* behind the experience. *What are we supposed to learn* from each experience we

Listen to Husbands, Children, or Invisible Forces?

encounter? If we don't learn the lesson in that moment, our soul will attract to us another person, or experience to help us learn the same lesson. This is why most of us can look back on our lives and see a similar pattern repeating. If you can say "Why does this keep happening to me?" it's probably a lesson you have not learned that is now showing up over and over. Again, everything is being orchestrated for our higher good and learning here. Spirit, and the Universal energy is there to assist us, not only with learning the lesson behind the experience, but also in helping us get *through* the lesson, if we open up and allow Spirit to guide us.

So there I was, leaning over my father's body, whispering those words to him. I wanted whatever karma or lessons we had to learn from one another to be done. I did not want to come back to another life and have to relive them over again. I wanted to cut the karma cords from him, so I could move on. I wanted his life on this Earth and our connection to be *history*!

Little did I understand then, that you can't just declare a karmic connection to be over with someone. I later realized I would attract many souls that would again assist in helping to teach me about my self-worth, self-love, and self-acceptance—everything I hadn't learned from my dad. It was going to be a very long, hard road of dealing with individuals, looking and acting different from my father, but showing up under stressful experiences, to help me learn these lessons over and over again. I had not learned the lesson; I was just simply saying I released *him* of all karma and energy. I could not understand in that moment that my learning was still continuing and would for quite a long while.

I was that caterpillar. I was changing and morphing and trying but still had a very, very long way to go. People were pulled in and out of my life and I was still trying to figure it all out. Having lost a marriage felt devastating despite knowing it was time to move on and I was juggling way too many things at one time. But somehow, Spirit kept pushing me. My lessons were in actuality only beginning and trying to open me up, and *trust* became a repeated theme.

In many ways I was still the child reacting to those around me, only stuck in an adult life with very adult responsibilities. But thank goodness, Spirit was growing me another way. I kept finding strength from somewhere even though I was still getting knocked down and still confused about many things. That rebel within me wasn't going down any time soon! It's a good thing, because Spirit hadn't yet forced me through the hardest of letting-go lessons in my life.

I had not even remotely realized that Spirit can bring you through trauma and teach you how unconditionally loved you truly are, despite what it looks like, when you have just painfully released some history; good or bad. I had not realized how Spirit was truly there to guide me and change me. Spirit was there to prove that I had to finally believe in this depth of true love and mirror it back to myself if I was ever to find peace. My destiny was really only still in the cocoon stage: I was working on my history.

Chapter Three
FINDING THE ELIXIR: MIXING SPIRIT WITH DAILY LIFE

CURRENT YEARS AND THE "NEW NORMAL"

*Love is the energizing elixir of the universe,
the cause and effect of all harmonies.*

—Unknown

My life really had become a balancing act between who to listen to, who to try to please, who not to disappoint and how to simply make it through another day as a single, divorced mom. I was learning things as quickly as I could, burning both ends of the candle and moving at lightning speed although I felt nothing more than the continual metaphor of being stuck in the mud, in many ways.

As I continued on my journey, there was a force pushing and pulling me toward learning. I wasn't even aware there were winds blowing behind me, putting just the right person in my path, at exactly the right moment. A little bit of unveiling at a time was happening, and my ego was both fighting it and trying to integrate it. Trust was still not something that was even remotely coming easily to me.

While I was living in that beautiful little ranch home, I was told of a medium, Bobbi Allison, who was amazing. She traveled to client homes for readings at that time, and she came to mine for a session. I had *no* idea what she was going to say, or what the reading would be about. Back then, I didn't understand the difference between psychics and mediums. She does both. Sitting at my dining room table, she talked about my deceased father being at my home, that he walked around the perimeter of the home, keeping it protected. I honestly didn't care. She validated so many things about him, his personality, our dysfunctional relationship, and kept saying how sorry he was for his actions here on Earth. Again, I didn't care. I was emotionless. I wasn't ready to delve into the damage done and the wounds within me. If I could put him out of my mind and emotions, then I was good.

During that reading, she was wonderfully comforting and loving, impeccably on point, and appeared to have a lot of knowledge about Spirit and why we were here on Earth. She told me that one day I would be doing mediumship work. I responded, "You're crazy; never going to happen." Although, I did share with her that I was getting very hot, electric pulses in the palms of my hands. It would feel as if my palms were vibrating. Whenever I'd place my hands on someone, they would always comment how hot to the touch my hands were. To me, they just felt like they were tingling with electricity. She suggested

Finding the Elixir: Mixing Spirit with Daily Life

I start to open my mind and see what I could learn about healing, energy, Spirit, and what to do with my gift. What I didn't understand then was these were already the whispers and winds of Spirit blowing me toward many mentors and teachers that would help me along this journey of learning.

Pat Longo was the first teacher that Bobbi recommended I work with. I attended different classes and bonded with others interested in Spirit, energy, and how the universe works. I learned about the energy centers in our body, the energy of those around us, how to meditate, how to ground and to protect ourselves. Some of the students I met early on were already learning how to read other people. I was learning how to harness the energy in my hands, and how to focus and push out healing energy to others. I was growing and learning each step of the way with everyone I met. I had no idea where I was headed, I just took these small baby steps and *trusted*—well, as much as I was capable of trusting! I stayed focused and in classes for about two years, but then something was prompting me to move forward. I had no idea where or how, but similar to my marriage, some force was making me feel like I needed to move forward onto something else.

So, my life moved along. I was working, learning, raising children, and trying to integrate my different worlds, and on most days just trying to get through 24 hours praying that something better lay ahead for me. Not that I didn't enjoy being a mom. I loved my children dearly, but still felt there might be something more. And during the next phase of juggling, this time it involved a new man, a new family, and still seeking more in the spiritual world.

The next chapter of my life begins with new love. Finally, after dating for many years, and finding all types of frogs that I was hoping to kiss and turn into princes, my last "If this one doesn't work out, I'm done dating" was with my Anthony. There was something different about him. And because I had never introduced anyone to my children while I was single, it felt safe to do this with him. He also had two children, the same ages as mine. Anthony was then fourteen and Christina, ten. After dating for a while, we introduced all four children together, and we suddenly created this *Brady Bunch* feeling.

Life felt very secure, comforting, and hopeful. I felt most at peace during those early years. All the pieces of my life's puzzle seemed to be coming together. He was also starting out anew, and we both wanted to create that loving, family atmosphere. The kids got along extremely well, and we created many, many happy memories together. I remember some time into our relationship, because I was taking the spiritual development classes, I had to at some point fess up to what I was into and what was happening around me. I remember sitting him down to tell him I had something important to share, and he might not understand. He looked very perplexed. Remember, as I was about to open my mouth, the wounded little girl inside me, who was always weird and saw things that other people around her never did, and who was degraded by her father—she was always present, letting me know I was broken and unlovable. And remember when I tried explaining my new spiritual studies to my first husband and he thought it was a "cult"? So I scrunched my face and reluctantly shared that I was studying spirituality and had healing ability. At that time, the concept of mediumship had not taken root. He looked back at me, perplexed, smiled, and said … "And?" It was like I had said to him "I'm going to make hamburgers instead of steak tonight," as I sat looking for some kind of awkward response from him. He accepted it wholeheartedly and was not weirded out at all. *Phew*, that was a load off my chest!

I had noticed there were these little telltale signs I was picking up about him, of his own gifts. He is extremely intuitive. I don't even have to show outwardly something is wrong. When I try to hide something isn't right, he'll pick it up and say, "What's wrong? Your energy just shifted." Many times I'd respond with, "No, nothing is wrong," and he'd look at me sideways, like he knew I wasn't being honest. No one likes to be read, and it would make me feel uncomfortable to have someone so attuned.

I remember once, in our early years of dating, letting him know that I felt he was also gifted, and could sense Spirit. He just looked at me and laughed. A big 6'2" Italian guy, a woodworker by trade, and I was telling him he had the gift? But intuitively, I could pick up he had something. One memory I have is we were sitting on my living room couch one evening, just chatting, and he suddenly said, "I just saw a man standing in the doorway to the den." I asked him what the man looked like, and he described my father to a "T." He had never met my father, and because I didn't have a great relationship with him, there were no pictures in the house in memory of him. It was weird how he described the dark, full head of hair, the flannel shirt he would always wear, and the cigarette sticking out of the side of his mouth, with his one eye squinted so as not to let the smoke go into it. This was even before I started to see Spirit, so the fact he validated my father was there was, uh, *creepy*. That just solidified for me that this man did have something special about him that even *he* wasn't aware of.

As our relationship grew stronger, we decided to purchase a house together, because the tiny little three-bedroom ranch, which my two children and I were so very comfortable in, became too restrictive with three more people added to the household. That small house I purchased after my divorce had turned into a home and had transformed with me, and I hated letting it go. But there was this push again, to move forward. I fought against that tide. Part of me understood this change would be for the better; part of me hated letting go of the comfort. That's what happens to us when we're upon the brink of change.

Change. Yes, we truly all hate it. We don't want to let go of our comfort, yet the tide and winds are pushing us in a direction too foreign for us to comprehend, and as a result, we resist and fight it. I was afraid and terrified of making a mistake. How many times have we each needed to make a change in our lives but were terrified that if we did so, would we regret it? I kicked, clawed, screamed, and cried my way through that change. My heart literally was attached to that small house. Even months and years after moving out, I would drive by the old house, slowly stalking it, and if the kids were with me, I'd ask over and over again, "Are you okay leaving that house?" The kids were unfazed by it, but for me, leaving was extremely traumatic.

A bigger, fancier new house with bedrooms for everyone, came with a bigger, fancier mortgage. The pressure of realizing we may have bitten off more than we could chew was overwhelming. I had crunched all the numbers a thousand times before, and everything worked out on paper, and I thought we were safe making the move. I wasn't in a place of trust then. I had to control everything in my life.

For many months, we crunched numbers, went over everything the new house would cost, and everything seemed fine. It was like we were being guided, or pushed in that direction, and all seemed well. Once we got into the house, the realization that something had gone wrong with the numbers was frightening. Yet I knew in my gut, as much as I didn't love this new house as much as my last little gem, we were supposed to be here for some reason, whether the numbers worked or not. With fixing up the basement to create a nice apartment, we ended up renting it out, to assist with the mortgage.

I was working in corporate at the time, taking the workshops and classes, learning and growing. Once the urge or nudge came from Spirit to start doing those practice readings, I was terrified but began asking friends if they knew anyone who would like to sit with a practicing medium—no expectations, please—and I'd go to their homes, very much like my friend Bobbi Allison had done for me all those years ago.

I wish I could say my confidence grew as the readings did, but the reality is, that broken little girl within me had a huge voice. She always reminded me of what I *couldn't* do. The fear of being seen as a fake was huge. With each reading, with each referral that came my way all on its own, Spirit was breathing life into something I had no capacity to see yet.

Many times we are given obstacles, opportunities, experiences that make us scratch our heads and say, "Why is this happening?" whether it's positive or negative. But the reality is, Spirit is seeing the highest picture possible for us. Whether it's a positive experience that falls in our laps and we're overjoyed, or a heartbreak or loss that brings us to our knees, Spirit is assisting from the higher perspective. We're not supposed to know all the answers at one time, because we would not be able to comprehend the entire picture. We are given these short little breaths that blow a particular experience our way ... *for our highest good.*

I wish I could say that my relationship with Anthony was always sunshine and roses, but the fact is, if we are here on Earth learning—there are going to be bumps in the road. We are the perfect pair to learn from each other. He had a stronger desire to always have me around; my nature was, and is to some extent to this day, to have more freedom, and independence. And, add to life some overwhelming stresses, and I want to bolt. There were moments when I felt perhaps we were the wrong match for the other. Between taking care of a family, working a 60-plus hour corporate job, the fear of finances looming over my head, trying to carve out time for my classes, learning, and practicing readings, I never felt I was giving him much of me. And I know he felt I wasn't giving much to him. Trust me, we fought, and sometimes I'm ashamed to say, the words got ugly. It was all a learning experience. As much as I felt controlled by his need to have me around a lot, it was my childhood tapes translating his actions as control and someone telling me what to do. That was not what he was doing, but he didn't get into a relationship to spend a lot of time alone. And I don't blame him. By the way, I call Anthony my husband, and he calls me his wife. Even though we are not legally married, we are a committed couple and have created a home and family together.

So, once actual, real, paying clients were coming my way, and I began doing groups, and still taking classes to learn and absorb more, it felt like I was rarely home. During the week I would work my day job, perhaps see clients in the evenings twice a week, and weekends were consumed with readings and groups. I had a hard time saying no to people and drawing healthy boundaries. I felt like I had to accommodate anyone who wanted readings. All this interest created more client referrals, and me pushing myself to do more readings. The wheel never stopped. This caused our arguing to escalate, which caused my fear and stress level to heighten, and all I could think of was running. Thank God I never did, but when you're in those moments of *I can't take another minute of this discomfort*, it was the only tool I knew that would alleviate the inner hurt. Little me was always screaming to run away.

Again, thank God I didn't run away! He is my biggest cheerleader. How the hell could I have gotten through all the changes in my life, if he hadn't been the anchor in the storms? Through the adversity, through the arguing, there was tremendous love. Another soulmate. And as much as I wanted to bolt at times, something was making me

Finding the Elixir: Mixing Spirit with Daily Life

stay. Spirit had a much bigger picture for us both, but how can you understand that as you're going through the discomfort and learning?

We were *working* toward finding a way, me *working* on my gift, him *working*, blending our families, both *working* (because life is work) and sure enough, if life hadn't been hard enough, two years into our relationship, Anthony's son, Anthony, was diagnosed with Leukemia at sixteen. What started out as a drunken night at a Junior Prom party, resulted in him passing out, being taken to the hospital for observation, routine blood work being done, and him opening his eyes in the hospital with his mother and father looking down at him.

Anthony had no clue what had happened. A week later, more blood work was done, and the diagnosis was given of ALL (Acute Lymphoblastic Leukemia). The only good news was that we were told this form of cancer had a positive 80% success rate with treatment. As his parents, we tried to stay hopeful, but someone has to make up that 20% and we were always afraid to go there. We were terrified beyond belief. But Anthony was strong, and went through his chemo treatments, and after a month of being in the hospital, he was released and received outpatient chemo treatments for a few years.

We had dodged the bullet, and teenage Anthony could rebuild his life again. He was on the road to recovery. When he was finally diagnosed in remission, we thought the nightmare was finally over. He had suffered too much, yet all we could do was stand beside him, powerless, watching him go through treatment. If you've ever had a child that is ill, the feeling of helplessness is overwhelming. It's an out-of-body experience where you don't know what to do next, or how to control the situation.

We're supposed to protect our children at all costs, right? How do we even begin to control what is not in our power to change? This was a learning experience in letting go of all the "should haves" in our life and learn to trust the tide. All we had in those awful months was faith and hope, and sometimes we had nothing but just knew we had to look like we were getting through it. Technically, Anthony got himself through it, because even though in life it didn't look like he was very strong or had a direction that he wanted to go in, none of us could have withstood what this poor soul went through. None of us. He did what was expected of him, he tried not to complain, he just wanted everything over so he could begin his life again. And that's exactly what this young man did. He fought the good fight and got himself in remission—a weight lifted off our hearts and minds. We were very thankful and grateful for every single event in our lives, because it meant we could still celebrate it with him.

As we settled into this new, larger home, and began renovating it to our liking, we'd notice there were always "things" happening in the house. Movement, shadows, noise. There was always something going on. My husband would stand in our kitchen, looking into the great room, and would see a young girl sitting on top of our armchair; then as soon as she knew she was spotted, she'd jump off and disappear out of sight. I never see spirits in this house; I only feel them. My husband actually *sees* them. He says there is frequently this woman who sits in one of our armchairs in the great room. He says she looks like an older woman that is somehow attached to the house. Maybe someone that lived here? Who knows? He sees her, I feel her energy in the room, but she never bothers me. So here we go again with spirits occupying the house and letting us know there are more than just the six of us living there. They may be sharing the house with us, but unlike the previous home, there is nothing fearful, scary, or awkward about the situation, so far.

One night, my husband was going upstairs to go to bed, and as he was climbing the stairs, he suddenly felt a lot of energy in the hallway upstairs. Remember, even though he says he doesn't have this gift, trust me, he does. As he got to the top of the stair landing, he called down to say, "Gina, you better tell who's ever up here and partying that I have to get to bed, because they're making a ruckus and I have work early tomorrow morning."

I remember replying from downstairs, "They're bothering you, so you tell them."

He's not a fearful man, and very open to Spirit, but he didn't understand he has a similar gift. That makes perfect sense. Spirit had paired me with someone who understands. Had this been my first husband, it would have been much more difficult for him to understand and appreciate this gift, or the teachings of the other side. It just wasn't in his DNA. My husband, Anthony, however, is different.

One night, after my daughter Christina left for at college, Anthony had been snoring for several nights, so I begged him to please go sleep in Christina's room so I could get some rest. Man, was her bedroom filled with energy. He told me the next day, that he tried hard to get to sleep, but kept feeling something or someone in that room. He said it was the energy of a little girl about five years old, and the little child was in the corner of the room and started giggling and he heard her say, "Hehehe, Daddy's sleeping," and begin to chuckle. He said the hairs on the back of his neck stood up straight. This is a man that goes to every scary movie with his daughter when they come out, and when he returns home and I ask how it went, his response is always the same: "Not scary." For him to be literally creeped out by the energy he was feeling in that room overwhelmed me.

On those nights that my husband is snoring exceedingly loud, and I can't take it, Christina's room is the only one available to sleep in. So one night, it was my turn to bunk there. Each time, I would toss and turn and still felt that same need to cover my head with the bed sheet, as I had done as a child in my parent's home. Sheesh, this house and bedrooms had activity too? It felt like wherever I went, Spirit activity followed me!

Even our golden retriever, Jojo, came to us in the house, after we euthanized him following a short battle with cancer. The day that I had taken him to the vet was excruciating. He could barely breathe for days, and I kept speaking to his soul, begging him to please pass on his own, because there was no way I could handle putting him down. I begged. Each day, I'd come downstairs and his breath was laboring. The veterinarian had said it would only be a few short days before it was time to let him go. And he was right. That Sunday, I knew he couldn't suffer any longer. I took Jojo to the vet, bawling my eyes out, and held him, and cried in agony, apologizing for his suffering, and thanking him for being such an amazing dog. He peacefully passed in my arms.

I had never had to put a dog to sleep. It was gut-wrenching. I could barely breathe. My little boy was gone after only eight years. This wasn't supposed to be. When I returned home, I collected myself for a bit, and sat on our front porch. Thinking of him, sobbing uncontrollably, I suddenly heard a "thud," the same sound he would make when he would plop his body onto the porch floor. I stopped crying immediately to hear if that sound was correct. I remember talking to him in my head, asking, "Is that really you?" And I heard the "thud" again. That was the first sign he showed us that he was not physically there with us, but his spirit was back in the house. Many times and years later, we would have the sliding door to our deck open, as we were going in and out to barbecue or spend time out there, and both Anthony and I would see his shadow, for a split second, running through the door. He was letting us know "I'm here, and I'm okay."

FINDING THE ELIXIR: MIXING SPIRIT WITH DAILY LIFE

Many times we "think" we see a shadow, or our loved one's face appear for a quick second, and we question was that really them. But because the vision doesn't stay very long, we discount it, as if we are making it up in our heads. Spirit has to create that vision for us, and it takes a tremendous amount of energy for them to do so. Which is why they can show us something for only a split second. If we're not careful, we're seeing the vision and discounting it as false. We're so conditioned as humans to *see* before we *believe*. If we can't see something in its entirety, we disregard it, and make sense of it by calling it a "coincidence." Every time you come across a coincidence, that is Spirit acknowledging you are seeing, feeling on another dimension, and they are right there beside you.

Well, once again I felt Spirit tugging at me. After years of dealing with our son Anthony's diagnosis of leukemia, and that storm calming, we had a bit of a breather in our lives. The urge and pull to go back to spiritual learning became even stronger. However, Spirit was pushing me in another direction. I remembered my reading all those years before with Bobbi and wanted to start taking classes for intuitive development as well as healing. After all, my hands were always still on fire. I always felt like I wanted to put my hands on someone in some healing capacity.

I had heard about Lorraine Austin, a Reiki Master Teacher on Long Island. She was a registered nurse and teacher who was teaching both Reiki and Intuitive Development classes. I decided to take her first level Reiki I class. When first speaking to her over the phone, and going over my background a bit, it turned out she was the same Lorraine that I had taken classes with several years before. We were both shocked and stunned when we realized who the other person was. How *bizarre* was it that after all these years, our paths would be reunited and crossing again.

These connections or re-connections are the weird happenings we label as *coincidence*, when in reality, it's Spirit shifting our sails in a particular direction. Of all the people for me to research about and look into as a potential teacher, it happened to be her? And she lived two towns over. Weird! She was an amazing teacher, so knowledgeable, kind, and had absolutely no ego or agenda. I learned so much from her. Reiki is a stress reduction and relaxation technique that promotes the body's natural ability to heal itself. It works off of the energy channels within our body that become stuck or diseased over time. Reiki was originated in Japan in the mid-1800s by a Japanese born Buddhist monk, Dr. Mikao Usui, and was later brought to the United States via Mrs. Takata. She lived in Hawaii, was of Japanese descent, and traveled to Japan to begin learning the principles of Reiki for her own healing.

Reiki is a natural and gentle "hands-on" healing art that helps the body heal on all levels – physical, mental, emotional and spiritual. It is done by unraveling stuck energy within the body by placing a practitioner's hands either on the patient's body, or just above the body, moving the trapped energy and allowing the body to get back in balance for it to heal itself. The Reiki practitioner becomes the *vessel* for Light and Universal energy to flow through them, and eventually flows out through their hands into the recipient. This energy and life force flows around us at all times, and through our bodies. The same life force that turns a seed in the ground into a plant, or heals a cut on our skin, or creates and grows a baby within a mother's womb, without us having to assist the process. It is the same energy that flows around us and within us.

Throughout the next few years I began to take more advanced healing classes with Lorraine and became a certified Reiki Master Teacher. I truly believed healing was my path, although I couldn't see far beyond what that would translate into. I noticed changes within me with each

Finding the Elixir: Mixing Spirit with Daily Life

level of attunements given (energetic openings) during each stage of Reiki. Something was shifting within me. Changes were happening; I felt like something was *opening up*. While taking these Reiki courses, I was also guided to take Lorraine's other intuitive development series of classes. I was learning about Spirit, energy, and how to channel that energy better not only for the benefit of others, but also for myself. I practiced Reiki healing on myself every day, and meditation became my daily ritual.

Can you see the opening-up pattern for me? First, I started exploring spiritual ideas and expanding my thinking, then I started learning healing, and then with each level of Reiki I started getting mediumship information, as I share next. It is the Reiki and learning spirituality that I credit for opening me up to mediumship, which then started my work doing readings.

With all the learning and classes and work, I finally began to get visions of loved ones on the other side. I would participate in weekly Reiki healing circles, where, as students, we were given the opportunity to practice on one another, and while laying my hands on the recipient, I would get flashes of faces, words, symbols. When we ended the healing session, I would *reluctantly* ask if something I had seen or felt made any sense to them. Every time I got the nerve to say something, it was always met with a resounding *Yes*! There were other students in the classes and healing sessions that were open to sharing images they received. I was envious of their confidence. That was not me. I was still haunted by my childhood, fearful someone would look at me as strange, or that the message relayed wouldn't make any sense and I would be laughed at. It didn't matter that each time I would validate information from a loved one, that it would be met with such appreciation. The very next time it would happen, I would clam up and pray ... *Please, please don't make me share this.*

As time went on, I shared my visions with my teacher Lorraine. She was always there to help guide me further along, help me polish my confidence one step at a time. I slowly had started doing mini-readings for people—at first, short readings for free, because I needed the practice. Slowly, referrals began coming through, and I would again *reluctantly* charge $25, then $30, then $40. Each time I'd raise my fee, it was like a sword going through my gut. I just didn't feel worthy, yet the referrals kept coming in. I had to charge, because these readings were taking me away from my family life. Not only did I have a full-time corporate position during the day, but now I was taking classes *and* doing readings at night. My energy was quickly depleting, so I had to start charging.

Clients were beginning to ask if I did group readings in their homes. Frightened and terrified of this prospect, I turned to Lorraine for guidance, and she willingly set up my first group reading in her office, of 10 people from her list of students whom I didn't know. In that trial, two-hour session moving from person to person, she said I brought through and validated nineteen souls on the other side. During that session, it felt like I was high or on some sort of speed medication. The energy whizzed through my body like electricity.

She was the right teacher for me at that time in my life. As each mentor was brought across my path, I was able to learn and absorb what that individual had been set up for me to learn. Then, just as in a relay race where you hand off the baton to the next individual, the next teacher would suddenly appear (no coincidences!) with their own particular knowledge. It was never of my doing or heading in the direction I wanted. It was always Spirit that gave me the wind at my back to make those changes. And, because I wasn't always a willing participant, they puffed and puffed behind me.

Finding the Elixir: Mixing Spirit with Daily Life

Along the time that I was studying energy, in one of my classes the name of a talented psychic medium, Paul Saladino, popped up. Of course, in a spiritual class, any time we'd hear of someone who was being recommended, we were all dying to see if they were the real deal. I had taken down his name and number and put that piece of paper God knows where. For several years, it was missing. I remembered his name was Paul, but couldn't remember his last name, and back then, the internet was not as savvy as it is today. Looking up "psychic medium" in the Yellow Pages was not a resource.

One day, clearing up some old papers in my endlessly chaotic filing system, I came across a little yellow piece of paper that was folded up several times. Opening it up, I saw his name and number. My heart smiled! I immediately called up to make an appointment. Of course, like everyone else, I was curious about my love life, curious about my children's future, but what I really wanted to hear *still* was *what the heck am I here to do with my life?*

From the moment I walked into Paul's house for a reading, I was excited. He's very on point and also very, very real. If you don't want to hear something about yourself or someone in your life, watch out, because you will hear the truth. Take it or leave it, Paul doesn't waste time, and he is very on point with his readings. From the first meeting with him, I knew deep down inside, *I will be having margaritas with this man someday.* Don't ask me where that came from, but we connected on another soul level. To this day, we still don't know who we were to each other in another life. Maybe siblings? Maybe spouses, but we laugh like crazy with each other all the time.

Once a year, I would treat myself to a reading with him. After several years of seeing him for my annual "psychic adjustment," as I liked to call it, and doing this reading and healing work myself, he reached out and asked to call me for some insight on something. I remember that day. Paul Saladino was calling me to ask me a question! The kids were making rambunctious noise in the house, and I was freaking out. We ended up having a lovely conversation, and I am very happy I was able to be there for him during a very rough patch in his life. I had no idea he even knew of me, let alone to reach out on a personal level. Since that time, we ended up being a part of each other's lives.

Paul is the head of the Soul Brothers/Soul Sisters organization on Long Island, of which my husband is a member. He also does huge seminars to benefit local community charities and children with cancer. A few years into our friendship, he reached out and suggested (very strongly) that I do my own event with another colleague, Laura. I was terrified beyond measure. What could I possibly have to offer anyone? But because the winds of change were blowing behind me again, I *reluctantly* (actually kicking and screaming) created this event with her. We had seventy-five people show up to listen to Laura and I tell our stories, and for me, that was the first time I did readings for such a large audience. Terrified out of my mind and hyperventilating, but I got up there. Then, *something else* took over.

That's how Spirit works. We step up in our lives, and Spirit takes over. To this day, whenever I'm getting up to speak or read in front of hundreds of people, I am frightened and anxiety-ridden. I can't breathe. Again, the wounded little girl is speaking to me, reminding me I'm not worthy of anything, and I'll probably mess this up, as my old tapes from childhood always want to remind me. But I force myself to walk through that fire each time, and once my mouth opens, some other force or energy takes over. It's actually frustrating, because I can hear myself speaking, but it feels like I'm hearing my voice speak someone else's words.

FINDING THE ELIXIR: MIXING SPIRIT WITH DAILY LIFE

When I'm doing seminars or speaking engagements, I usually have no idea what's going to come out next, and I've given up even having an outline, because my brain can't recall a thing I've practiced over and over again. Whenever I get up in front of a large crowd to read for Spirit messages, I always joke to others that instead of several souls coming to me at once, wanting to push through in order to have some Spirits to "open up with" to the crowd, all I hear are the sounds of crickets.

Each time I walk off the stage, my little broken inner child speaks up again and says, *You made no sense, what a waste, you screwed that up.* I walk away thinking I have no business getting up in front of people. My husband always reminds me what a great job I did, how I spoke to the crowd in a way that was endearing and genuine, but he's my partner, he's supposed to say that, right? It wasn't until the last recent seminar that I was invited to participate with Paul Saladino that I perceived something different. He had invited W. Paul Young, author of the bestseller *The Shack* (also adapted into an award-winning movie of the same title) to join the panel of speakers. For the first time, I received a recording of my speech. I was talking about grief, how we all handle it differently, and how our loved ones want to help us communicate with them from the other side. I remember freaking out before it was my time to go up, because each time I'd think of something amazing to say, it would literally slip out of my mind. I couldn't hold a thought to save my life! Over 550 people in that room, and I was going to get up on stage and turn out to be a hot mess! Again, I got up, and something took over. Words came to my brain, I spoke them in my own voice, and had *no* idea what the next sentence was going to be. Again, I came off the stage with the same old tapes running through my brain. *That was crap, you should be embarrassed. Paul Young heard you, and he must be laughing.*

Months later, I received a video of that seminar and I finally watched myself. I was shocked. I could physically see something take over me. My words were fluid, my sentences all made sense. And there was actually a beginning, middle, and end to the speech that was all cohesive. Watching and hearing myself, I actually thought, *This has to have been Spirit talking, because I don't have the capacity to speak that way.* For the first time, it dawned on me there is a force behind each of us that won't let us fall. We think we're going to capsize, but in reality this all-knowing energy won't let us, *if* we let go, trust and believe it to be there. In that moment of stepping on stage and getting mic'd up, I had to step aside and allow Spirit to step in.

Paul Saladino was that next mentor and teacher placed in my path, as I have been talking about. The baton of Spirit was passed to him, to help me get out of my own way and get up in front of large crowds. Had Spirit not driven him to push me out of my comfort zone, I could not do the large speaking engagements I do today. He was the sail that Spirit used to direct my path a certain way. It was no coincidence that I was given his contact information many years back in one class, only to find it hidden amidst papers years later. It is no accident that he was pushed to get me up in front of people speaking and reading for large crowds.

This was all part of the higher picture that I couldn't see for myself. I was looking to know the specifics of my life, how things would work out, and see the bigger picture. Yet Spirit was guiding and blowing me in directions, and across many mentors and teachers, that were there to help direct me to the next level.

There is nothing special about me. Spirit is directing me, as they are directing you, but all too many times, we are looking in the wrong direction, or we're so focused on the overwhelming big picture around us that we forget to see the magical moments of the breeze whispering across our path leading us to the next step. I will talk more about this in Part Four.

I am indebted to each advisor and supporter that crossed my path, at exactly the right moment for my learning. Had they left it up to me, God only knows where I'd be. But remember, Spirit gave the nudge. If I had not taken the painful wheel and kept going full speed ahead, I would not have made it to here. This is why we *must* step up. We can't leave it to others. We have to take control of our lives—not by manipulating others and situations, but by allowing the love of Spirit and Universe to chart our next path, and trusting to take the next step as shown to us.

As you can tell by my story, it is because of each experience and person in our lives that we learn and grow to the next level. We are actually all here to help one another develop. It's up to us to watch the winds shift and change and understand something far greater is coming our way. We just need to smile in the face of that wind, knowing something is happening for our highest good. We need to embrace it, to find that perfect elixir—the mix between Spirit and our lives—and know that if we step up, in the end all hard lessons are there for a purpose and don't simply exist to torture us, as I talk about in Part Three and Part Four.

I truly hope that some of my brutal honesty and true stories will help you understand that life can be tough. I mean really, really tough. But don't they say when the going gets tough, the tough get going? Most days, anyways!

In balancing all of these emotions, the roller-coaster rides of the day or even the moment, I did manage to continue to get directed and truly began to hone my skills. You will read more about this in Part Two as I share with you all the important pieces of information like the differences between a psychic and a medium, who to trust, who to run away from, how my business has evolved, and how to start to open up your mind so that you, too, can receive the gifts the Universe is waiting to give to you. Because the point is, there is one universal law and that is that all goodness, all from Spirit, is for the best and highest good for each of us.

You will hear me talk a lot in the next sections of this book about love. About Universal love, unconditional love, that no matter what, we are *truly* loved and I do mean it. However, I understand that until we succumb to it we are in that roller-coaster battle between who to listen to or try to please, or who hurt us, or how we've been wronged. And the list goes on.

But the lesson I am here to share is that if we stop fighting the undercurrent (which is really ourselves), allow change to happen, and let go, we will find that magical blend, the elixir of life which is *Love* from the Universe. It is what harmonizes us. It is what picks us up when we don't have an ounce of energy left. It's what holds us when we think we are alone, and it is what will bring us through the greatest pain and suffering any human should ever have to endure. Hang on, because Spirit has a lot of love still to share with you, and as one of their messengers, I assure you the ride has only just begun!

Part Two

Knowledge and Knowingness Equal Enlightenment

The Tool for Anchoring Your Life Voyage

*Awakening is not changing who you are,
but discarding who you are not.*

—Deepak Chopra

Since the beginning of time there is one thing that we as human beings, Homo sapiens (physical bodies with the ability to consciously think), have in common, and that is that somewhere in our thought process there is the ability to think beyond our five senses and use reason to determine our next steps—or at least try to. We are able to think about past and present and even dream of the future. Unlike animals—that absolutely do feel, learn, and have souls and connections after death—we as humans have the ability to take more control over our own destinies and definitely have the ability to choose which circumstance, with what levels of pain or happiness, we wish to experience over the long haul. And, although you may not believe it this minute, all of this is done through our own free will.

We have the ability to attach thoughts and ideas and throw in a mix of emotions to form "judgments" about our lives and those of people around us. This judgment is not necessarily correct, but it does teach us to look further. Put your hand on a hot stove and get burned—feel the pain—and tell me how many times you are going to purposefully make a point every day of touching that hot burner. As a result, with pain, we are moved into a direction to think, to judge, to determine how to stay away from pain. This is an innate gift.

We are innately gifted with this ability and taught quickly to learn that this getting burned is not good and we should not do it again. This consciousness exists because we are learning what it is like to live in a human body and what to do or not do to make it comfortable and even feel good. Not that we always listen, mind you, because if it comes to a hot fudge sundae that will taste, oh, so good, but spikes our blood sugar through the roof leaving us with diabetes, versus drinking a green juice that heals our body, we often choose the hot fudge sundae. Yes, we've all been there. "I deserve to treat myself," you say. "I just suffered a let-down, or a major loss, or a major illness, or even worse, a death.

I deserve to spoil myself." And you are correct, dear reader, you *do* deserve to treat and love yourself when you are in pain and to do the things that will help you move back to having the will to heal again.

The problem is that as conscious beings, we often move the temporary treat, quick pick-me-up-feel-good into full blown self-sabotage and end up in the end only hurting ourselves. This is not the way it is supposed to be long-term. We are here to nourish, love, spread love, and be loved. That means even loving the bodies we were born into.

When it comes to understanding how humans flourish, how we vibrate, how we grow, the most important lesson is to learn and constantly work to become a living being in knowledge, in knowingness—or as some may say, in enlightenment. That ability, once we accept that it exists, is also innate for us to embrace and is there to help our journey here become far easier to master and enjoy.

To learn to seek and find knowledge will help us heal. Will it take away the pain? That's ridiculous. I don't believe that. *Nothing will bring Johnny back*, you may be thinking, *ever*. Well, the truth is that when knowledge of this incredible guide, or our angels, or Spirit or the true Source are on this journey with us, the time in pain and grief is lessened and a feeling of oneness, *knowingness* of true love does overcome and eventually release the waves of tears and internal tantrums that face us in the first stages of our loss.

"Then how do I find this knowingness?" you may ask? "How do I find this peace?" It starts, quite simply, by learning that we are not alone, that there is more to us than just a body and that we are all connected to our loved ones and animals after death. If you knew you could talk to Johnny to learn what happened, or why they left you, or see how much fun you really had while you were with them, versus focusing on the moment of death, don't you think you would heal more quickly?

There are now actual sociological studies that prove that the term of grieving, which is so different for all of us, is lessened when a person can put a spiritual belief and understanding, knowingness, behind the purpose of such a tragedy. This is one reason why mediums are becoming more popular and readily accepted. More and more people are acknowledging there is an afterlife, there is a God, a Source, an energy beyond our comprehension and that soul connections continue, sometimes even over many lifetimes.

Now, I'm not telling you to run and just learn anything that is out there—and I'm certainly not telling you to believe a lot of the junk that is spewed on a daily basis on the TV, in ads, on the internet, but I am telling you to explore, check back in with your heart, or maybe even Spirit so you can learn discernment. What is that? That is the ability to determine fact from fiction and determine what is truly good and loving versus what is a set-up or actually harmful and created to hurt your body, your soul, your loved ones. The checking back with your heart is there to protect you, warn you, and even override the lies that our head wants us to believe.

For years we have existed getting "dumbed down" by those in charge like politicians, marketing companies, sometimes religious dogma, sometimes even well-meaning people who feel safer with what they are familiar with versus allowing themselves to grow. They can't move out of their comfort zone to even think of expanding their belief system or realizing they can heal more quickly—physically or even psychologically. Some are even happy just being unhappy.

That is not you. You would not have picked up this book if you wanted to continue living in pain. You are reading this to find a way, to learn how others have made it and to try your best to move forward versus feeling stuck in that moment of insurmountable loss. This is why I am presenting to you the most important and crucial part to your healing process: knowledge. The knowingness that you are never alone. That you are here for a purpose. That your loved ones are still with you—and even constantly sending you messages. That all of you are unique and divine, and that all answers and truths are within you or can be brought to you. The purpose of life is not to live in suffering and misery. It is to live a guided life of unconditional love, health, and even enjoyment.

I am asking you to keep an open mind as I present this material, to understand that I am a true medium, certified, yes, all checked out and validated, and that I am here to do good, to help others and to share my gifts. I am not a "bad witch." I'm not someone whose skills should be hidden. There is nothing evil or sinister about getting help and hearing from your loved ones. There is nothing wrong with discovering they are truly wonderful where they are now (no matter how they died) and that they love you beyond your wildest imagination. The timing may feel painful, but everything in the end is perfect in its purpose and this includes timing.

I am here to show you, teach you, share with you things I fought for years—fighting the inevitable, as I said in Chapter 1—how my work as a medium and how my life as a mom who lost her son has learned to cope and grow and still have the highest hope that tomorrow will be a much better day—that the sun will always rise after the storm, and that there is love in every part of our beings that can never be broken, even when their bodies leave us. I respect and honor Anthony when I honor where we all originated—the Universe—and when I concede it's not my will, but that of God. While learning to trust in what I don't quite understand, I still honor him because that's what each of our loved ones wants us to focus on.

In Part Two, I am going to start with a little history and terminology so that we are speaking on the same wavelength and so that you can start to embrace this knowingness, this knowledge of truth and light and learn that this is a gift within all of us. Now, despite that being true, not all of us decide to exercise it because it may not be the profession or life-calling we choose. We may choose to be that mathematician, that most-needed car mechanic, the nail esthetician, but we all have a connection to Source, to God, and are all guided and watched over by Spirit guides, and yes, even angels. We are so loved that we are constantly being guided.

I will repeat, we are *so* loved that we are *constantly* being guided. But, the first thing that is asked of us is to open our eyes, open our hearts, and open our minds, because only then can we move from pain, grief, misery, misdirection, and continuing to put our hand on that hot burner every day, to a knowledge that we would much rather live without pain and actually live a life full of great meaning, intense love, and immense joy.

Granted, that will not be every day or every moment for *any* of us. I'm not painting a candy-cane life. Life is a very hard dimension to be in, and there are triggers and pains everywhere around us. However, I am saying that if we open up to the truth that our loved ones are with us, that there is purpose and meaning in their lives and even deaths and that understanding the true working of how they (and Universe) communicate with us, it will make our time on Earth much easier, with much less suffering.

Then why, when it comes to emotional pain, do we allow ourselves to dwell there over and over? Why is it the first thought we wake with and the thoughts we go to sleep with? How does it consume every moment of my being and every pain in my heart? Imagine this—what if by just hearing from a loved one you never thought you would hear from again, or seeing a sign, or smelling a smell, or seeing a movie or hearing a phrase, you learn to know that they are with you at that moment? How do you think that would change the way we grieve?

I can tell you, for a fact, it does. If I had not had the privilege of this gift when Anthony was dying, as painful and heartbreaking as every moment still is six months in, I assure you I would be way more of a wreck. I am here to share the incredible news with you, that knowledge is power; knowledge from true love is light and a lightness of being. All I am asking of you is to try to open your mind by allowing yourself to find ways to start to heal and start to allow peace and happiness back into your life.

This is why I call knowledge or knowingness the actual *tool* that will *anchor* your life. While there are many pieces (instruments and learnings) within that create that tool, they make that tool useful and valuable and are all necessary. Once you open your mind to a different way of thinking, a different way of feeling, you will find an automatic movement toward healing and eventually peace. These pieces, these instruments, are knowledge tidbits of truth to help you awaken. I am going to talk you through these pieces. From the very brief history of psychics through the years, the difference between psychics and mediums, who to trust, how to make the best use of their various services, how to break through the concept that we are more than just a body—we are Spirit in body and have access to all forms of information that may not be visible to the naked eye, and how they are there to be tapped if we ask and are open.

I will even walk you through, perhaps for the more advanced, how to help you understand why we come to this Earth, connect with the people we connect with, work through karma the way that we do, what it really is, and how to uncover it in the most basic ways. Most importantly, I will then show you how these new learnings, that make up the tool of knowledge, can actually help you deal with grief.

There are many books and resources that are now available and in my Bibliography I list the ones that helped me immensely. However, at this moment I am revealing, with the pain that I have just again gone through, can relate to you in this moment. Spirit is helping me, along with Anthony, of course, and encouraging me to provide some hard-knock learnings – not necessarily the step by step or 101 instruction manual learnings, but guides, directions, *processes* that you can use to help move you toward releasing the pain.

Will you ever be whole again? Will you ever heal from the death of that child or loved one? Will you ever forget? Will the pain ever truly disappear? The quick answer is no. You may ask, "Why should I even bother?" Because a new level of understanding and appreciation and love and even remembrance of the beautiful moments will start to take hold and eventually override almost all the pain and grief. You will truly move from an individual who exists in heartache and pain in many parts of their lives to one who is more enlightened, more in love with the universe, more in awe of the miracles than you can ever, ever believe. And once you get this deeper understanding, be prepared to change—from the inside out.

I can't wait to take you on this journey and share with you all the amazing angels, Spirits, energy, and things there are to learn as you start to become one with knowingness. Because it is then, and only then, that you anchor yourself with the daily ups and downs from the turbulence of what we call human life. And with this willingness to learn, to hunker down, to anchor, the most amazing whispers from the heavens and your loved ones will blow through your heart to prove that death is *never* final. You are loved unconditionally, and every moment and every being plays a vital role in the universe as part of Source.

Welcome to your awakening!

Chapter Four
Psychic or Medium? Wait, There's a Difference?

If it's the psychic network, why do they need a phone number?

—*Honoring the brilliant* Robin Williams

The struggles we endure today will be the 'good old days' we laugh about tomorrow.

—Aaron Lauritsen

Now that you have read a little bit about my journey in Part One, I hope it is clear that mediums come into their gift from many different walks of life. Mine was a jagged path and one I often tried to avoid because I didn't want to be different or weird. Nonetheless, we all arrive at our gifts through various life learnings, and some people even come from a long generational line that makes them extremely open to Spirit from the youngest of ages. The benefit those individuals have is that while they are learning and growing, their ideas are praised and encouraged, and they are not made to feel alone or different. I did not

Psychic or Medium? Wait, There's a Difference?

have that benefit and when you are told it's time to visit a priest, you know it's time to zip your lips!

Along with us originating from all walks of life, one of the top misconceptions is that *all* psychics are mediums, and that is simply *not* true. The truth is a saying in our industry: All mediums are psychic, but not all psychics are mediums. The difference? Mediums talk specifically with the deceased. That is their gift. Psychics on the other hand, pick up energy around you to discuss past, present, and future probabilities. Some work with Tarot cards, others just sit and read the client's energy. How does this all work? Well, a medium is open to *all* energy around you, picks up the radio wavelength vibrations of your loved ones in Spirit, and is open to the energies dealing with past, present, and possibly future. But as mediums, we are only given the future probabilities *if* Spirit wants to share that information. Which is why if someone asks "*When* will I marry?" sometimes Spirit does not feel the need to give that answer.

Psychics on the other hand, can tell you about your life, but will not be able to connect you to loved ones on the other side. It all works like a radio frequency. We've all listened to the radio stations in our car. Some stations come in very clear, others as we move around, come in more static. As mediums and psychics, each is picking up on a different frequency, and each loved one that comes through to a medium also has their own frequency. You can imagine, while doing a reading and picking up all sorts of energy, how depleting that can be after several readings in a short amount of time!

The difference between psychics and mediums are decisive so this sometimes drives me a little nuts. People throw inaccurate terminology around and it just confuses the public more. I was even recently told about an individual who did a YouTube video and was communicating with dead famous people and she just called herself a psychic. She never clarified she was a medium. I want you to know the difference because as you look for answers in your life, since we are long past the Yellow Pages—you know, those huge five-inch-thick books that list businesses on yellow paper that have now disappeared because we just check the internet and do a search—well, if you are looking for someone who talks with the dead, you are looking for a *medium*!

As an aside, I also joke that I am most definitely a medium because I'm not a predictions kind of person. That is someone more psychic than medium. I can't even predict what I'm going to eat for lunch tomorrow let alone *predict* the outcome of the future of the world! However, I do call myself a *Spirit Medium,* because I am always connecting with Spirit, who will validate certain events in a client's past and present. That is the way they acknowledge they are always with us. I always tell my clients that if you get anything out of the reading with me, it is that your loved ones prove they are always with you. They see every part of your life experiences, as well as validate things you have been thinking of but haven't shared with others. They are *never* far from us!

An exciting and beautiful thing is that through the years the role of mediumship has drastically changed, even in the last twenty years. People are more open than ever to healing and hearing from their loved ones. They are looking to release pain in a very difficult world and most people now believe in a life after death, or at least something spiritual above guiding us.

In 2017, the Rasmussen Report, which is a national telephone and online polling system, quoted that "62% of American Adults believe in life after death. Just 17% do not, but 20% are still unsure if there's an afterlife."[2] This is a huge difference from fifty years ago where the

Psychic or Medium? Wait, There's a Difference?

statistics (although varied from numerous sources) ranged more in the 20% range for people who believed in an afterlife. This is good news for us because it means that people are coming around to the fact that there is more to life than just our physical bodies. It encourages people to think beyond and to ponder what is happening spiritually around us and to confirm that something actually happens after death. It helps us sort through the feeling in our hearts that we really must have a soul and that soul might be connected to others beyond what we can see right this minute. And, in the beauty of the Creator, it definitely helps us in the grieving process when we have that moment of *knowing* or hearing that our loved ones are still with us.

All of this belief in the afterlife is also good for mediums to share their gifts—not that a person has to be receptive or even believe to be helped. Now, for a fun fact relating to whether or not mediums can really talk to the dead, which I assure you we can, "In the U.S., belief in communication with the dead rose dramatically in the 1800s along with the rise of Spiritualism, a religion founded on hoaxed spirit communication by two young sisters in Hydesville, N.Y. Despite the fact that the sisters later admitted they had only been pretending to get messages from the dead, the religion they helped start flourished, claiming more than 8 million adherents by 1900."[3] That is a huge jump in beliefs and although it was started for the wrong reason, it helped people ask questions and seek answers, and like I said, all knowledge is good knowledge, because it helps you seek the truth.

Trance states and séances were all the rage back then. Ever see the movie *Ghost* with Demi Moore where Whoopi Goldberg is pulling a con and pretending to be a table-moving, spirit-possessing hoaxer who surprisingly turns out to be able to communicate with the dead husband played by Patrick Swayze? If you haven't seen it, it will bring a smile to your face! It turns out Whoopi has a real ability to speak to the deceased, and in the end, she helps bring peace and resolution for the characters by helping them communicate from "beyond."

Putting hoaxes and movies aside and talking about the tried and true mediums, by 2005 still only 21% of the population believed that people can actually communicate with the other side[4], the dead. Despite the fact that 61% of people were leaning toward the existence of an afterlife, speaking to deceased loved ones is harder for people to trust. Today it is only really gaining additional popularity because most people who watch TV have now seen John Edward communicate with deceased loved ones, and who hasn't heard of Theresa Caputo in her show *Long Island Medium* as she walks up to strangers or does readings for people where she communicates with those crossed over while shocking even skeptics?

The truth is soothsayers, seers, healers, psychics, and mediums have existed from the beginning of time. Whether it is shamans, or the Oracle of Delphi from 600 BCE, or Daniel and Jesus in Biblical times, or Nostradamus from the 1500s, Baba Vanga from the 1900s, the list goes on. One thing you can count on, other than death and taxes, is the fact that we have *all* questioned at one point in our lives why we are here and what is going to happen in our future!

Seer, sage, soothsayer: These are all words for psychic. They describe an individual who can foretell what is happening around you, as well as the future. They use the energetic aura, or energy fields, to pick up information. This can be past, present, or future, because there is no linear time when it comes to the spiritual universe. The purpose they serve is connected to our humanity, and our desire to always want to know what is going to happen to us in all phases of our lives. And, again I stress that there is no linear time. The sooner we try to wrap our heads around the fact that energy exists in all levels and all time frames

Psychic or Medium? Wait, There's a Difference?

at once, the easier it will be to break the illusion that time is only from birth to death in this body, in this life.

The scary part is that since the beginning of time as conscious beings on Earth, our humanity has been controlled by our ego. This ego puts time in a linear fashion. This ego brings fear. This fear prevents us from staying in the flow of *trust*. This fear from ego causes us to question every move or piece of our lives. Every person, every decision. As humans, it is unfortunately in our DNA not to trust; therefore, wanting the answer to every experience becomes the desire.

Daily, most people's thoughts are focused on "Tell me who I'm going to marry, and when," "Tell me if I'm going to be famous," "Tell me how many children I'm going to have, will I be rich, will I be happy, will I die young … ?" and on and on. We are saying to the Universal Life – I don't trust the process. We are yelling, "I'm afraid I'm always going to be alone, so please give me a ray of sunshine and hope so I can continue praying my life will be better than it is."

We just don't trust the process of Universe. The funny thing is, even if a talented psychic tells you how it is, you pretty much ignore it, because ego isn't ready to hear it. I often say not one psychic was ever able to tell me my future, because I had to find it on my own. Well, back in Chapter Three, you read that Bobbi Allison tried, God bless her, and I just was not ready to hear! And, in my defense, in the end we do all have to determine our own future, our own destiny. We do have free will.

So while psychics are individuals who use the collective energy of the Universe (angels, guides, archangels, etc.) to obtain information from the individual's aura about past, present, and future events, mediums connect directly with your loved ones that have crossed over, to obtain evidential information from their lives, validating specific information that is shared with the client—or as we say, "sitter." Evidential information about your loved ones cannot be made up. Your dad's name is John, he did die of a heart attack, and he left his collection of carved pipes to you. How can a medium make this up or know about it? Some skeptics say they "guess" at it or do cold readings of the person's body. How does someone know about a pipe collection from reading body language? It's ludicrous.

And, while we are clearing up terms, since I am talking about the collective energy of multi-dimensional beings, I call that Spirit and it is neither he nor she. You will see that throughout this book, I reference Spirit as *they* because technically it's a collaborative of many souls, many energies co-mingling. It is not only those collective angelic beings that surround and protect us, but also the energy of your loved ones in Spirit. Everyone and everything works for the Source, together, *and they speak together.*

In the world of mediums, they can even be divided into further categories by the way they communicate, whether it is physically or mentally. There is the physical mediumship where the person actually lets his or her person be taken over by the deceased Spirit and allows them to communicate a message. It's what Whoopi Goldberg was initially faking in her séance scene. This is not to be confused with a "channeler" who may actually "leave their own body," in a sense, and when they return after the communications, may have absolutely no knowledge of what transpired. Some people are familiar with Edgar Cayce, who went into a trance and gave readings to heal people. At the end of the session, he didn't remember anything, but his assistant transcribed all his messages so that letters of instruction could be sent to the sick patients to follow and heal.

Before I divide the talents and differentiate more about the physical and mental delineations of the gift, I want to stress no matter *how* the material comes through, the point is that it is there to help the client validate that their loved ones are right there watching over them—sometimes more than we might want, but in a good way, and with no judgment! In my readings, clients are amazed at the evidential information Spirit shares about their current lives. Remember, this is not about me, *I am just the channel*, so I can't take any credit for the validations that come through! I remember one mother in Spirit that was coming through in a reading, validated a favorite fur coat she had had here on Earth, and how she knew the daughters had cut it up to create and make pillows. The daughters gasped in horror! "OMG," they said, "is she okay with that, or is she pissed?" I reassured them that she was okay with whatever made them happy.

Other Spirits on the other side love to validate how they know their loved ones here sleep with a favorite tee-shirt, wear a specific ring that they describe in full detail, or know of the special ways in which they have been honored. One client has a beautiful nine-year-old son, who had passed in a tragic car accident. The mother was distraught with extreme grief and guilt, because it was an unfortunate freaky accident that happened on her watch. He was her only child. Her son came through in the reading full of energy and love and acknowledged the beautiful lanterns she had lit and released over the ocean in celebration of his birthday. He also asked her to please release any guilt she had over his passing, because he was at peace and loved her very, very much.

Spirit loves to validate the beautiful gardens created in their memory, or how something was planted in their honor. One mother in Spirit even confirmed to her daughter I was reading that all the houseplants she had tended to over the years were dead because the daughter never watered them! I love when clients, upon hearing this kind of information, look up toward the ceiling and say, "Sorry, Mommy." That shows me that even if they don't see specific signs on their own, in their everyday life, that in that moment they feel the energy and presence of their loved one right beside them, enough to actually speak back to them knowing they are in the room with them. That warms my heart every time. To be able to make that connection for them in that moment is not only healing for them, but heartwarming for me.

Another client of mine was shocked to know that his father in Spirit, who had been working on creating a ship replica model before he passed, knew that his son had finished it and was displaying it on their dining room table. At a group reading I was doing at a client's home once, a father Spirit kept showing me sawdust on the dining room and living room floor of the house I was in—the floor covered in sawdust. I couldn't understand what that Spirit was showing me, and I just relayed the information as his father was showing me. Turns out, the father was validating that when his son had purchased the house, the previous owner was using it as an indoor workshop and the entire floor when they walked in had work benches, sawhorses, and was covered in sawdust! That family howled and laughed so hard, because of all the things their father would validate, it was sawdust on the floor? *Yes*! That is how Spirit works. They want to bring up the crazy stuff that nobody could possibly have access to.

Turns out, for that son that I was reading, another Spirit had shown up that he wasn't expecting at all. That happens too, and those are the ones I *really* love. Turns out this younger male soul was validating a gunshot, and his message was, *I don't blame you and please do not have guilt over my passing*. Turns out, the gentleman I was reading for was a retired detective, and over twenty years prior, had critically shot a young man in his mid-twenties in a high chase pursuit. The young man was taken to the ER and later died from complications of that gunshot wound. That detective held such tremendous guilt over that tragedy for all those years. Talk about a validation! The client was beyond shocked that the young man, whom he thought of every day, had come to give him a very healing message.

These are the kind of confirmations that Spirit wants to talk about so you as the client know for sure that it truly is your loved one here with you. After all, how could I know about a fugitive, a gunshot, or a ship that was completed and displayed? Again, it's not me. I'm just the channel, but when it amazes the clients I channel for, it amazes me too! I sit in awe, just as they do! That's why I love my job!

You can see that with mental mediumship, the medium relates what they see in their mind's eye, or feels, or even hears. It is what some people call telepathy. It is here that it is further compartmentalized with what is called clairvoyance (seeing), clairaudience (hearing), clairsentience (physical feeling and emotions), clairsalience (smelling), and clairgustance (taste). For the clairvoyants, it could be seeing a movie in their head, a photograph, an object, a color, anything that the deceased wants to share with the sitter to define who is "talking" or sharing their message.

For clairaudiants, they can hear the person's voice as if the deceased were speaking to them, or it could be a favorite song or music that is played in the background, the sound of a whistle, an advertisement, a phrase that gets the point across. When a Spirit lowers their voice to me or changes their octave and wants me to mimic how they sounded, it's a validation to the client that this is their loved one. And many times the client will remark, "That's exactly how my mother would speak."

For the clairsentients, who work with sensing—emotions, feelings, empathy—their psychic impressions work through the ability to sense the emotions of the loved ones they are reading for. We can feel the pressure of physical pain the deceased carried in their life, as well as sense the happiness of a particular memory, or the pure regret of something that Spirit wants to apologize for that happened in that life. Sometimes for a clairsentient it is even something like a chill, a breeze, seeing a flash of light, or even getting goosebumps! Goosebumps is a big one and sometimes the clients even get them—validation that their loved ones have just moved through them to have their presence known. For some, the first time this happens it can be shocking or even scary, but when you start to accept it, there is a wonderful feeling of awe and love left in your whole being.

Clairsalients use the sense of smell, like a perfume, a flower, a type of food or spice used when cooking, and even tobacco or pipe smoke—something that triggers a memory that then the medium can share to help the sitter recognize who is really coming through with a message. The sense of smell is usually very strong with a medium, which is why it's a strong clair that Spirit loved ones often use. I will even smell burnt popcorn if the Spirit loved one wants to validate that they burned popcorn in the microwave each time! And, just last week I read for a group of women whose mother had passed. She showed me baking something that smelled like Irish soda bread, but to me was spread out in a flat Pyrex dish and looked like flat banana bread. What the heck was this? They validated their mom would always bake her Irish soda bread in a large, flat Pyrex dish and she always cooked it brown like banana bread. You've got to love when you smell great stuff!

The above descriptions of "clairs," as we say, are just terms to help you understand the various aspects of the gift. A lot of mediums have a mix of senses that we get at different times, depending on the experiences we have had in our own lives. This is what helps us comprehend the message and then describe it so we can share it with you.

Believe it or not, there are even those loved ones who work through us with the sense of taste, known as clairgustance. This can be a funny sensation and can even make us hungry! A client whose mother used to make sauce every Sunday for the family will show herself standing at the stove, but then when I ask what she's making, I will taste the actual sauce in my mouth! Or I will taste lasagna and the client will confirm that was her father's favorite food that he couldn't eat toward the end of his life. Another strange example would be tasting pistachio ice cream, which used to be the Spirit's favorite ice cream when they were on this plane. Instead of just showing me a picture of what they are up to, I literally get a "taste" of it!

Again, the Spirit will use the modality of Spiritual language, the various clairs as discussed above, that pertain to the memories of the individual medium. They will extract that memory or sensation from our bodies, memories, or sensations. If we have the memory of the vision, smell, taste, Spirit will use that memory/feeling/sensation to validate things about themselves. They are literally riffling through the "card catalog files" of my brain and body to pull out similar memories so I can interpret them and present them to the client. Spirit is always using the vibrations and energies within our bodies to communicate, because they no longer have a voice or body to communicate with.

One Spirit father energy in a reading for a small group of his family members was showing me the number "8," and then pounding one fist into the other, hitting it hard. He kept showing me this over and over again. I had *no* clue what he was talking about, and I again, explained it exactly as I saw him doing. To me, the number 8 either represents the 8th of a month, or the 8th month of the year (August). That's it.

I said to the clients in the group, "Your father is showing me the number 8, but then pounding one fist into the palm of the other hand really hard, over and over again."

They laughed and said, "Yep, that's Dad. Every time we'd go gambling, he loved his craps table and would say, 'Bet on the hard 8.'"

Because I don't gamble and have no clue how to play craps, Spirit figured out how to get the validation across in a way that I could understand *and* relay to his loved ones. Spirit is *very* creative that way, but they can only use the memories or experiences the medium contains within their memory bank. There is a lot of charade-playing when we're attempting to translate what that Spirit is trying to say!

The next two forms of mental mediumship are not discussed as much but have very important roles. They are claircognizance, or clear knowing, and clairempathy, or clear emotion. When you are claircognizant, you have an inner knowing about something or someone. You just know it. There are no words spoken, your whole body confirms this with the message or information just being there for you. An example would be someone telling you the exact opposite and your brain may try to wrap around the *supposed* truth of what they are saying with *supposed* facts, but your head and your knowingness, your heart, know different and better. Another example would be you and your sister meet the same person, and she says what a great lady she is, and you turn around and say, "Are you *nuts?*" You felt the energy of that person (clairsentience), and something is telling you that person is off (claircognizance).

Many speakers, writers, artists, and inventors naturally use their gifts of claircognizance. As you open up to understanding that Spirit exists to guide you, this will become stronger and you will be able to start listening to your heart more and your mind or ego (or even other people's egos) less. There is even the process many creative people use called automatic writing. This is where you are sitting with a blank piece of paper in front of you, holding a pen or pencil lightly and all of a sudden something comes over you and you are writing away, perhaps even with your eyes closed and often in a different penmanship than your own. For a musician this happens in front of their instrument, like a piano or guitar, and for a painter in front of their canvas or paper. Through the centuries creative artists have even named these moments as from their "Muse," but this very well could be the collective energy of Spirit.

Clairempathy is more about gut feelings, like when two people have had an argument in a room, and the empath comes in hours later and can "sense" something happened. It gets confused with clairsentience a lot. Clairempathy is more a *perception of the feeling*, not the actual feeling, like if you know someone is grieving, you can sense what they are feeling, but you can't actually feel the emotion. Whereas Clairsentients can actually *feel* the raw emotion, heartbreak or anger. With clairempathy, a person can actually psychically tune in to this emotional experience, this "gut" feeling of a person, place or animal. It's a type of telepathy to sense or feel the attitude, emotion, or ailment of another person or entity. An example would be feeling the devastation of a client whose family member just passed away, or sensing an issue or a pain in the medium's knee (not the actual pain itself) which symbolizes the pain your client is carrying in that same spot in their body.

In one reading, a young girl came to me, and we connected to her boyfriend who had passed over. He made me feel the gunshot toward my head, and then suddenly made me feel her horror in that moment. He had been in the military and suffered from severe PTSD (Post-Traumatic Stress Disorder). One day, he couldn't take the mental torture anymore, and in front of her, pulled out his revolver and shot himself in the head. He made me feel her horror, shock, and terror. I couldn't stop crying, as the feeling of what she witnessed went through every fiber of my being. I always ask during a reading that Spirit allow me to only see the emotion, not go through the emotion myself. I need to connect to the clairempathy part of the moment but cannot function in being a clear channeler if I am going *through* the pain of that emotion. However, in that moment, the Spirit actually placed me behind her eyes, and I saw the entire visual, and felt the insanity and terror of that moment. It was too much to bear as I sat there crying, unable to stop. It took a few minutes for me to calm myself down and continue with the session. Spirit rarely gets through to me in that way, but this Spirit was very clear he wanted me to see what she felt, so he could acknowledge the sorrow he had for making her witness this. I felt it, all right.

I think there is a certain bond that you create with the client when they feel someone else finally knows the pain they have been suffering through. You can't fix it, but sometimes just the recognition from another human being, which is more than just sympathetic words, can help move you through your pain. That is why Spirit will use our energies as mediums to feel, sense, hear such difficult, painful and even violent re-enactments. Some Spirits on the other side can get their sorrow, heartache, and apologies through much more effectively if they use the medium's senses to get a point across. That young man who pulled a gun on himself wanted me to feel what he saw in her eyes as the event was happening and the horror that poor girl witnessed. It wasn't enough for him just to say the words, he wanted to let her know exactly what he was sorry for. He re-enacted the whole scene so I could just share in her pain for a short amount of time.

Spirit is always all-knowing, and the healing that happens in these readings astounds me to this day. It's all about the healing. It's not about *Guess what I have tucked away in my pocket for you to confirm? I put it there before I arrived for the reading.* Spirit could care less about validations like that. They want to get to the healing messages that will help lighten your heart, let go of the regrets, and help you move forward with your life.

Finally, when it goes back to physical mediumship, there are the rarer forms of presence when one can manipulate physical energy and create reactions on our physical plane—such as raps, ectoplasm, levitation, and materialization. I want to address them because I always want you to stay focused on the Light. By knowing and acknowledging what they are, you can get that knowledge and then hear in your heart when you should stay away because the energy is malevolent, or when you are working with benevolent energy. I assure you, you want to stay on the side of Light!

Raps are like a form of knocking that the spirit sends to answer questions like yes or no; ectoplasm is an actual ball of energy light that manifests which comes from the energy of the Spirit acknowledging they are in the room; levitation is when a table or even a body can be raised and float in thin air with nothing else holding it. And, last but not least, the actual materialization of a spirit that can happen during a séance or with energy so strong it can be seen in the physical realm as a ghost. For me, I have never seen this type of mediumship, other than what's been shown on TV or the internet. Am I open to acknowledge it actually exists? Yes, but do I have this gift, or find any healing reason to do this? No. It's not my thing. The most Spirit has shown me is the very specific taps, noises, footsteps they take in the client's dwelling that confirms those noises are their loved ones, or even the occasional orb or filtered light that appear in client pictures. The Spirit loved one is validating in that moment, when everyone huddled to take the picture and thought it didn't come out right, it was actually their loved one letting them know "I was saying cheese, too!" But, other than those two examples, that's about as crazy as my readings get when it comes to the presence of physical mediumship. But remember, I am working in the Light and have no idea where those other physical mediums are deriving their gift from.

The above list of physical manifestations may occur, but the energy itself is neither positive or negative, it is the intention with which the energy is used and its purpose, to hurt or heal, that is the issue. There are those who have that gift who are benevolent; it's just not the type of gift I have. There are also those that truly do have darkness in their hearts, so please don't be naïve when it comes to choosing someone to work with. My work is of the Light, and as I said before, clearing my energy field before readings so I am *only* receiving information that comes from the Light is always my first step. Those that practice other modalities of energy work, whatever you may want to call them—witches, pagans, séances, Ouija work—it's not what I do.

I serve the one Source, God. Funny true story, I have a group of female friends, my Spirit Soul Sister group, most of us in this line of work: psychics, mediums, tarot, astrologer. We are Sisters in Spirit. We all became friends because of this line of work and just give support to one another as we each move along our individual paths. It's nice to have a commonality with people who often feel very much alone or different. We offer support to one another as friends and occasionally get together. One year, our beloved friend Bobbi returned from Colorado to do a few events back in NY, and we all got together right around Halloween. I threw a little dinner party at my home, and, of course, the decoration theme was Halloween, as it was right around the holiday. I decorated the table with pumpkins, lanterns, silly Dollar Store spiders. I made these cute little decorated black witches' broomsticks from Michael's craft stores to give out as party favors, because I always love a party favor! Another friend of ours brought little paper witch hat kits she picked up. It was a coincidence, since no one knew it was

Psychic or Medium? Wait, There's a Difference?

a Halloween-themed dinner. We sat around the table eating, laughing, and doing these fun little crafts. We took a picture together, each person holding up my silly broomsticks, wearing paper witch hats, and we looked *so* cute! Of course, these pictures were posted on social media. Well, guess what happened?

Listen, people get concerned. I get it. They get fearful, and more than a few people really wondered if we were trying to imply we are actual witches from the dark side. Does having innocent fun and poking fun at ourselves make me or anyone else in that group a witch because we created a fun-themed party and took pictures? No. This is where more education about the work we do would be helpful, and we ask the public to not be so closed-minded. And, so you know there are still some Christian sects that will not allow themselves or their children to participate in Halloween because they fear worshipping the Devil? That is absolutely their right of religion, and we all honor that. However, there is not an ounce of evil-heartedness in our group. Hundreds of years ago, we would all be labeled witches or warlocks, because of our special gifts—but trust me, my line of work is within the Light of God, not to any other energy other than Source.

I have to laugh when I hear these crazy statements. If I were someone who was emotionally entwined with what others think or say about me, it would bother me. Remember, I was the young girl who always wanted to be accepted and liked. I had no self-love or self-acceptance. Now that I've learned those lessons, I accept that everyone is entitled to think what they want. Whether it's something negative or positive—oh well, it's their business, not mine, so why worry about ridiculous things that aren't even true? Wow, it took me many decades to learn this lesson!

On the other hand, people ask me about Ouija boards over and over again. I hate them. Let me emphasize again, I *hate* them. Why? Because not only do I know they open you up to negative, dark energy, but I have, unfortunately, witnessed it myself. It's a fun board game, right? No. It's a modality board to contact spirits and other entities through the use of a planchette that is moved around to spell out messages. The emphasis is "other entities," because it opens up and exposes you to everything—good and dark.

When a medium or psychic begins their work, hopefully they have meditated, cleared their bodies and minds of all negativity, and have connected themselves to the grounding of the Earth as well as to the Divine energy from above. We become a channel of light, guidance, and information from Spirit. A Ouija board is a portal opening to communication, but what you are communicating with, who knows?

Decades ago, when I was first learning about Spirituality, I had a friend of mine who was really into Ouija boards. We decided to do a "séance" type of session together. We were sitting in her sunroom one evening, and decided to pull out the board. This sunroom was completely surrounded with windows, twelve of them. We lowered the shades of each one, lit candles, and she began to say words—who even remembers what she said? As we started to use the Ouija board to ask questions, we kept getting stupid, silly answers. I would ask her, "Are you doing this?" She would ask the same of me, each swearing we were not pushing the planchette around. I was getting weird vibes from this. All of a sudden, all twelve of the roller window shades in that sun room snapped up at exactly the same time. It was as if there was someone at each window and simultaneously all shades were pulled up straight at the exact same time. I remember throwing the chair from behind me, and running out of the sunroom screaming. Was that a coincidence? Nope. That was some trickster energy that just wanted to play with us and since then, I've refused to use or even get near one. Please do not think you can contact your loved one you miss using this tool. Please go to a reputable, experienced medium that can channel correctly.

You can see that there is much involved and much to take into account when you are dealing in the spiritual realm. The good news is that some of this is now even making it through scientific communities and moving from an unknown art into a documented statistically provable talent. And, factually, "The study of mediums by scientists is certainly not a new undertaking. During the late nineteenth century and early twentieth century, there were quite a number of eminent scientists engaged in such exploration. Such well respected researchers, including William James, Sir William Crookes, Sir Oliver Lodge, Frederic Myers, Charles Richet and many others conducted exhaustive research that utilized scientific experimental protocol. Despite the overwhelming evidence confirming communication with discarnate entities, their findings were not embraced by mainstream science." Nonetheless, by 1976 the role and acceptance of psychics and mediumship had changed, and the profession started to be studied in a more scientifically measured manner. This is a welcome change for people who are *different*, like me.

If you think about it, 1976 wasn't that long ago. I was only thirteen at the time, which shows how truly new my profession is and explains why I did not have a lot of mentors early on in my life! This is the year a committee was formed by the American Humanist Association called CSICOP, but pronounced Psi-cop[5], the Committee for the Scientific Investigation of Claims of the Paranormal, and its purpose was to look at all claims of psychic occurrence non-biased, with an open mind, and attempt to be objective to define what the psychic phenomenon really was without dismissing its existence or validity. These drew the very famous and greatest thinkers, like Carl Sagan of the astronomy world and B.F. Skinner of the behavioral psychology world.[6] This truly helped parapsychology make a positive turn and thereby encouraged other "accepted" scientific institutions to study and pay more attention to the field. It's also groups like this that eventually led to the creation of the Forever Family Foundation that I will speak more about in the next chapter, because it is a way that I feel is easier now to discern truly gifted people from those who simply pretend and then con wonderful people out of their money.

The most important point I want you to remember, as you try to keep an open mind, is that each medium is vastly different from the one beside them. Just as an artist can use different modalities to express their gift (watercolors, sculpting, chalk), each medium uses the experiences of their life, their beliefs about the afterlife, and conveys different flavors to readings.

What one medium will pick up in a reading is vastly different from what another medium will pick up. I have found in my readings that loved ones enjoy telling funny stories or memories from when they were alive. They enjoy the laughter part of the reading and are always cracking jokes or wanting me to share something funny. Laughter allows the client to understand, the Spirit is not focusing on their death. They are focusing on the *living* part of life, and the memories and laughter always keep us going in the darkest of moments.

It is pretty amazing when we look back to times that weren't always easy—like the time when I was eighteen and in college and my used Mustang would leak heavy amounts of oil. I was working part-time and going to school. I had no money to fix the engine. I would check the oil level sporadically, but it wasn't at the top of my priority list. What was I thinking? The problem would magically just go away? I had absolutely *no clue* about the consequence of not making sure there was oil in the car. So one day, coming home from classes, and about five miles from home, I saw this enormous cloud of white smoke coming out of the tail pipe. Did I stop? Nope. I didn't know what was happening, so I just kept pushing the gas pedal to move forward. Finally, the smoke turned black, and the engine seized. Yes, I burned the motor dead. Now the entire engine needed to be replaced—talk about irony, and this was not funny at all.

But now I look back at those days with a great deal of "man, those were the days," feelings. Even though that was a very stressful time in my life, I look back on what simpler days those were. All I had to do was go to school, go to classes, and take care of a car. *Sheesh*. Those are the stories that Spirit shares with the client—ones that in the moment were not one bit funny, but told from the perspective of the deceased loved one, and re-connecting, they can actually make you laugh off your chair! It's good to have a sense of humor, especially when most of us carry such deep burdens. The struggles that we have endured are not only moments we laugh at and enjoy now, but they are an arsenal for the medium to help connect their client to their loved ones and make them experience, hear, and feel them in a way they had thought was lost forever. What a gift that is!

Chapter Five
MEDIUMSHIP YOU CAN TRUST

CERTIFYING THE MESSENGER WHO BRIDGES LIFE AND DEATH

*Life and death are one thread, the same
line viewed from different sides.*

—Laozi adapted from teachings of Lao Tzu

For me, the entire purpose of mediumship is to confirm there is life after death, and that our loved ones are always with us. It is to be the bridge of communication for all between life and death. The reading provides a level of comfort to the client as their loved ones describe not only events that happened while they were alive, but also validations of events happening after they passed—to prove they have never left us. As you can tell from my stories in the previous chapter, Spirit enjoys sharing memories of their past, to further confirm this is truly their loved one in the reading with them. Spirit enjoys providing comfort to us, saying, "Even though you think you can't see or feel me, I am always watching over you."

It is such an honor for me to have this gift, and I have worked hard for it, but it also makes me very protective of my clients, the mediums around me, and the bad name the psychic community can get. The sad part is there are corrupt people out there in all professions, looking for a quick con, who will take you at your lowest and not give it a second thought. The grieving are especially vulnerable. That is why I am here to share how you can actually find a trusted medium, how some of our beloved TV shows are double-edged swords, and how we can really benefit from the many truly skilled and loving psychics and mediums out there whose soul (ha – sole) purpose is to help others heal.

We've established that psychics and mediums all work a little differently and come from all walks of life. Now we need to learn that like other professions each has a varying degree of skills. As you read in my story, for the longest time I didn't even have confidence in my skills and it has taken years for me to build confidence and feel validated in my own gifts. Even now there are times in front of large audiences, before Spirit kicks in, that I get nervous and wonder what in the world I could possibly have to offer. The good news is that I still forge ahead!

To continue my story from Part One to help you gain insight on how to validate a psychic and medium, I want to walk you through my story. In the earlier phase of learning about my gift, taking classes, and honing my skills, I started dipping my toes in the water. I had the opportunity to do the group reading that my teacher Lorraine put together for me, and it was such a success that it led to new readings and new clients. I started charging $25 on up until my skills got so good that I could command a higher amount. Within a very short time of doing these discounted readings and working a corporate job, it became apparent I could no longer burn the candle at both ends. It was super scary to even think of leaving corporate. The benefits, security, 401k, were holding me hostage. And the salary, oh yeah, at this point of working in corporate for over twenty-seven years, I was financially doing very well. How would I give up that security?

Some of my co-workers knew what I did on the side, but because my job was my livelihood, I could not let it get out that I was a medium. Who would understand? I was a manager and had a code of ethics to follow not only within my job, but outside life. I was extremely fearful that it might get out. But the pull to leave corporate was overwhelming. Finally, I made a pact with Spirit, and said I would leave when my readings could match my corporate salary. That took three years.

I actually arrived at my salary number fairly quickly, but I kept pushing it, because the idea of leaving what I had always known was terrifying. Remember the big house with the big mortgage? Well, there is no room for irresponsibility, especially when children are in college. I had moved from my accounting position into the sales department and could have easily stayed there and finished out my years until it was time to retire. But again, the tides and winds were pushing me, and I knew what I really wanted to do in life was help people. I wasn't doing that in my corporate world. I left my job, said goodbye to that life, and have not looked back once.

Spirit kept promising me that if I would just take the leap of faith, it would all work out. Since then, I've never once had a month where I couldn't pay my expenses. And within a very short amount of time of doing readings and groups, I had a year-and-a-half waiting list for private readings.

Then one day, the winds of Spirit came blowing again. Remember my friend Bobbi Allison, whom I spoke of earlier, who had done the reading for me all those years ago? Over the years we stayed in touch and began getting to know each other better, and our friendship developed into the loving and warm closeness we share today. I truly love this woman. She knew the double life I was living and knew one day I would leave corporate, although remember, I had no concept something like that would ever happen for me. She called me on a December evening, and said she was supposed to do an event with the Forever Family Foundation on Long Island. They are a not-for-profit, organized fifteen years earlier, that tests mediums' efficacy and accuracy through their own blind test process. Not many mediums make it onto their list of acceptable mediums to refer. There is no membership fee to belong. You apply for consideration to be tested, go through their mediumship application and review, are tested blindly by several people on their panel, and you either pass or fail. Passing their certification process means you will be referred on their website for people who want a list of reputable mediums to contact, and all our work for them is on a volunteer basis.

I had been doing readings for such a short time, but Bobbi called and said she was ill that day, and could I cover for her that evening. People were coming from long distances to have a large group reading, and it was already too late for the foundation to start calling people to cancel. I was terrified. How was I going to do this? I reluctantly said yes, because my husband kept forcing me to do so. Winds of change blowing in my direction, and I am digging my heels in silently screaming *no*! What a shocker.

I arrived that night and did the reading for the group. Afterwards, the president of the foundation, Bob Ginsberg, thanked me for covering so last minute, and may I uncomfortably say, said I did a fantastic job.

He said I should seriously consider going through their mediumship certification process. It felt like he was speaking Chinese. Certification? Testing my skills? It was all completely foreign to me. I finally got the guts up, asked for their certification application, and it took me another three years to get my confidence to finally apply.

Three years. I was always beating myself up, seeing the application on my desk, and saying *Okay, when the spring rolls around, I'll send it in. Okay, when the fall comes around, I'll really send it in.* Three years of procrastination. What was this fear about? It was, again, the little wounded girl inside saying, once you apply, you will fail, and then you'll really be a fraud.

The week before my actual certification testing, I learned there would be panel members on the board who were going to call me and I would be giving them each a fifteen-minute reading over the phone. All I knew of them was their first name. They were allowed to answer only yes and no to what I confirmed in their readings. They had their own check-off and marking system that I was unaware of. The morning of the test, I was going down into our finished basement that I had turned into my office from the apartment it once was. I was terrified. All my fears were choking me. How was I going to get through this? No one could help me. I was getting dressed, going over this in my head a million times, trying to calm myself, and I again turned to Spirit and asked for a *huge* sign that I wasn't going to fail. *Please Lord*, I would ask, *don't let me look stupid.*

When I opened the door that led to the office, right there on the rug was a huge 6 inch feather. White and gray. You couldn't miss it. It *never* could have been there before, because that's the door that leads up the stairs into our kitchen. I pass through that door a hundred times, and no one else goes into my basement office, just me. This was not a small feather, it was *huge*. I picked it up, smiled a huge smile, and left it on the desk right before me as a reminder I wasn't alone. If Spirit brought this to me, they would bring me through it. I had to remember that this gift is not me. I am a channel for the work Spirit needs done in this lifetime.

We are always co-creating with Spirit. Whether it's owning your own business, working in corporate, being a painter, or even being a parent, Spirit is always working through us to create the life we want. Those big opportunities that come our way are jewels and gems from the Universe. Yet, when presented with big opportunities, many of us turn them down, because we're afraid to move forward. Spirit is always guiding us, always moving us from one spot to another, but our fear as humans overwhelms our decision-making, and many times we pass up those opportunities. We may notice the winds of change are blowing around us, but we remain stuck because the *what-ifs* of life are too much for us to handle. Again, if we can't see it, we can't believe it to be true. After doing those five readings blindly, it felt like I had given birth. Loads of energy expended, and it would take three weeks to find out if I passed.

Do you know what? After taking that test, and not knowing if I failed the certification or not, I honestly wasn't concerned any longer. If it happened, wonderful, I would be happy. But if I failed, I was okay with that outcome as well. The test had been taken, literally and figuratively. My test was not actually reading for people and passing; the test from Spirit was, *Do you trust us and have faith?* And I walked through that fire and knew no matter what the outcome, I would be okay. A huge weight had been lifted from my shoulders. I had walked through that fire, and could face that fear, and I was extremely proud of myself! Thankfully three weeks later, I received the letter stating I had passed the certification test and would become a certified medium with the

Forever Family Foundation. Such a big accomplishment for me, and it meant I could work with an amazing foundation that continued to teach about the survival of consciousness after a body expires from this world. Spirit had been guiding me this way, from that first night that Bobbi called to help cover for her. Spirit had been guiding this, from the first time I had met her seven years earlier; even if I didn't connect all the dots, they sure were. Spirit is always planning and blowing the winds in the direction we need them to go.

The entire reason I wanted to be part of the Forever Family Foundation was to help allay the public's negativity about and disbelief of mediumship. I wanted to show that there are science and numbers and validations to our work and focus on proving that consciousness survives death. This foundation is backed by scientists. There is even a new science, referred to as afterlife science, where they discuss "near death experiences, after death communications, life after life (death), and reincarnation."[78]

The importance of this foundation is that there are still divides and differences as to who believes what. You have religious individuals who may feel there is a heaven and a hell, or other religions that believe in reincarnation, and opposing atheists who believe when your body dies, that you cease to exist at all. There are the more neurological sciences that believe that it is just the brain acting in a reactionary way. And "Traditional scientific thinking most often discounted the possibility that consciousness could survive physical death, instead asserting that since consciousness was a by-product of the brain, when the physical brain ceased to exist so did consciousness. In other words, our thoughts, memories, and soul were forever extinguished."[9]

I know that this is not true. Our consciousness does survive death. Our souls continue (because they are energy, and energy never dies) even after the body expires. The problem is that disbelief exists because it cannot be studied in science labs, or cannot be expressed quantitatively, for the most part. What we cannot see, we have difficulty believing. Unfortunately, this is a true detriment from our humanity. This is why I truly encourage you to check this foundation out at www.ForeverFamilyFoundation.org and learn more about how they are trying to protect the public from frauds.

As for my level of accuracy, I had been receiving more and more validation through the years, and this is why I could leave my corporate job. In this specific certification testing as mentioned above, a medium is given five individuals to read. Believe it or not, they used to have candidates sit in a room, blindfolded, and the individual sat in front of the medium, and that is how the readings were conducted. During the testing process, candidates are graded on the number of "hits" – correct answers received. The sitter is only allowed to answer "yes" or "no," nothing else. Over the years, and due to technology and the internet, and now that they have mediums all over the country that have been certified, the process is done over the phone. You know nothing more than the person's first name, as they introduce themselves. Then for fifteen minutes, the medium reads them, and the sitter scores how many "hits" or correct answers were given about the deceased. The medium is never given their score. They are only told if they passed or failed. Again, I still thank Spirit to this day for allowing me to pass! In the end, following an organization like Forever Family Foundation, or the Windbridge Institute which are organizations that test mediums in secure environments, to confirm they are gifted and are connecting with loved ones on the other side, is a great way to find a reputable medium, especially if you don't know where to turn.

The next best way to find a reputable medium is often word-of-mouth from other trusted friends and family who have had their own successful readings. Definitely find out more about the medium you're looking to book and dig deeper to find out who they are. With information on the internet, reading reviews, whether it is on Facebook or their websites, or modern social media, this can sometimes help you out. No matter what, you want to look for referrals, and always look for those who work with integrity, with the Higher Light, and really be aware that there are a lot you should stay away from. You wouldn't just throw your body to a quack doctor to repair; why would you throw your Spirit to a quack psychic or medium? There are a lot of charlatans out there, all willing and wanting to hang a shingle outside their door, and the average person does not know who or where to turn to for advice. This is why an authentic psychic and medium receives most of their clientele through word of mouth and recommendation, and the reason why I was fully booked with over a year-and-a-half wait list.

Since I'm on the topic of validation and the evolvement of mediumship, here goes my next reality check! Many, many times I am asked about other popular mediums that have become a household name like James Van Praag, Theresa Caputo, and Tyler Henry, just to name a few. How have their successes affected our profession and livelihood? In my heart, I believe it's been a double-edged sword. I am very thankful and grateful that these pioneers walking before us have trail-blazed and started to open the minds of millions of people and help get us out of the "gypsy" state that intuitives were once classified as. Their exposure has opened doors and allowed more spiritually-minded people to be able to spread the light of healing through our work.

Now, the double-edged sword. Since the excitement and popularity of these shows, as great as the positive side has been for our gifted mediums, we also have the negative. Through every crevice, crack, or opening have come sneaking out of the woodwork, every type of intuitive, medium, psychic, healer—many claiming they can help you to either connect to your loved ones on the other side or give you psychic insight. It has become a money-hungry business opportunity. You don't need a license to do this work, and there is no written code of ethics; just put out a shingle and start getting clients. Because of this low morality, I have heard horrendous stories about psychics wanting thousands of dollars from clients to remove spells that they convinced them were creating havoc in their lives. Spells? What? The fact is, the only negativity you are experiencing in your life is the cause and effect of what you already feel inside and are calling, energetically, to you. We will discuss Law of Attraction and how energy works in another chapter.

The idea that someone can take a spell off you is preposterous. No candle to burn, no jewel to purchase, nothing is equipped to take negativity *off* of someone. I am so angry when I hear that this stuff goes on. And because the emotionally hurt are going to these charlatans, they are desperate for anything they think will help them. And these opportunist people are champing at the bit.

I once had a gentleman call me for a reading. He had heard of me from someone he knew that recommended my services. When I spoke to him, he asked what my fee was. I told him, and he asked if there were other things I sold. I told him no, and I don't like to read for clients more than once a year. I don't want anyone becoming dependent on one person for a reading or for guidance. He explained that he had gone to someone that charged him $2,500 to remove a spell that was placed on him and wanted another $2,000 to help the love of his life come back to him. I warned him that anyone that would abuse a gift, like this woman was doing, was not working in the Light. She was working with some sort of dark magic and I suggested he please stay away. But he continued to ask what else I sold to help me do my job and was perplexed that I didn't charge more. I told him that's not how my gift works and asked if he wanted to make an appointment to see me. He seemed reluctant and said no.

This poor man. He had been conditioned to give someone a lot of money, so he could be fixed. This is part of the double-edged sword that scares me and people don't have the right information about what this gift is all about. If you're not feeling relief and happiness and a feeling of hope after a reading, think twice about going back. If someone is telling you that you have to come back for multiple readings over and over again, think twice about going back. Now, I'm not talking about intuitives that help clients through traumatic events in their lives, similar to how a psychologist works. Bottom line is, some intuitives work with helping people over a succession of visits. Rome wasn't built in a day, and some traumatic events cannot be spiritually healed overnight. I'm talking about the physics that say you *need* to see them more often. Follow your gut; don't just listen to someone tell you what they want you to do. If it feels right to see them again, do it. But if not, don't fall prey to their greed.

Therefore, does having the exposure of television help? Yes, for those that want to remain in the light and serve, in whatever that capacity is. We have a strong community of psychics, mediums, tarot readers, healers, and astrologers here on Long Island. It's a large community for such a small area of the United States. There are many that work in the Light I was talking about. And there are many who want to compete with each other, get the next better deal or TV/radio gig, and are in this for all the wrong reasons. When I see or hear of that competitive streak or talk and rumors running around, I just smile and say to myself, "Gina, stay in your lane," because that is the one being guided by Spirit, and that's the one that keeps me serving in the Light.

This gift is not about me or my ego. This is about hearing the call of Spirit, and stepping up, even in my fear and uncertainty, to serve in whatever way Spirit deems it to be. Not my way, their way. Please be careful. When deciding to go to someone, a personal referral is always the best resource! As I mentioned, most of us doing this full-time have arrived to this place by just that—hard work over many years and referrals from one client to another. And many times, if I can't accommodate someone because of my extensive client list, and I can feel this person really needs to speak to someone right away, I refer them to my colleagues that I have tremendous respect for.

My husband Anthony thinks I'm nuts doing that, but honestly, again, it's not about keeping clients for myself. It's about the work in spreading the Light and the healing that is needed. Where we share and give back out to the Universe, Law of Attraction again, says it comes back to us tenfold. Why not recommend others that I know do an amazing job in this field and help this person get the healing and validation they need right now? This is all part of the whole, and I discuss this in my chapters about karma (Chapter 11) and the Law of Attraction (Chapter 12). I think it is also this level of honesty, integrity, and true love for healing that brings you the right type of recognition and will bring you work even when you might not see it right in front of you.

The Universe really does have your back! Don't forget, the winds and energy of Spirit are always seeing things from a much higher perspective, yet as humans we are always seeing things from the horse-blind perspective. One day, another friend and medium of mine, Laura Jackson, contacted me to say she had just done a reading for Gwyneth Paltrow's assistant and they were putting together a guide for Mediums, Intuitives and Healers on their website magazine GOOP.com. They asked her for several names she would recommend for the article. Of course, she reached out to the small group of Long Island-based mediums that are certified through the Forever Family Foundation and let me know she had given out my name, and they would be contacting me. What was my reaction? Guess—I think you are getting to know me now! *Scared* out of my mind. This was a huge opportunity, as well as a huge chance to fall on my face. I was contacted by her assistant, Elise Loehnen, as they were setting up "test" readings via phone with all the mediums to be featured. Since they didn't know us at all, they were finding people from all around the country who were interested and willing to have a phone session, and based on the outcome of that reading, the decision would be made if we were going to be featured on GOOP. All Elise shared was the person's first name and what predetermined date and time the call would be set up for. That's it.

I honestly don't even remember the girl's name I read—Katie? Kathy? Kimberly? No memory of it, but what does stay cattle-prodded in my mind was the fear that consumed me. At this point, I'd been doing readings for quite some time, and yet, when big opportunities came up like this, I became frozen—almost the same paralyzing fear as if you stuck me high up a mountain and asked me to look down. That same incapacitating fear of heights I have is the same fear I experienced in situations like this. But I knew this was being brought to me for whatever reason that Spirit needed it to, whether it was to pass the test and be featured, or to get through the fear by walking through the fire *again*. Either way, there was a higher purpose.

I remember the reading going well, and this girl's mother on the other side validating it was her. The mom brought up the great guy her daughter was currently dating, and how much he treated her like a princess, and how he loved to do adventurous activities, like hiking and outdoor sports. I could hear her smiling on the other end of the phone. But when I brought up her mother's crossword puzzles, she started to cry. She remembered her mother loving to spend quiet time doing crossword puzzles and it brought back a flood of emotions. She just started tearing up. Funny how the smallest of memories can trigger such a huge response.

As a medium, I will receive signs, symbols, pictures, short movie clips of things the loved one on the other side wants to validate. Often times, what that sign or symbol means to me is completely different than what it may mean to my clients. For me, seeing the woman doing crossword puzzles would seem inconsequential. And in the past, I would judge and think, *Should I even mention this*? But to that young woman, it meant the world. That's why as a medium, as insignificant as something is that Spirit is showing me, I share the information, because it might mean the world to that person.

There is no filtering with readings. As the Spirit shows the memory or message, I explain it exactly as they are showing it. And most of the time, it is meaningful to the client. But this means having to take out our human self from the reading, and just allow ourselves to be channels of Spirit. What they show, is what the client gets. And Spirit is also pulling memories from my past experiences, to help convey their validations. They may show me my cousin's old blue Chevy to recount a story from their own life. Or they may show me a large long-haired dog like our departed golden retriever Jojo, to help express that a similar dog is on the other side with them. I make sure that I don't spin my experiences the way I perceive them, but relay the messages as they are given, and allow the client to make the connection and validation.

The article featured in GOOP.com continued to explode my reading list. It was featured almost two years ago, but I still get clients that are just seeing the piece now. What I love about this experience is that I've gotten to read for clients all over the US and in other countries like Germany, Sweden, Australia, Mexico, Spain, Dominican Republic, and England, to name a few. The interesting clients I've met, their lives, loved ones, and stories have been incredible; such a gift to help so many people that I am humbled by the experience Spirit brought my way. Again, when Bobbi Allison told me fifteen years ago that I would be doing this kind of work, it made no sense. Now it makes all the sense in the world. I was meant to serve. I thought, as a child, that I was going to be serving via studying medicine. When that didn't take root, Spirit brought me to a completely different path, always serving, but in a way I could have never imagined myself. What a gift!

As you may be able to tell, there has been a consciousness shift happening in our Universe over the past ten years. Living in this stress-induced life, we make the mistake of looking outward to ask why we are really here, what this life we are living is all about, and what purpose we have. We need to move that inward. We need to understand the relationship and power between body, mind, and soul. The sooner we can acknowledge that there is more to us than what we experience on this earthly plane, and ask to get validations from Spirit, the more we will have stronger experiences with our loved ones who have crossed over. We will learn that we are not experiencing this life alone. We are always guided by Spirit. Thank goodness; because of this forward thinking, and the mediums and intuitives that have walked before us, we as mediums are seen with greater credibility. Those of us that have this inherent gift are able to practice it, and the world is becoming brighter because more people can add to the light and consciousness of this world.

Our world *needs* healing, insight, and help learning through peace and love. I am very grateful that as a medium, I can practice a gift I have had since childhood. What would have happened to me if this was the 1600s? I would have been burned at the stake as a witch for sure or stoned to death. As a medium, being able to give healing and hope to the clients that come to us is the most rewarding job on Earth.

With readings, the client is assured of life after death, through validation that their loved ones are around them and in peace. Giving characteristic specifics, events that have happened in that loved one's life while they were alive, as well as things that have happened since they crossed, are all accessed to validate they are still with them. That is very healing! Who doesn't want to know that the loved one their heart aches for is acknowledging the tie their son wore in honor of their grandfather for his graduation? Or that a client is still using her mother's lasagna pan and still thinks of her every time she pulls it out to use? This is how our hearts begin to heal, when we know whatever we are going through, our loved one is saying *I'm still here with you*. It helps explain life, love, and loss on a whole other level.

As a recap, what did I say at the beginning of this Part? "How do I find this knowingness?" you may ask. "How do I find this peace?" We need to use the tools available to us to get us to feel it in our hearts. To "know" we are never alone, no matter who around us is trying to convince us otherwise. It is to embrace our own clairs that we are all gifted with but are either too afraid or too busy to pay attention to. Those tools can be psychics, mediums, our own intuition, signs from the universe, taking classes, connecting with mentors, reading a book, and the list goes on.

It starts, quite simply, by learning that we are not alone, that there is more to us than just a body, and that we are all connected to our loved ones and animals after death. If you knew you could talk to Johnny to learn what happened, or why they left you, or how much fun you had while they were alive, and to remember that versus the moment of death, don't you think you would heal more quickly? The truth is that when we acknowledge this incredible Universe, or our angels, or Spirit, or the true Source, we accept a oneness with all. When we understand our loved one's Spirits are on this journey with us, the time in pain and grief is lessened and a feeling of oneness, *knowingness* of true love eventually releases the waves of tears and internal tantrums that face us in the various stages of our loss.

This love is what ties us together and allows us to understand that life and death truly are just one thread viewed from different perspectives. It gives us hope and I'm hoping it keeps you moving to this next section, Part Three—the rough one, on what it is like to grieve.

Part Three

GRIEF

AFTER THE WIND IS KNOCKED FROM YOUR SAILS ...

DEALING WITH UNSPEAKABLE TRAGEDY AND PAIN

When you survive loss ... everyone is quick to tell you how strong you are, and how tough you must be. But actually, no one has a choice to survive grief do they ... it's not optional. You just have to cry in the shower, sob in your pillow and pray you will make it.

—Zoe Clark-Coates

Grief. Yes, that ugly one. That feeling that is so deep and so painful: The one that I am in the midst of now. It is the relentless pain that is making it very hard to write these chapters and some days see the point of writing this book at all. It has only been six months since we lost our beloved Anthony and I can't tell you the number of triggers, tears, tissue boxes, "firsts," and full-out breakdowns I have had. It's normal, I know that, but it doesn't feel right.

I do feel the same human emotions as you. Picked on, hurting, targeted, unloved in moments, angry, broken, unhinged—you name it, I'm going through all these roller-coaster feelings. As a matter of fact, I keep avoiding this chapter and just rereading it now is making me want to throw this book across a wall and throw in the towel. That's how we feel at times when we're in the grieving process—I don't want to do this anymore. This is a totally normal reaction.

Who wants to hear my painful story? Who else cares? Why would I even torture myself by constantly bringing up these memories and then be crazy enough to think I could write about it so soon? This wasn't supposed to be *us*. This wasn't supposed to happen to *our Anthony* who had already gone through way too much to make it through his first two remissions. This is all a bad matrix dream and, *Oh, God*, I just want to wake up back to his early healthy years, the life we were making as a new Brady Bunch family. Yes, I want to tap my Dorothy red shoes and go *home*.

But I'm going to be brave. I'm going to believe that what I have to share might help you, and I'm going out on that really high ledge, scared to death of heights, to tell you the rest of our story. 2017 began a year-and-a-half process that would change and rock our world to the bitter core. After years of being in remission and feeling great, our son Anthony began to not feel well, and could not get rid of a chest cold he had. With new blood work tests being done, on October 5, 2017, Anthony was re-diagnosed with leukemia. Our world shattered. Here this poor young man, who had just started up his life again, was being re-diagnosed after nine years in remission. Nine *years* in remission. You read that correctly. Why couldn't this have just lasted? Why were we the chosen family to be tortured again? Surely, God and karma were making huge mistakes. Life was again a blur.

This time, it wasn't as "simple" as being in the hospital for a month and getting outpatient treatment. This required a bone marrow transplant, and even then, they never spoke percentages of survival. As afraid as we were at the first diagnosis in 2008, this one created a living and breathing fear out of every pore in our bodies. If you've never seen a loved one have to go through the process of stripping away their immune system via chemo and radiation, it is a suffering no parent wants their child to experience.

As Anthony systematically went through the process, we'd always say, "We wish we could take this pain from you Anthony, so you wouldn't have to suffer. We wish we could trade places with you." But all we could do was sit back and watch, cry, and not let him see we were crying.

Something felt different to me this time. I was still being hopeful that he could beat this, like he did the first time, but since I was doing readings full-time now, my schedule was a bit more flexible and allowed me to stay over at the hospital at night. Something kept telling me, as tired as I was, staying over, night after night, I had to do it. Between me, his mother and father, we all took shifts. Anthony was very anxiety-ridden, and being in the hospital with all the treatments and procedures he had endured all these years made him very fearful, and he never liked to be left alone. Even though he was twenty-six, there were times we were almost still dealing with the sixteen-year-old that had first been diagnosed. He always wanted someone in the room with him. Poor thing, frightened out of his mind, wanting to live life normally as all his friends were doing. This wasn't fair.

While he was being treated in the hospital, one night he announced that his girlfriend was pregnant with a child. Well, here we go again. I guess he really wasn't as sterile as the doctors thought all those years ago, and grandchild Number 2 was now on the way! With the wonderful news that his sister Christina was a perfect match as a bone marrow donor, and knowing there was a baby on the way, things seemed to be lightening up and we had a lot of hope for his future.

We welcomed Christian in March 2018, a few weeks before his daddy received his bone marrow transplant from his sister. Thank God the baby was delivered in the same hospital that Anthony was being treated in, and he was allowed to be transported down to delivery to welcome his son into the world.

Gifts like this felt like precious little gems from the Universe, and we were ecstatic! We prayed, and our dear friend Bobbi Allison (God bless her) helped us reach out to prayer groups, to everyone in the healer, intuitive, and medium community. We had thousands of people praying for Anthony's recovery and that's exactly what he got! He received his bone marrow transplant in March 2018, and at the 100-day mark after his transplant, his spinal fluid was examined and there was no more leukemia. Words cannot even describe this feeling of euphoria and happiness that filled our hearts! He was getting a second chance but had to be careful because sometimes the body will reject the new marrow cells from a transplant, so it was always looming over us. Could this happen? Would he be targeted again? Or, this time, was he truly healed? It sure looked that way.

He started again, back at life, working, and taking care of his newborn child. In November 2018, right after Thanksgiving, after weeks of feeling ill, not being able to breathe, with it getting worse and not letting us know, Anthony was admitted into the hospital. Quickly he went from being in the cancer unit to going to the ICU. Within days, they were talking about temporarily putting him on a ventilator to assist his breathing and allow the meds to start taking the infection away in his lungs. This meant sedating and intubating him. We kept vigil by his side, night and day. He was never left alone. After ten days of sedation, they were hopeful they could remove the ventilator and have him breathe on his own.

We kept praying by his side, talking to him, begging him to please get better and fight whatever was happening within him. I remember they had backed off the sedation, to see how he was faring on his own. One day as he lay awake, I was talking to him, stroking his hair and saying, "We need you to hang on and fight this, Anthony." He just shook his head back and forth, as if to say *no*, and a tear fell from his eyes. *Oh*, the *unbearable* pain of that moment. Not being able to speak, yet his eyes told the whole story.

The pause in the ventilator lasted only days. He could not breathe on his own, and when the doctors advised that putting him back on the ventilator meant they couldn't promise he would come out of this, he didn't care. He was so done; you could see it in his eyes. He didn't want to suffer anymore, and asked to be reintubated. We got to spend four days trying to do something, and yet doing nothing but watching him suffer. He was put back on life support, and as his body fought to stay alive, we kept praying, begging, please don't leave us. We are unbelievably grateful he wasn't experiencing any pain. He didn't even know what was happening around him.

We were there holding his hand, stroking his hair, putting lotion on him, whatever we could do to stay connected with him. Then his body and organs began to fail, his breathing became more labored, even with the ventilator supporting him. Finally on January 4, 2019, his body just couldn't fight anymore and finally gave out; he took his last breath and passed.

His father was in the room that day. Something had told him not to go into work. Usually, I would spend the night with Anthony, and then leave around 1 p.m., as his dad would come home from work to spend the rest of the day with him. Something told him that day to not go to work and just stay at the hospital. My husband said that at one point, sitting in the chair beside his hospital bed, something told him to stand up and go over to Anthony's side.

He started stroking his hair, talking to him as he always did, and at that moment, he heard the heart monitor flatline. He sensed in that moment something was calling him over to his son, and just as he had been there in the delivery room when his son took his first breath of life, so had he been there to see and feel his last breath. Anthony's Spirit was already speaking to his father even before his father knew what that was.

I had been at home that day, waiting to read a few clients and then join everyone at the hospital as we had done the entire year before. That afternoon, when I was meditating to prepare for clients, along with my usual Spirit guides that show up to let me know we are ready to start working, suddenly I saw Anthony appear, all dressed in white. In my meditation, I asked him what he was doing there. Alongside him was standing his grandmother Linda, my husband's mother, who had crossed over twenty-plus years before. I remember saying to him, "What are you doing here? You're not supposed to be here." He just smiled. When I repeated my words, "Get back to where we know you are, in the hospital, we're waiting for you to recover," his response was clear as day. "Go back to what? That?" He pointed down to a lifeless body. "Go back to that diseased body? No way, I'm very happy here, at peace and no longer suffering." And he smiled that beautiful smile. As soon as I finished the meditation and got ready for clients, my husband called to say Anthony had gone into cardiac arrest and they were trying to revive him.

That was Anthony's sign and way of saying, "I'm whole, happy and at peace." He was coming to me, so I could let everyone know his suffering was over, and he was thrilled to finally be okay. Did I race like a mad woman to the hospital, wanting my vision of him to not be what I knew it meant? You bet I did. I kept saying hold on, hold on, hold on. As I entered the hospital floor, into ICU, my husband was standing there, and said, "The doctors tried but were not successful. *He's gone.*" I fell to the ground, his mother and aunt already there, all of us huddled together, wailing. The pain of his suffering, the anguish of his life snatched from him, knowing we would never see him raising his new son, the pain of memories never to be made with him again. So much pain. So much anger over the unfairness of it all. Why does this stuff have to happen? What is the purpose and why did he have to suffer so much? All for what in the end, for it to go down like this? Where is the justice?

We ask ourselves these kinds of questions when going through traumatic experiences. We want to compare what we're going through to a "fairness" meter. This isn't fair, but why, how come? We hear these kinds of excruciating stories happening to other people, and we say "Aww, how sad for that person; I am praying for them." But when it hits our backyard, suddenly we don't want to be suffering like everyone else. We want justification for *why* this horror has happened to us.

Whether it's a child dying, or a spouse walking out on us, or a sibling that no longer talks to us, or being fired, or a parent that abused us, we want the justification, a reason as to *why* this is happening. We think we're being punished for something. We think we have done something to cause this or acted in an inappropriate way, or committed a sin, or brought this upon ourselves. How could any just God or Higher Source ever let us suffer this way? It just doesn't make sense.

Why do we have to go through all this punishment? The truth is there actually is *no* punishment from Spirit. Yes, there is pain that we experience. Yes, in the ego part of our minds, as humans, it has us suffer and question and fight with the big *Why*. We wonder if we made wrong choices or experienced a terrible calamity and were in the wrong place at the wrong time. We suffer the "karma"—the lessons. Sometimes we may even know why things have happened to us, but most often, we are still looking at that "fairness meter," and comparing ourselves to others who seem to have that golden horseshoe with what looks like an easy and blessed life.

So, what is this karma thing people talk about? Karma is the after affect (the effect of the cause) that we suffer in this life. Whether it was a conscious decision or mistake on our part, or something that is done involuntarily against our wishes, we suffer the karma (the effect). The karma is the "lesson" of the event. Why did a partner abandon me? Perhaps your lesson is to acknowledge you are whole and lovable, even though you have been left. Why does my son not talk to me? Perhaps your lesson is to learn to detach from the pain of that child not being in your life. Why did I lose my house? Perhaps your lesson is learning to let go and trust in something higher than yourself that will always take care of you. Why did my child leave me so early in life? Perhaps your lesson is about accepting "what is," not what we want it to be. Not that I have all the answers, *please* do not think that I do, because I don't, but wish I did: Answers for myself as well as clients that come to me asking the same. What I *can* tell you is, I'm always trying to push through our collective pain and ask the "why" of what the *lesson* is supposed to be. Because I know and understand, no matter what the experience, there is a lesson of learning behind it—learning for our souls as humans on this Earth.

It helps to understand karma if we understand soul contracts. There are soul contracts we agree to before incarnating on this realm. Each soul on the other side confirms and contracts who they will be to each other, and the specific roles we will each play on Earth. You be the mother, I'll be the child, we will love one another, but then I'll leave tragically and you will learn how to survive, learn, grow, and help others through this pain while I am no longer here. Your soul will learn just how strong you really are, because your heart will be pushed out of your chest, and yet, you will continue living and being strong for both of us. The soul on the other side says, "Yes, I will do this." Then we arrive on Earth, live out our lives, and have no knowledge of the contract we agreed to. Suddenly the hurt, loss, sorrow become the primary focus. And we disconnect from the lesson. But it is the lesson that is bringing the particular experience to us, for our ultimate growth. What we should be focusing on, rather than the pain, hurt, betrayal, is *what is this experience trying to teach me about myself? What* am I to learn from this experience? Trust me, I am *not* making light of losing a loved one, especially not a child. But all lessons and experiences are being brought to us for our highest good. What appears to be a punishment is actually a contracted experience we agreed to on the other side to learn. Sometimes I want to know what line I was standing in on the other side when I agreed to overwhelming pain and torment in this life. But as a parent that lost a child, I remember what we said to Anthony over and over again, that I stated before: "I wish I could take this pain away from you, so you wouldn't suffer." Well, guess what? That's *exactly* what happened. He is no longer suffering. He is in complete peace and light, and we are here suffering. We just didn't realize when we said those words to him, how it was to play out. But now when I fall into those times of despair, I remind myself over and over again, the suffering is ours, just as we promised.

While we are being shaken to our core and feeling like nothing makes sense anymore, it is Spirit's way of helping us learn, let go, and trust. What? Let go and trust? How, especially when in such pain? (And you know me and my issues with trust!) I understand this is a lot to integrate early on in the grieving process, especially to those who are new to these ideas. That is why I deal with this in more detail in the next chapters. The point is that if we allow ourselves to properly grieve, we can make it through the tragedies that we were contracted to experience and still move on to live a beautiful, loving, and rewarding life.

Bottom line, if you are still breathing, you are here to learn. Do not allow any crisis, trauma, or hurtful experience to steal the love and joy still left in your life and kill your desire to press forward. You are still here to learn, to experience life—the heartaches as well as all the joy still left. Continue to know you are being supported by Spirit in a very loving way. You are never alone. And if you have been brought to the trauma or had your heart broken, it is because you are loved, and you must go through the experience, in order to learn and come out stronger on the other side. But we forget about the learning because we're here having a human experience, not wanting any pain or difficulty in our lives. But that is exactly why we arrived here—to learn. To get through the experience, move through the ordeal and pain, to realize we are strong enough to continue living and pressing forward. Do not allow the suffering to steal your joyful heart. (Easier said than done—trust me, I know). As long as you are here breathing, the Universe, the God source your soul originated from, wants you to continue to breathe, live, and love.

I hope you can see that in the end, as proven by the devastation and grieving over our son, I'm really not that strong. I'm truly not any stronger than you. I am going through the sobbing and the tissue boxes and the flailing and the raging and all the things that are happening to you. And, by the way, I am still praying every day that I'll make it, my husband will make it, and that our family will make it. Many, many days, it still doesn't feel like we will. Yes, I can intellectualize the *whys* and *how comes*, but the whole point of grief is to let the heart start to heal in its own time irrespective of what the mind tries to process. And, our hearts, after all, are just plain *broken*.

Quite frankly, what is the justification of a child dying before their parents? I don't know the answer to that. But I do know that I have one edge, the one I want you to be open to. It is to know that when not one ounce of strength is left in your body, they will be carrying you. That is, Spirit and your loved ones. From a safe, happy, beautiful, perfect place, being in total peace and harmony, they will be watching you from above, sending love to you from above and even sending messages to you from above. How do I know? On top of what I do for a living, I can already say that in the short amount of time Anthony has been gone, besides my faith becoming stronger than it was before, we are also learning more about Spirit, their signs, and how they want to communicate with us from the other side. That is why I feel honored to share with you next where they are now, what they are doing, and the signs they are sending to us that become visible even on this Earth plane! In the midst of your deepest grief, they can manage to get an "Oh, wow" or even a smile from you. That's how powerful they are, and that's how loved you are.

What I'm about to share with you next will leave you realizing that you can't make this stuff up!

Chapter Six
WHY DID THEY LEAVE ME AND WHERE ARE THEY NOW?

The death of a beloved is an amputation.

—C. S. Lewis

So, where do our loved ones go after passing, and are they in pain or suffering? Those are questions I am most frequently asked by clients. Trust me, I am *not* an expert on this. I can only describe to you what I am shown by Spirit on the other side. The reality of death is just an illusion—an illusion of being separate from who and what we were on this plane. The energy of our souls never dies. Energy changes form, but it never dies. The fact is that as we move from the shell of our body vessels, our souls still exist.

There is only the illusion that we are separate, when in actuality, their souls are always around us, wanting to show they haven't left. This is very similar to the energy of water. Water has three forms: solid (when it is frozen), liquid (when it is melted), and vapor (when it is heated). Water, H2O, takes on different forms, but the energy is always transforming from one state of energy to another, as do our souls. The true reality is that our loved ones have never left us. It just becomes impossible for us to fathom they are around, because we can no longer touch them, hold them, speak to them. But they are still there, saying, "I'm here with you."

Whatever the cause of a person's death, the actual moment we take our last breath is pain-free. At that moment, despite any pain the body may be suffering from, the mind is completely free of that distress. As Spirit has shown me thousands of times over, there is no pain for the soul entering life, and there is no pain exiting life, even though the circumstances of their passing could be viewed as traumatic. The soul slips out of the body, usually hovering above it. Your new soul's energy will feel very light, like a feather. But for a brief moment, you will still feel a connection to that body, as there is still this silver cord of energy attached to the body below. Soon that cord dissolves, ending the connection to the body. That's why many souls, on the other side, can describe to me the exact events of the accident, tragedy, or loved ones surrounding their bodies as they were passing. They describe to me that the soul is lifted out of the body a few milliseconds before the last breath is taken, which is why there is never any pain for the soul, just the body, but at that point your loved one's soul is not here feeling it. This is the protection the soul has from all pain.

Now, imagine what it is like as you are floating around your body, feeling the presence of loved ones on the other side, wanting to greet you! As you have moved from the heavy pain and difficulty of the old body, to the energy and force of floating and free of all suffering. You are finally as free as a bird! To the soul, death feels absolutely amazing!

When my husband suddenly got the feeling to get up out of his chair to go over to Anthony right before he took his last breath, that was Anthony's soul that had already exited and was still tied by the silver cord. That is the way he used the energy around my husband to make him get up and go over to him. He had already left the body and was at peace, but was still attached by that silver cord of energy. That's why in that meditation I had earlier in the day, Anthony was already traveling to the other side, seeing the perfection of heaven, and no longer wanting to suffer. Our souls choose certain exit points to leave this life. Thank God, we don't consciously know when they are. But that was the moment Anthony decided, *I've had enough of this pain – I'm out.* It was his way of letting his father know, *I'm leaving.*

How does the soul transition? Some have reported moving toward the light, others have shown walking through a fog state, others have shown walking over a bridge. It doesn't really matter. To us, if you want to exit off a highway, you have to use an exit ramp to do so. On the other side, there is no "have to" anymore. And once transitioned over, whatever your ailments were on this Earth, whatever you may need to become whole, is granted to you immediately—because you *are* whole. No more breathing issues, no more heart attacks, no more difficulty walking or speaking. No more cancer, no more disease. All undesirable effects of our life on Earth, we come to understand, is just a short period in the huge and expansive timeframe of our soul. It's a revelation of, "Aha, that's why it happened," and we suddenly have the ability to see our suffering not from the perspective of being the victim, but as the soul that understands the reason "why" we left the way we did. Wouldn't it be wonderful if our loved ones would show up after they passed to enlighten us here so we could understand? Wouldn't the grief be made easier to get through if we knew the "why"? Unfortunately, and what prompts our anger, tears and questions as we sit in pain, it's not up to *that* soul to give us the answers. It's up to us to determine them on our own.

WHY DID THEY LEAVE ME AND WHERE ARE THEY NOW?

The newly arrived souls are mesmerized by the beauty and magnificence of "heaven." They have often told me in readings that there are no human words to actually describe the brilliance and magnificence of their new surroundings. They show their energy is connected to the energy of the colors around them, the grass, flowers, and light. Suddenly everything around them is buzzing and alive and they have become *one* with everything that is. Everything becomes part of the whole and everything is about loving energy. That's so difficult for us as humans to comprehend because we know about separation. I am me, and you are you. We look, act, sound different, so how can both of us meld together? That is what I was explaining before about our energy never dying as we become One with all that is. Many times in a reading, a soul will show up, validate themselves, and the client says, "But I never met that person because they died when I was a baby." That is the collective consciousness of the whole that is showing up, the energy of the soul revealing, "Even though you don't know me, I am here always beside you, guiding you."

The level of heaven that you arrive at is determined by how you lived your life here. Troubled souls, who killed, maimed, or tormented others on Earth, arrive at a very low level. The highest levels are reserved for those who are spiritually evolved. Think of Mother Theresa. The rest of us fall somewhere in the middle. When we arrive to the other side, there is a lot of learning for our souls to do. We are given our "life review" where each of us must watch the events of our life, as if on a monitor, and the higher angels and guides on the other side will then stop the video tape, so to speak. We are shown those moments when we didn't choose wisely, wronged someone, or said something cruel. However, now we are placed in the receiver's position and made to "feel" what it felt like to be on the other end. This is where the soul, that now has 20/20 hindsight, is able to feel the pain inflicted to that person and is made to learn how they could have reacted, or chosen differently. This is how our souls learn, if we didn't get the lessons here on Earth, and many of us just don't.

It's important to note that no one gets away with anything here on Earth, despite what it may look like to others around them. And this is the karma that I spoke about earlier. Whether it's here on Earth that someone's actions come to haunt them, or whether they see it for the first time on the other side, all souls are forced to learn from the human experience. Some learn faster than others. As they learn the meaning behind the experiences and lessons, they move up higher on the spectrum, with the intention to always become more "enlightened." And I have always been shown that the higher elevated souls are able to go down to the lower levels to visit other loved ones, but lower energies have not yet earned the right to travel up, until they do the work themselves.

As we are made to feel the negative effects of our actions on Earth, we are also made to feel the love and kindness we showed to others. Experiencing the joyful feeling of giving love to others makes the learning process easier to handle. But there is a tremendous amount of forgiveness our souls must learn—for ourselves. Learning to forgive is a tough lesson here on Earth, as well as in heaven. Feeling the hurt inflicted on others, and then having to forgive ourselves, is the soul's purpose in learning.

And, as each soul is learning on the other side, they are also living. They are reuniting with loved ones passed before them, even beloved pets! The happiness and joy these Spirits show is sometimes unbelievable. They always want their loved ones to know they are no longer suffering, they have been reunited with family and are enjoying all the things on Earth they were not able to enjoy while they were on this plane. They laugh, commune with family, travel, do sports, cook.

WHY DID THEY LEAVE ME AND WHERE ARE THEY NOW?

Whatever their passions were here on Earth, they are showing doing the same thing on the other side, except now that they are souls connected to all that is, all they have to do is imagine doing something and they are suddenly transported there. Want to travel to Italy? Boom, think it and they are there. Want to play a round of golf? Think it and boom, they are on the putting green. Everything is instantaneous, loving, and peaceful. If you're wondering if your loved one is okay and no longer suffering, think of them being the beautiful, perfect versions of themselves in heaven, having the time of their lives! Lucky them, right?

As for children who never had a chance to complete their life on Earth, things work a little differently. Whenever a child Spirit shows up in a reading on the other side, they always show me about the "age" they passed. Remember, linear time is relative only on this human plane. Time does not exist on the other side. They "validate" themselves by showing me their ages. Some young souls that passed as babies will show themselves still as babies, but then may show me actually being an older age that they want to be on the other side. For example, I had a woman who lost one of her twin boys a few months after birth. The boy was redheaded, unlike his brother, and he wanted to show me what he knows his mother would remember him as, a six-month-old baby. But then he transformed into being about five years old, running around and playing catch and t-ball with his grandfather on the other side. He described exactly what he looked like. Turns out, the brother that remained here, looks like his mother, and the soul on the other side was an exact replica of his father; red hair, freckles, hazel eyes, and all. He said he was very happy playing with all the other children on the other side but said when it's his parents' turn to cross over, he will show up to greet them as the infant baby they knew, so they could recognize him.

Linear time is held only on this Earth. We are young, and then grow old. There is a chart and pattern to how we age. Age does not exist on the other side. Many gentlemen who suffered, or grew old, present themselves much younger—perhaps in their military uniform, or their wedding picture, or even young, in high school, leaning up against their favorite car as a young man. The soul only validates how they passed, what they looked like, but then shows how they really want to be seen and feel—*for eternity.*

How amazing must that be? To be free of all human ailments and disease. Just as Anthony showed up all dressed in white, a nicely trimmed chin strap beard, glasses hanging from his t-shirt, all smiles and extremely handsome. No longer suffering! That's what we have to keep remembering. They are no longer suffering. The pain is just ours.

My girlfriend Kim Russo's mom, Maryann, passed ten weeks before Anthony. We didn't even know he was ill at that time. I went to her wake, never having met the woman, to pay my respects. Kim is a very well-established international medium, and on my way out, said to me, "If you get any messages from Mom, please let me know," and we hugged goodbye. It was either that night, or the following night, her mother kept appearing in dreams. Remember, I never met the woman. She appeared in one dream, sitting at a kitchen table, laughing and howling with her sister-in-law, who had crossed over before her. When I shared it with Kim, she validated that's exactly what she and her aunt would do when they were together. Another evening, in another dream, she was sitting on the side of a major highway out in the hot sun, very young, with a big sunhat, sitting on a beach chair. As I drove up next to her, to see why she was sitting there and if she was okay, she just smiled and said she was waiting to log in the times of the circuit-racing bikers en route as they passed her. When I shared it with Kim, she said her mother lived right by a major highway in Florida, and race bike riders were always using that route. The last dream, her mom appeared in this very beautiful, flouncy white top, her hair and nails all done, makeup and lipstick perfect, smiling and again looking so young. As she smiled, she said, "Tell them I'm OK and having a great time." Kim validated she knew exactly what blouse her mother was referring to and that it was one of her favorite blouses she loved wearing. She had also had a vision of her mother wearing that same blouse a day before she came to me in the dream. Great validations!

These are all signs and visions of how happy they are on the other side. Sometimes through our own grief and heartache, we so desperately want to see our loved ones in dreams, because having them ripped out of our lives is so painful. But many times they will appear to others that we know, to give us the message they are okay. Just as when we go on vacation, and arrive, we call back home to say, "We're here, we're okay and see you in a week." Our loved ones will do the same, but if they are blocked from getting through our thick heartache, they may decide to appear to others. This is specifically why Kim's mom came to me right away after her passing, because Kim was still in the midst of her heartbreak, so Maryann came to me!

Listen, if you have a dream about someone's loved one, even though it may not mean anything to you, please reach out to them to let them know the message given, or what you saw in that dream! Souls will give us visitations to let us know they are still with us. Not everyone gets dreams, and I don't understand why. I wish I did. But those dreams of them that we can remember with complete clarity weeks and months later, are visitations. A message to us that their souls are whole and at peace. We must always remember that, as we trudge through our grief on this side, wanting constantly to be reunited with them.

Now, having shared all of this I do have to address the possible elephant in the room. There are some times as a client that you want a reading and are very clear that there are certain people you just *don't* want to hear from! You read that correctly. You were relieved when they died, even though you may not be able to tell anyone that, and the minute their name comes up you get agitated or even angry. To make my point, this happened to me at a Breast Cancer fundraiser I had done on Long Island. I walked up to this woman, told her a husband was standing right beside her, and his name was Joe and was standing there with an apology. She immediately yelled out, "Tell that bastard I don't want to hear from him!" The crowd roared with laughter. I have to admit, so did I. I wasn't expecting that reaction. I continued to relay the message of his apology, how he was learning on the other side, the angels were showing him his life review and he was *so* sorry for his lack of learning here, and the hurt he had done to her. She refused to listen. Her response was, "I don't care!" Again the crowd roared. Boy, was she funny! She was there to hear from her sister, not the husband.

But as a medium, we have no control over who comes through, or the messages they want to share. I tried explaining that Spirit will show up with the messages that need to be shared, not what we want to hear. When the husband was able to validate a few experiences in their life, I thought for sure her heart would melt, and she would be open to hear his message and healing. *Nope.* She was not interested, and that's a shame because this was an amazing opportunity of healing this soul wanted to help with. He wanted her to understand what went wrong here, and how sorry he was. It's up to us to either be open to an apology and forgiveness, or not. As I said before, forgiveness is a tough lesson to learn, and this woman was not open to it.

I honor and respect client wishes, but it is such a shame when a client cuts themselves off from their own healing. Do you understand the importance of this? Yes, you don't want to hear from that person who traumatized and perhaps ruined your life for a period of time, but, if they have grown and are showing life from a different perspective to you, as well as apologizing to you, you owe it to yourself, not them, to try to find compassion and forgiveness. Please come into a reading willing to grow. And, if you are dragged kicking and screaming to some channeling event and get "read," even if you don't believe in this hokey-pokey stuff, all the more reason you want to open your ears and wake up to what is being shared. The Universe is screaming at you in love by any means necessary!

Many times clients will come in for a reading, and they say they are not there to connect with loved ones on the other side, but are there to discuss their life direction and purpose. I always ask these clients to be "open" to loved ones appearing, so they can then confirm what they see is happening in that person's life and can validate this person is never alone. When a client is open to this kind of communication, not only do they allow that loved one to give whatever message is needed for healing, but most of the time, that loved one is saying, "I see where you're headed and I am trying to help you." When Bobbi Allison came to my house for that reading, and wanted to talk about my father being there, I was like these clients. I didn't want to hear anything from him. I wasn't *ready*. When clients tell me the same thing, I gently talk about that loved one, ask the client to please be open to receiving whatever messages are coming from the other side. Most of the time, they focus less on the *person* coming through, and more on the *messages*. Bingo! It becomes a very healing, loving session. It's all about the healing; otherwise, why am I even doing this? To validate what the last words were said before the person passed? Or to validate that you brought a piece of their lace doily with you in your purse? Yes, that does come through on readings, and I get that people want the validations of the individual, but isn't it more important the soul acknowledge something they should have apologized for in this life, or show this client the soul sees everything they are going through and they are not alone? This is the kind of healing I always ask Spirit to show me. Let this client walk out feeling lighter in spirit for having had this reading and connecting to the other side.

Even the clients that come in specifically to connect with loved ones in Spirit usually get some amazing validations that their loved ones see what's happening with the people in their lives, or what is happening around them now. I had a mother Spirit show up in a reading, and she immediately gave me the name Michael and pointed down here on Earth. The client having the reading said, "Yes, that's my son." Her mother in spirit said, "I am watching over him, I know you're afraid for him, but please do not be. I am watching over him." The mother Spirit validated about the anxiety, depression, and drinking this boy was doing. She saw from the other side her daughter fearing something horrible would happen to him and she was saying, "I'm here, I've got this, please don't worry." Spirit is always in control of the reading. Whether the person wants to hear from a loved one or not, I follow the direction of Spirit. However, because I understand some people are not ready to hear from some souls on the other side, Spirit and I work together to gently get the messages and points across to them.

The truth is that we never actually lose contact with our loved ones if we choose to open our minds. They are trying to contact us regularly and in many different ways, although the pain feels like that of having lost a limb, as C.S. Lewis brilliantly stated—because it is an amputation from our lives. There is an uncanny significance to this phrase and loss. Have you ever heard about people who after losing a limb still seem to feel it or experience it? It's called phantom limb syndrome, and it's a sensation that up to 80 percent of the population feels after an amputation. It's as if the limb is actually still there and people often go to scratch it, use it, touch it and then realize it is gone. Well, I want you to start to think of the loss of your loved one like this. The limb,

Why Did They Leave Me and Where Are They Now?

the person, is gone, but it is actually still there, and if you pay attention you can actually feel it, sense it. That is why in the next chapter I start to help you see, feel, and pay attention so you can actually learn to read the signs they are leaving for us everywhere we go.

Chapter Seven
VISIBLE AND INVISIBLE EVER-PRESENT SIGNS

LEARNING THE NEW LANGUAGE OF LOVE

*When you are sorrowful look again in your heart,
and you shall see that in truth you are weeping
for that which has been your delight.*

—Kahlil Gibran

Now that our loved ones are crossed over and have left us, what is the first thing we want? *Signs*! We can't hear them, touch them, hold them, yet we desperately want to connect with them because the holes in our hearts are beyond shredded. The issue now is that here on Earth we communicate through sight, sound, touch, smell, taste. Our human bodies learned all these human modalities and linguistics as we

Visible and Invisible Ever-Present Signs

grew and assimilated with our other human relatives. But now that our loved one's soul is on the other side, they no longer have the ability to communicate with us in the way to which we have become accustomed. They have to figure out, and we have to re-learn, how Spirit is now communicating to let us know they are always with us. Remember the "clairs" I spoke about in the previous part? Well those are all energy vibrations mediums use to get impressions about your loved ones. Sense of smell, sense of seeing, sense of knowing, etc. Guess what—mediums have this gift, but so do *each* of you. However, as mediums, we've learned and homed in on this gift.

Your loved ones are always trying to use the *energy* around you to let you know they are there. The visual of a red cardinal always perched outside your window when you're washing dishes—that's a sign. The dimes you find in the weirdest of places, like inside your shoe in the closet—that's a sign. Your loved one's birthday or significant number here on Earth and you see it everywhere you go—that's a sign. When my father passed over fifteen years ago, I knew and understood about signs. I remember having a conversation in my mind with him one day, and basically said, "If you want to prove to me you're around, don't send me pennies and dimes, I want you to show me one-dollar bills." I was sarcastically wanting him to prove he was around; after all, how often do you see dollar bills? For this reason, I chose a sign that I knew would be difficult for him to produce. Everywhere I go now, I often see dollar bills. Sometimes I'm able to pick them up and keep them, other times it is the word "dollar" spelled on something right in front of me, or a plate or mug with a dollar bill picture on it. One time, while driving and talking to my dad, going over things I should have said, or some memory of the past, I stopped at a stop sign intersection and heard in my head *Look up*, and as I did, I saw I was at the street intersection of Dollar Street and Dollar Avenue. He was letting me know he was there listening!

My dear friend Suzie's son Justin passed away five years ago, from a tragic car accident, at the age of twenty-seven. She was never able to say goodbye to him. Funny thing is, I actually met her at a restaurant event I was doing, right after he passed, and she had come to me there for a reading. From then on, we became dear friends. One year, she was doing a beach memorial celebration for Justin's anniversary of passing, of which I couldn't attend. I was thinking of her, her family, and him the entire morning. I kept asking him, "Please send a big sign you're aware of this celebration." As I entered Starbucks to get a coffee (I'm typically a Dunkin Donuts kinda' gal), at the register I heard *Look down*, and right in front of me was a package of chocolates called Justin's. *Wow!* I never met this young man, and yet he was giving me the sign for his mom, to let her know he's aware of the celebration today. Now I've heard Starbucks carries this Justin's brand of chocolates, but I'm not a Starbucks customer. Yet that day, he arranged for me to enter one, to specifically see that sign. No coincidences! Justin is always sending signs to his mom. She takes these most amazing pictures of the sky, clouds, and sun, and he is always putting an orb with angel wings in the picture. She must have 500 pictures and *all* of them come out like that. That is a sign from her boy! Yet most of us would just look at the picture and think nothing of it.

Oh! And my client Laurie's son Jeremy passed of cystic fibrosis. She and her daughter came to me for readings every now and then. Jeremy was a huge Superman fan. One day, a few weeks before Christmas, and about a week before his mom and sister were scheduled to come to me for a reading, I stopped at a local Walgreens pharmacy store by my home to pick up a few things. I grabbed a cart outside and as I was pushing it toward the entrance of the store, I saw there was a Christmas ornament in the cart someone had left behind. Weird. When I picked it up and turned it around, it was a Superman ornament. I just *knew* this was from Jeremy! When his mom and sister came to me for the reading the following week, I pulled out the ornament and they started crying! Unbeknownst to me, his mother had created a small memorial Christmas tree for her son, and had all different Superman ornaments, statues, pictures all on that tree in memory of him. And the kicker is—the family is Jewish and does not do Christmas trees! This was his validation and sign; he knew about the special Christmas tree and was adding to *his* collection. How awesome is that for a sign and validation! You see, we don't just get signs from our own loved ones, we get signs for those all around us. Sometimes we're looking for the book to fly off the shelf as we walk by to validate your loved one is in the room, but Spirit can be very powerful and also very subtle as they lay signs before us and before others. Stop saying this is just a coincidence. There are *no* coincidences!

I stand by my belief that *all* death for those remaining is painful: Where there is great love, there is also great pain. I am at the moment resonating with the people who feel losing a child is the worst and with Dwight David Eisenhower who said, "There's no tragedy in life like the death of a child. Things never get back to the way they were." That is the truth. Of all the pain, discomfort, and loss in my life, the death of our son Anthony has been the worst pain imaginable. No doubt the death of a child rocks your world. Does it matter if our loved one was ill over time, or suddenly passed by accident or of their own volition? Each type of passing brings with it, its own "could have, should have." The bottom line we all hold similar is, they are no longer here for us to hold, talk to or laugh with. The finality of their passing is what hurts the most. We will never have another tomorrow with them again. For the loved ones that died early, we will never know what they would have become in their adulthood. For those who passed in their prime, we will no longer be able to share the memories and milestones of their lives. And for those that passed after a full life on Earth, we will no longer have them by our side as we have become accustomed to. Every passing brings with it a feeling of loss, fear, guilt, hurt—all human emotions that we do not like to face, and now have to face for the rest of our lives, alone.

I am by no means an expert on loss. No one is. And we each grieve in our own unique way. But what I have come to learn is that great loss, as in that of a child, brings with it also a very lonely road. Others are fearful. They have fear of saying something to us that's wrong, fear of not saying enough, fear of not having the right words to make it all better, fear that they can't imagine our pain. And, what do these very well-meaning people do? They say nothing at all. Better not to stir the pot, not open a wound, but allow the ones grieving to just do their thing. What becomes our pain and cross to bear, becomes our pain all on our own. And grief is not something that most of us can share with our family and friends, because they won't understand the full magnitude of our loss. It's just another lesson learned in trusting in the process, even when the world feels very lonely on this one-way road by ourselves.

It's a sad, sad truth. We walk in the shoes others can't go to in their minds or in their nightmares. Their terror of losing a child, is our reality. They can avoid it, but we can't. It frightens them, as it probably used to frighten us before we had to bury our child. Terror, loneliness, sadness, crying become our new reality. We walk and talk and try to deal with the trauma as best we can, but we're just faking it. "Fake it until you make it," they say. That is what we're doing.

When Anthony first passed, all of my medium and psychic friends told me the very big signs he was going to give us to prove that he wasn't far from us. I just assumed they were being kind, to help us during those initial very tormenting days. The fact is, Anthony, as with every Spirit on the other side, is trying to connect with us through Love.

Visible and Invisible Ever-Present Signs

And since love never dies, they are always trying to give us signs they are with us. Since Anthony passed at age twenty-seven, from the first day he was gone, we began to see #27 on almost every license plate.

Coming home from the funeral parlor one day, there was a car in front of us that had 2735 as the license number. My husband said, "Oh look, there's the 27 again, but the 35 doesn't mean anything."

I looked at him and said, "Are you kidding me? 3,5 is the month and date of his baby Christian's birth - March 5th." From then on, we saw 27 and 35 on most license plates.

We had gone to a plaque store, to get a plaque made for his urn at the cemetery crypt. As his mother, his dad, and I were standing waiting for the man to inscribe it, all of a sudden a white feather fell from the ceiling and was floating right in front of his mom. She gently allowed the feather to fall into her palm, and of course, we all started to cry. That was a sign. A few days after Anthony's passing, my husband went into New York City with his Soul Brothers group, to give out survival bags to the homeless. On his way out of the city, feeling very numb and missing his son, he began to think of Anthony and asked him for a "sign."

Coming out of the midtown tunnel, in NYC, a white van passed the bus my husband was riding in. The name on the van was "Father and Sons, Inc." Anthony knew his son was with him. He smiled and when he opened his eyes again, he looked out of the window of the bus and he passed a building with a big sign on the roof. The name of the company was Typhin Steel. Anthony was a huge Pittsburgh Steelers fan. This boy bled black and gold, he ate, slept, dreamt of this football team. My husband has lived in NY City for his entire life and has come out of that midtown tunnel thousands of times, and never saw that sign before. What are the chances Anthony would have him look exactly in that direction when asking for a sign? Anthony was using the power and energy of Love to help his dad see these signs. To let him know, "I know your heart is hurting, but I am right here beside you." Steelers license plate frames, Steelers car decals started popping out of everywhere. We're located in New York; Pittsburgh Steelers fans are hard to come by. Suddenly we were seeing Steelers stuff everywhere we looked.

When we'd get into a car, suddenly songs would come on the radio to let us know he was with us. Lyrics literally took our breath away, as we would talk about him, and a song like "Without Me" by Halsey would suddenly come on. One night right after his passing, we met with his girlfriend Nikki and our grandson Christian. We were in Friendly's ice cream restaurant enjoying dinner and a song came on—"Shine" by Collective Soul. This song dates back to the early 1990s. My husband said that earlier that day, he had posted on Facebook a picture of Anthony as a young boy about four years old, and had posted the words to that song alongside his picture and explained how he used to sing that song as a little boy in the back seat of the car, whenever it would come on the radio. Anthony reminisced about hearing his son's little four-year-old voice bellowing out the lyrics "Shine, heaven let your light shine down." What are the chances that we were sitting together with our grandson, enjoying a meal, and *that* particular song comes on? That was a *sign*! He was letting us know, I know about the post on Facebook, and I am right here putting that song on the restaurant play list. Amazing! Did we all begin to cry? You betcha!

An incredibly huge sign Anthony showed us was a short while after his passing, when we went to visit his first son Austin in Pennsylvania. We were all in the car driving to get something to eat: Austin, his mom Cassie, her husband Tim, Anthony and myself. We weren't really sure where to go, and finally Cassie said last minute, "Let's

Visible and Invisible Ever-Present Signs

go to Friday's," a restaurant chain we're familiar with on the East Coast. We parked in front of the restaurant and walked to the front door. There parked right by the door was a bright all-yellow Dodge Charger with a huge black decal on the side of the car that said *Steelers*, and more Steelers decals all over the back window. It took our breath away, and we just had to take pictures. What are the chances as we are visiting his son, and deciding where to eat, that we would end up somewhere that a huge Steelers sign would show up? Yes, the Pittsburgh Steelers are a Pennsylvania team, but we were just outside Philadelphia, which is huge Eagles fan territory. This was Anthony's way of letting us know he was there with us too. Wow, just remembering that day still gives me chills!

How do we connect to Spirit so they can give us their own signs? First of all, you must be open to receiving signs. When I first gave my father the sign of a dollar bill, I wasn't open, I was taunting. It took me several years before I started seeing the sign. That was on me. I believed, but then I didn't believe. Not that I didn't believe in Spirit and signs. I didn't believe he would send me that sign. Hence, why it took so long. As humans, we are definitely a "believe it when I see it" species. We question everything. If we are looking for a sign, and something pops up, we categorize it as a "coincidence." We're used to communicating with our eyes, mouths, and ears, we don't understand Spirit wants to have something appear that seems weird to us and make us say "huh," but it's actually our loved one creating it to show they are there.

Remember the "clairs" I've spoken about? That's the energy of the senses that Spirit uses to communicate. Spirit can make you *feel* their presence beside you. You can't see them, but suddenly, inexplicably, you just feel like they are sitting right beside you. You can only feel them. Yes! That's a sign. If we're somewhere and we smell a perfume or scent of lilacs and it reminds us of our mother. Yes! That's a sign. One day a few weeks ago, I had gone to the doctor's office for a physical, and on my way out, a flood of memories suddenly popped into my head about Anthony and being in that damn hospital. As I was pulling out of the parking lot, there was a truck parked there that had both a Steelers sticker *and* a Yankees sticker on the car window. Two of Anthony's favorite sports teams. Could that be categorized as coincidence? I guess. But what are the chances I was at the doctor's office, thinking of him at that time as I was walking out, and seeing those two validations of him that he was there? How does everything align perfectly like that and we dismiss it as a coincidence?

Because my husband had such a huge bond with Anthony over sports, not having him here, not being able to text about the latest team trades, scores or players, has been very hard on him. When the first NFL draft happened after Anthony's passing my husband was devastated. On the first day of the draft, driving home from work, he was talking to him in the car, crying and letting him know this was a tough day without him here. How much he missed him and didn't know how he'd get through all the tomorrows without him. He was traveling home on the parkway, saw up above a traffic sign flashing "delays ahead" because of an accident and decided to drive off and transfer to the Expressway. All the while he's talking to Anthony, and saying, "Please let me know if you hear me and know how hard this day is for me. Send me a huge sign. Show me a Steelers logo somewhere." He specifically asked for *that* sign.

As he merged onto the expressway, a huge Mack truck passed his car and began to drive right in front of my husband's vehicle. On the back of the truck was a huge sign. It said Pennsylvania Steel Co. My husband smiled and thought, *Wow…nice sign.* The word "steel" was in that sign. Not exactly what he had asked for, but it was close. But as he went around the truck and started to pass it, he looked at the truck

Visible and Invisible Ever-Present Signs

driver's door and wouldn't you know it, the driver had a Steelers logo on the door! There was the very sign he had asked his son for, not ten minutes before. Had the traffic sign not flashed when it did, then my husband wouldn't have gotten off and switched to another expressway, and he would have never passed that truck, and never seen this sign. Of course, this blew him away and he cried, sobbed, you know, snot coming out of his nose kind of crying! *This* is how Spirit works! Does seeing that sign bring our loved ones back or stop the pain of missing them? No. But it begins to give us a higher understanding that if they can produce signs like that, they are with us and hear us! Their souls don't end. They are just with us in a different form.

Do not be afraid to ask your loved one for a very specific sign. A yellow rose, a blue feather, a scratch-off, a significant number pertaining to them. Whatever is meaningful to you or them. Ask them for the sign, letting them know that is what you are wanting, and then be open to allowing them to bring it to you. It may not be immediate like Anthony's sign to his dad, but give them some time to show you that they can hear you. Anthony shows me the word *HUG* on license plates. What is the probability of seeing that word on license plates all around me? When I'm in the car, that's what he shows me, and I am so blessed and thrilled each time. Do the same for your loved ones. Give them the sign, trust it's coming, and then be aware of allowing yourself to see it. Spirit wants to prove to you they are always with you. Give them this opportunity to do so!

Allow yourselves to be open to these types of signs. Allow yourself to have conversations with your loved ones and allow your loved ones to speak back with you. Will it sound like their voice is being heard from outside your ears? No. It almost feels like you are answering back for them, or you are imagining what their response would be. When I'm in the car, and a crazy song comes on and I feel lightness in my chest, I can almost "see" Anthony sitting right beside me rocking and dancing in his seat, pretending he's dancing in his chair. I don't see him actually sitting there, I see him in my mind's eye. You can too. When we assume we're talking to our loved ones, many times we don't believe it because it's foreign to how we're used to communicating. But when we're talking to them, and they're either giving us signs to show us they are there, or we're talking to them in our head, they *are* there talking to you. That *is* them right beside us having that conversation. Do not dismiss it as either a coincidence or just our imagination. Spirit is trying to use our senses to communicate. Allow them to let you feel their presence, or smell them near you, or hear their voice in your head, or even get a small chill up your back with goosebumps for no apparent temperature change reason. That is the way they are giving you a hug, saying, "I'm right here."

So many times, I am asked about how time works on the other side. What has been described to me, via readings, is that there is *no* concept of time there. On Earth, we live in a linear world. Monday comes before Thursday, 11 a.m. comes before 3 p.m., and February arrives before October. Everything is linear. For us there is a past, present, and future. We *all* understand this linear thinking. Realize, though, that on the other side, the concept of linear time no longer exists. What was in the past, is now in the present and is also the future. Everything is living and *all* is a part of the whole, even our loved ones' souls. We become part of the whole and time no longer exists. In a reading, if a loved one gives information about what they may see happening to someone here on Earth, there is a dilemma of translating that concept of "time." Spirit may show us a number "6." Is that six weeks, six months, six years? It's hard for Spirit to translate that, because time no longer exists. But as humans, we always want to know the answer of time. How long do I have to wait? How much longer before I get a new job? When is my soulmate arriving? When will I have a baby?

Visible and Invisible Ever-Present Signs

And we don't want to hear the answer is "6," when that makes no sense to us. We want to know the linear time involved. But if that is all Spirit is showing us, we can't just assume they are talking days, weeks, months, years. This is where dealing in time is very difficult for a medium because we're interpreting for Spirit on the other side and trying to translate it into a human language the client understands. Instead of worrying about the "how much time" question, just allow Spirit to acknowledge it may or may not happen and then just *trust* the answer. Be open to the information Spirit wants to share in your session. Do not go in with preconceived ideas of how the information should flow. You will get a much more healing session if you allow Spirit to speak in their new language: Love.

All I can reiterate is that you need and want to be watching for signs, paying attention, making notes, and getting ready to be astonished by the new language of love they are teaching and showing you. It is through connecting the dots, agreeing there are no coincidences and moving through life knowing they are just beside you and their love is ever-reaching and ever-present that it will truly help you work through your grief. You will start to enjoy the interactions and look forward to their "proofs" of existence beyond the current world you live in. You may even heal more quickly than you might have before when you believed there was no purpose behind this level of suffering and that life did not exist beyond this plane.

Chapter Eight
GRIEF IS EXACTLY LIKE FEAR

I never knew that grief, is exactly like fear.

—Author CS Lewis, in his book
"A Grief Observed," after he lost his wife.

For those of you that have been struggling through your agonizing grief, and have been in your darkest depths of despair, or even just entered it, I wish you courage and solace through your journey. This will not be an easy road, but if you allow the forces of nature to guide you, it can be a learning experience beyond your wildest imagination. From this pain, you will enter into a stronger *knowingness* of yourself, your soul, and your purpose. I don't make these claims lightly. Grief and fear can either swallow you up alive, or they can propel you further ahead.

Isaac Newton's Third Law of Physics states that "For every action, there is an equal and opposite reaction." Simply put, this means that for every interaction and experience we encounter in life, there is an energy associated with that experience (negative or positive). This duality of forces is always in play and is acting on either side of you. The magnitude of that force on one side equals the size of the force on the other. Since this duality of energy is around you at all times, you can either lean toward the darkness, fear, and despair (the negative side) or move toward the light, love, and compassion (positive side). The magnitude of the dark energy will literally swallow you up whole, if you continuously give in to it. Similarly, the magnitude of the force on the positive side will propel you to understanding, peace, and learning.

I often compare our problems, grief, loss, and troubles to the story of the caterpillar and the butterfly. We've all heard this story a thousand times—the caterpillar that metamorphoses within its cocoon, struggles to break free, and then flies away as a completely different form than when it started. In the process of growing out of its encasement, and having to break free, the butterfly is required to work, struggle and endure, in order to be free. If someone were to snip the cocoon to assist in the process, and if they snipped too early, the caterpillar would not be half caterpillar, half butterfly, it would actually just be a liquid entity that had never formed properly. If someone snips the cocoon as the butterfly is struggling to break free, the butterfly would fall out, unable to fly. It needs to go through the process of development and struggle. It physically needs to do that in order to transform from a caterpillar to a butterfly.

That is the law of nature. There's no getting around it. That law of nature works in the same way for us as well. And within that law, the by-product of those forces is either death of ourselves, or renewed life and purpose. When we are struggling through that darkness and wanting it to end, we are depriving ourselves of becoming stronger. We want the easy way out. Someone please snip this cocoon of pain so I can escape. We ignore our feelings or want to suppress our anger, hurt, sadness. We are preventing ourselves from the benefit of the struggle, which is there to get us beyond to the individual we are meant to manifest into. By resisting this struggle, we are preventing our labor and pain to allow our cocoon to open from within, and for new life to emerge and begin anew.

There is no doubt that the struggles you have endured in life are real, and tremendous, no question. But where there is great loss and pain, also comes with it the potential for great love and understanding of the whole picture of the Universe. That struggle is the catalyst for your transformation here on Earth. It's not meant to take you down; it's actually the same struggle as the butterfly pushing its way toward freedom, bringing you through to a new level.

I'm sure you can look back on your life, to all the experiences you've endured, and remarked at how strong you were to get through them. How did you get through that? With the same strength of taking one day at a time, until you finally arrived at a point in your life, when there was no struggle. This is the same lesson that comes up each time as we continue with our battles. The pain you endure for loss of your loved one, whether it's physical loss of someone, loss of a job or relationship, or any other catalyst creating the suffering—that pain is the cocoon holding in your transformation and manifestation. The learning comes through breaking free of that pain, allowing yourself the full emotions, and then letting go, flowing with the winds of Spirit so they can assist you in your transformation. This will enable you to spread your loved one's courage, their dreams, their love in this life, not their individual pain, not your pain, but *love*. When you let go and surrender to the pain, is when the heart can begin to mend, to move forward out of your agony and back into *love*. It's always about *love*.

Love: being and sharing love, is where your freedom lies—in expressing the love you have for your loved one and for yourself and not focusing on the pain. Your loved one is no longer bound by the circumstances of their passing: They are free. You are being asked to stretch out of your comfort zone, as the butterfly does, and emerge from this cocoon of pain.

In our loss, especially the loss of our child, we have to remind ourselves to flow through those moments of excruciating pain of missing them, let that pain go, and allow ourselves to flow into the love we have for them. What does that mean? It means that in that moment of excruciating pain, we remind ourselves that this sharp heartache will ease, if we let go. Breathe through the emotions. But in that moment of terror and sadness, we can't see our way out, so we hold on to the negative forces, the ones that remind us we cannot breathe because our loved one is no longer here.

We are not being asked to let go of our loved one and their memories; we're not letting go of the individual that we miss every second, but we are asked to flow out of that pain. Everything is unfolding in Divine order. Pain is *not* the path to freedom. It is, however, an emotion that as Spirits having a human experience, what we have collectively chosen and agreed to follow here on Earth—letting go, trusting, flowing, and coming out of that excruciating pain and allowing us to connect to the love.

The point is, our loved ones on the other side want us to feel only the love, not the heartache. It is our job to awaken to the truth of the experience that only love begets more love. Only the Light of Love can clear away the dark corners of pain. We want this world to be one without pain, and when it crosses our doorstep, we can't handle it, so we want it eliminated quickly. But as humans, we have chosen to learn from pain. How many of us learn when life is flowing well? Not many. It's in the struggles that we learn, "Aha, that's the lesson." Your lesson is to trust the forces around you, the winds of Spirit that are trying to help you learn through this experience and not allow it to debilitate you. (Well, at least for as little time as possible.)

I always compare the process of our pain and grief as similar to a train needing to pass through a very long, dark tunnel. As the train enters the tunnel, there is a sudden darkness, heaviness surrounding it—the light of the surrounding day and sunshine no longer searing into the windows, warming our skin with light. The train is pulled, pushed by a force guiding it through that tunnel. Each second as it passes, it seems as if the darkness will never end. If you've ever sat on a train going through a dark tunnel, there's a little bit of a trepidation, a quietness, a feeling of unease as you immediately pass through the darkness. That train is being pushed and propelled forward. As it continues forward, all we see is the darkness, and perhaps an emergency light whizzing by us as we continue through the tunnel at very fast speeds. This is similar to the darkness that we endure when we begin to grieve the loss of a loved one.

Being propelled and forced through that dark tunnel, wondering when this darkness, the heaviness, the unknowing will end. The force of our experience is pushing us through an uncomfortable situation. The energy and Light of God and Universe pulling us through to the other side. Beckoning for us to continue down the path with each second that we take, propelling us further. But to what? More darkness? As with a train that eventually passes through the dark tunnel, back into the light on the other side, so does the Light of the Universe beckon to us: *Come toward me, keep going. Don't stop. We want you to release the pain and move forward.*

It's encouraging you, cheering you on, like a parent watching a child who goes from crawling to taking their first steps; you are there.

You can do it! Don't stop. I'm here to catch you! In this process there is the constant energy that surrounds us, asking us to continue to move forward even in the darkness when we don't understand where we're going to end up once we come out. The same force that propels the train to continue moving forward, out into the Light of day, or through more storms on the other side, Spirit asks us to have faith, keep moving, don't stop.

The dark tunnels are just a passageway to another side, toward growth, toward more life, toward even more heartache at times—sorry to say. We don't know where it's bringing us, but that life force energy is asking us never to stop. The train moving us from one place in our world, to another, that inevitable Force that keeps reminding us to never stop. There is a meaning behind every pain, every experience. There's always learning for the soul to do.

Our job is to keep moving forward, no matter what the storms are around us. Our loved ones want us to keep moving forward, because they are still a part of us. They are watching and guiding us and know that as humans we don't understand the meaning behind their death—but they ask us to keep moving forward despite the pain and emptiness in our hearts. Like the train, we are constantly moving forward and we will emerge into the sunlight again. We may feel stuck in many moments of our grief, but there is always the light at the end of the tunnel. Always.

My husband Anthony lost his mother over twenty years ago. They had a very special bond, and after a long, painful battle, he lost her to that wretched disease of cancer. I didn't know him then, but he would always talk about his loss and staying in bereavement for two full years after his mother had crossed over. He said he was like a zombie walking around just doing his daily motions, doing what he needed to do as a father and husband. Going to work, taking care of the kids and the house. Very robotic; just a zombie as he dealt with his pain and suffering. He didn't know how he was going to go on without her, or how he would get back to that jovial, loving, and engaged person he had been.

Yet, already, within just a few months of our son's passing, he notices a distinct difference from the grief process of the loss of his mother to the loss of his son. He and Anthony were very close; they texted and spoke almost every day about what was happening in sports, and since our son Anthony was into football, baseball, hockey, and basketball, they shared their passion for sports 365 days a year about whatever team or player of that particular season. Their bond was deep. And while Anthony's pain as a father is excruciating, there are actual moments of clarity, of peace.

My husband even laughs and smiles at times. Even he notices the difference in processing his pain from twenty years ago. In those moments of letting go and enjoying life around him, he is letting in the Light, even though he's still going through that dark tunnel of pain. Nothing stops us from having to go through that tunnel, because it's part of our human path and existence to feel pain.

So what changed from his mother's loss? Tools. (Remember the start of Part Two!) Tools of understanding about the other side. *Knowingness*. Understanding how Spirit communicates with us that I know twenty years ago he wasn't aware of. When he's thinking of our son intensely, it's usually on his long drive to and from work when he has more time to think, when he's listening to a sports talk show they were fans of. Suddenly, a significant number, 27 (his age), 14 (month and date of passing), 35 (his son's birthday), and 91 (his birth year), show up on a license plate driving right in front of him. He hears the songs that start playing on the radio as soon as he turns the car on. The songs that play over the loudspeakers as we enter a restaurant or store. A specific Steelers car emblem on a vehicle driving right beside him. There are numerous signs our Anthony is sending him. He didn't know about any of this twenty years ago. (Thank God he's been listening to me all these years!) There are now occasional moments when he smiles and when something is really, really funny, he will still belly laugh. Of course, when I see that, it just makes my heart smile because in that moment, I see a glimpse of who he really is and how he is trying to come out of this darkness. Already in just a few months of our son's passing, he has the tools to help him get through his grief in a different way that he never had decades ago. The tools and understanding are imperative to helping us get through the grief. We will never forget our loved ones, and the hole in our heart will never go away, but we can still let in the Light, a tiny bit at a time, to help us get *through* it.

As humans, we compare the significance of losses, like comparing the loss of a mother versus a child. Many people have said to me I miss my loved one but of course it's no comparison to the pain that you must be feeling having lost a child. I don't necessarily buy into that. I know many will disagree with me on this, and that's okay. But hear me out. We could have had *very* special souls in our lives whether it's a sister, a mother, an aunt. It doesn't really matter what their relationship is, we can share very strong bonds with that individual. It's a bond of love. When that bond is broken, regardless of what the title or the relationship was in this lifetime, we mourn them, we're in pain. It also doesn't matter how long we've known them. The lost fetus, the stillborn child, the crib death—it could be only an instant but that love connection was so strong it felt like we had cared for them forever—and perhaps we had, many, many lifetimes ago.

Now before I upset anyone, we do *expect* to lose a parent or an elderly person before a child, so I suppose it is ingrained in us to have this loss seem much more shocking. As humans, it is our ego that becomes trained through time to believe that there is a natural order of things and then to assign a value—an often inappropriate judgment—to them. For example, we assume that all humans should be born healthy and live a long and prosperous life. Nowhere are we taught that in actuality humans come to have an experience and come with an actual "time stamp," time contract, life-experience, or hardship contract that may expire before they die of old age.

In this world today we are even beginning to accept that as we age, we one day will start taking medications before our eventual demise and death, and only pray that we will have lived a long life. We pray that our loved ones do too, with a minimal of suffering. But, remember, this is all ego. If we change our way of thinking and realize that the super-conscious, *Love*, exceeds all boundaries and goes beyond any linear phase, then we accept that all *Love* is equal. When all love bonds are equal, then the level at which we suffer, no matter who or what died, is connected to the depth of the bond and has nothing to do with the title/relationship of the deceased.

An individual can have a very close relationship with their sister where they are literally each other's soulmates. And suddenly that sister crosses over. What is that remaining sibling to do? They feel the loss of that person on such a deep level. Their bond was intense. Her mourning is powerful because the love was real. And that bond of Love has been broken on the physical level. And that is what we mourn. That is what we cry and sob during the day or call out to them in the middle of the night. We want the pain to end. All we can do is remember the loss of the person, the body, the voice, the laughter, and then the realization, like a bolt of lightning to the heart, that this loved one is no longer here.

Yes, we do have a million memories. But in that *moment* we want to be able to *touch* the person, see them smiling, hear their voice and laughter. And because that option has been taken away from us, we cry in hysteria and our heart is forever shattered—no matter what the relationship. Once that bond of love is broken because that individual is no longer here, does it really matter whether it was a child, a sister, or a mother? We miss what we miss, which is why I do not judge people's emotions and feelings. As a mother who's lost a child, should I be standing on my soap box and claiming my pain is greater than yours? Love is love, and the way you loved your family member or friend is completely unique to you. It's not for me to judge, or compare whose pain is greater than the next.

Now, there may be many who disagree with my feelings and understanding, and that's fine too. I would never say to a parent who's lost a child, whether it be from illness, accident or of their own will that their neighbor who lost their parent is grieving the same way. Never. This is torturous beyond comprehension. What I am saying is, to a person who lost the most important person in their lives, whomever that loss is, their grief is just as palatable. Just as fierce. We all process grief, fear, and agony in different ways. So to my husband who didn't have the tools available to him twenty years ago, getting through the pain of his mother's death was excruciating. And his loss is immeasurable now, believe me, but he's already understanding a bit more of the entire picture and is now connecting more to the "signs" that his son is always there.

Also, remember that as a medium, I have had many client readings, where a loved one, grandparent, uncle, or aunt are validating they are around them during the session and the client remains very non-emotional. Then I mention a beloved pet suddenly appearing on the other side, validating what they looked like, or some characteristic trait they had, and suddenly the client's eyes well up with tears. In the beginning of my practice, I found this very odd. Loved ones did not provoke the emotional reaction of loss, but the pet did. This is my entire point: I began to understand that Love is Love. The bond the person had with that animal could have been for them very similar to the bond someone else has to a sibling. Who am I to judge? When I am meditating, grounding, and preparing prior to a reading, all I ask is that the client receive whatever is needed for their highest good, and for their peace of heart and mind. That's it. If they don't get much out of a loved one showing up in the reading but do get peace of mind because their beloved pet showed up, okay, so be it. It is *their* bond of Love that Spirit wants to validate.

I grapple with the spiritual part of me that understands the bigger picture, and why things happen the way that they do—the realization that we are actually spiritual beings having a human experience and existence on this Earth, and the many varied lessons that come along with this choice to incarnate here at this time. There's that spiritual part of me, and then the human, physical part that doesn't understand the *why* of losing someone that we love, the unfairness of it and how it wasn't supposed to be this way or happen that way. I grapple with both sides. One side understanding, the other one screaming out loud that the pain and loss of our son is too much, and this should not have ended the way that it did.

I allow myself those moments of crying, of giving in to the pain, and allowing it to bring me to my knees. But then like the rest of you who have lost someone significant in your life, we have to shake off that pain and move forward. As difficult as it may be, we have other loved ones in our lives to take care of. We also have to take care of ourselves. And if we allow ourselves to be swallowed by that pain, then we are missing the whole point of the experience: to bring us to a place of understanding that there is a higher power that is guiding us in every moment. Even *if* we don't get it then. And even though experiences are not fair, remember the "fairness meter"— there is growth happening in this world, and that pain is allowing us to be open to the love that already exists in our lives, and to be present in our lives for those that we still care for. The pain of losing a loved one actually forces us to learn the meaning of life that's still going on around us.

All too often we go through our lives blindly pushing through the motions, similar to how my husband Anthony went through life twenty years ago, after his mother's passing. The loss of a loved one stirs up our emotions and reminds us how fragile life really is, how we should be in gratitude for each breath we take, as things could always be worse than they are—even with the loss of a child. Our lives and situations could be far worse. Yes, let me repeat that again. In comparison to millions of people suffering all over the world, our lives and situations could be far worse. In our loved one's loss, we are reminded of the gift of life that brings with it pain and suffering, and the tremendous love and compassion we can show for each other. In my office, on one wall is a plaque sign that simply reads, "Each Day Is a Gift," because that is all we have in this world. Today, and the gift of breathing, living, and loving. Only for today.

So during your grief, you will transform as a person, and your actual grief itself will transform. Give yourself all the time you need to get through this. It isn't a race. My husband Anthony always says, "Others think this is a sprint, but for us, it's a lifelong marathon, and they don't get it." That's correct. Others don't understand every level of our grief, and they don't have to. It is we who need to be gentle with ourselves and understand that our grief makes others very uncomfortable. And that's okay too.

Remember, this is *your* journey.

Each death and loss is unique. Be tender with yourself, show yourself love and patience, even in the midst of your despair. Remember you are still living and breathing, and what your loved one on the other side wants, more than anything, is to see your heart shine. And for those who know of others who have had tremendous loss in their lives, as someone who is currently grieving, just let them know you are thinking of them.

Please do not try to fix the situation, because *nothing* can fix bereavement. Only time can let the light shine back in our hearts. We just need a kind phone call, compassionate text or email, or to just sit and hold our hands. We're in this tunnel of darkness, and we're afraid. We just need to know someone is also thinking of us, and saying I'm sorry, I wish I could change things, but you're not alone. Darkness begets fear, fear begets isolation. When in darkness, everyone doesn't want to feel like they are alone. Hold space for us; there is no need to fix us. But most of all, thank you for reaching out and trying to connect, to help. That's all we can ask for.

Before I finish this chapter, I want to share with you a beautiful lesson that even I forgot about until I transcribed the speech on grief I gave on October 27, 2018. I was so honored to be invited by Paul Saladino to be part of the Paul Young Seminar – you know, *the* Paul Young of *The Shack*? Not only was I crazy thrilled but I was—yes, you guessed it—scared to death, pardon the pun. When I finished, I doubted I had done a good job, but then this came in a video months later and even I was surprised! Remember, Spirit talks through me; therefore this was not technically me speaking. Even I was impressed by the message, re-hearing it at a time I probably needed it again.

Here is what I channeled that day as I stepped up to the stage, not knowing what the heck I was going to say:

Grief Is Exactly Like Fear

Please raise your hand if you have *never* lost anyone in your life. Everyone look around; there isn't one arm raised, yet when we go through this grief process, we think that we're completely alone. And we don't understand the people we pass at the grocery store, getting gas, at work, have also lost loved ones. We're so programmed to continue life, continue on. Afraid to bring up that grief during the day, afraid to bring up those memories, for fear we're going to fall apart.

Author CS Lewis, wrote in his book *A Grief Observed*, after he lost his wife: "I never knew that grief, is exactly like fear." And that's a powerful statement. How is grief like fear? We're afraid of this intense pain after having lost someone. We're afraid the pain will never go away. We're afraid we'll forget about the memories of our loved one. We're afraid people will forget her laugh. We're afraid people will forget his eyes, or the way he made people smile when we were in a bad mood. We're afraid of that fear, and the fear is terrifying. As our previous speaker stated, we feel powerless. We feel as if something has been taken away from us. And as humans, we're not used to handling that feeling; we're not used to not being in control. And now someone we love has been ripped out of our lives and we're left with that hole inside while we're dealing with the grief.

As a medium, I love to connect clients to loved ones on the other side to validate that life and soul and energy always continue. It's not important to me, as the medium, to validate that you stuck a lucky ticket in your pocket that your father used to carry all the time. Nonetheless, if it brings you some peace to confirm your loved one's energy is there with you with that validation, then I hope and wish that the message comes through for you.

The reality is, your loved ones are not really impressed with the magical shows or tricks or wanting the medium to confirm what was I thinking today, or what the special nickname they used to call me when they were here. They're more concerned with how you are living your life now without them. Continuing to love without them. Continuing to feel the emotions of life without them.

Unfortunately, when we lose someone, we completely shut down. And everything around us becomes this whirlwind, like a tornado happening around us, similar to what Dorothy in *The Wizard of Oz* experiences as she clings onto the little house that has taken her up and away. We lose all perspective. We just hold on to what we only know: the fear, the grief, the loneliness of our raw emotions. And what we're actually doing in the midst of that grief—we're missing all the signs and symbols and ways in which our loved ones are trying to let us know, I'm still here.

Let's talk about the example that the previous speaker Adam gave of his friend Michael who had passed. As Michael's girlfriend noticed Adam on the beach one day, and was walking up to him to say hello, his friend Michael's picture mysteriously popped up on his phone at *exactly* that time. Out of *nowhere*. That was the soul of his friend, letting him know he was there. This is the synchronicity of events that should take our breath away. The ones we call "coincidence" when they are not coincidences at all. They are Spirit, using whatever energy they can to get our attention.

Everything is happening in divine order. Everything is specifically ordained for your benefit. Even the loss of a loved one is the part of the process of letting go, of learning to trust. I will admit, when I went to go see the movie *The Shack*, every time the character Mackenzie (Mack) asked a question to God, "Why," "Why, God, do you allow pain and suffering like this," I was waiting with bated breath for the answer. I wanted to hear the answer. We all do, right? I wanted to hear, what does God respond with? Why do tragedies happen? I was sitting on the edge of my seat, waiting. And the answer always came from a place of love. Of a place of letting go. A place of trust.

Growing up in a household that was very dysfunctional, I learned at a very early age not to trust. So, I grew up not trusting. Therefore, that's a very comfortable, common reaction in life for me, not to trust. When something scary happens, I immediately go to the childhood tapes and say to myself, don't trust, don't trust this situation. And yet, when I was watching the movie *The Shack*, that whole feeling of trust, of love, of letting go and releasing was experienced. And in that flow of releasing is where we start living again. Where we start smiling again, we start laughing. Where we start reminiscing, not from a place of triggers and pain, but from wanting to remember a beautiful memory because it makes our heart smile.

Your loved ones on the other side, their energy and soul continue. Not in the physical form like we are here. They transform into energy. The way I like to explain it when I'm teaching classes is to explain how energy works on the other side. Think of a large ocean, and we scoop up ocean water in one cup. Then we scoop up water in another different cup. Each cup represents the vessels we are here on Earth, our Earth bodies. Within each cup is the energy of the ocean, which represents our soul within our bodies, which is the energy of God, and of the Universe. These two detached cups of energy are kept separate from each other, because the vessels they are housed in are different. Our bodies are each different from one human to another. We grow up thinking we are all different, because we see only the outside of who we really are—the vessel or body. We go about our lives on this Earth feeling disconnected, because we see ourselves as different from every other person around us. Finally, once we die, our souls leave the physical body, and like the energy within that cup, get poured back into that large ocean, from where we originated. The cup is poured back into the ocean of life. The water of one cup merges with the water of the other. The energy of the souls co-mingle on the other side. We return home. Once the water is poured from each cup, and merges, can you tell where one soul is versus the other soul? No, because they are now all *one*. This is what the energy of love, of God, of Spirit is on the other side. This is how it works.

Your loved ones, when they are showing a medium a specific validation of their life, they're kind of generating a mirror image of who they were in this lifetime. They are very different on the other side. As energy, they are balls of light. They're always moving about and experiencing love on a level they cannot even explain in human words. When a loved one is trying to describe what heaven is like, or what it's like to see or feel God, they say that God is in everything, love is a part of everything. It's a part of the colors and flowers, it's in the wings of the butterflies, it exists in the blades of grass. They show me their soul is one with the whole. There is no feeling of separation the way we experience life here, separate and different from each other. There, everything is part of the whole. Just like pouring that glass of water back into the ocean, the water contained in that cup, becomes one with the whole. That's how your loved ones show life on the other side.

Grief Is Exactly Like Fear

Grief is hard. And it's especially hard when very well-meaning people share some crazy statements because they want to help you feel better. They may say things like, "There's a reason why everything happens." When you're in the midst of your pain, the last thing you want to hear is that there is a reason why you lost your loved one! Maybe down the road, as you start to deal with your grief, start to go through the process and steps in healing, you may come to a better understanding of why your loved one left the way they did.

It's difficult because we have that void of wanting to connect with their voice, their hug, their touch, their smell. We want to connect with that human part of them. So, Spirit says, OK, we're going to connect, but it's going to be on a different level. Instead of actually hearing my voice, we'll have conversations together and you'll think you're making up my part of the conversation when in reality it really is me speaking back to you. As humans, we're so used to hearing things outside ourselves. And then we have conversations with our loved ones in our head and we think we're making up their part of the conversation. You're not making up the conversation on your own. Your loved one is actually feeding you the feelings, the emotions, the words. They are making that connection, because they've never really left you. Even though we can't physically see them beside us, or touch them, they're constantly giving us the signs they are there. Very common signs are pennies, dimes, butterflies, feathers. A sign of our loved one's picture suddenly popping up on your phone just as you're thinking of that person—that is a tremendous sign! Yet most of us shrug it off as just a very weird coincidence.

Spirit loves to laugh, so when they see us sad, depressed,

and upset because they are no longer here with us, it weighs on their heart. When you sit down at a table, or among friends or family and you reminisce and remember about the crazy stories or memories of laughter and fun, it lightens their soul. They commune with your soul. Their Spirits and your soul become one, and it makes them so happy. When you share the crazy stories about how your mom used to always burn the garlic bread, and now every time you smell garlic bread and think of her, she smiles with you.

The messages they also bring up is, yes I am gone, and no longer with you, but please make peace with your brother. Please call your father, don't be angry with him. Let go of what your son is doing that you don't approve of.

They are constantly trying to send us love and remind us through the energy of God, of the Universe and Holy Spirit, that we are all connected here, even though we may not understand how. They're constantly reminding us, as humans, we still have work to do here. And they remind us, "Yes, we still love and belong to one another, and even though I'm no longer here, I still need you to do the work that you're meant to fulfill here." In the movie *The Shack*, after Mackenzie's young daughter is kidnapped and murdered, he still had family to take care of on Earth, to love and watch grow. When we allow our grief and fear to bring us underwater where we can't breathe, we're no longer living, and that makes our loved ones on the other side very sad.

I remember whenever a loved one would cross over, and I'd ask them for a sign. I would get a sign, but not trust it, so I'd ask for another sign to confirm the first one was truly a sign. And then I'd ask for 2 out of 3 signs. It was a process that went on and on and on. Now, I don't even play around with the signs anymore. I give each Spirit loved one a very specific sign I want to see from them. Something weird and out of the ordinary is what I'm thinking of, so when I see it, I know *for a fact* that Spirit heard me and gave me back the sign I asked for.

As an example, for my father, I ask for a dollar bill. There's nothing special about a dollar bill; it's just something that I don't see and haven't found often in the past. Because that is his sign, and he knows it's what I'm looking for, he gives me that exact sign in the weirdest of places that I would never expect. Now I see dollar bills everywhere, because that's the way my father shows me he's always around. So help yourself during your process of grief, and give your loved ones a very specific sign you would like to see. Don't worry about making it too hard. There is no sign Spirit cannot produce in some manner. Make it something out of the ordinary, something you don't normally see. I have a client of mine that shared her mother used to love putting paperclips on everything. Because of this, she decided to ask her mom for paperclips, but remembered I said make it a bit harder, so when you get the sign, there is no mistaking it was your loved one giving you back exactly what you asked for. So, she asked for white paperclips. This woman shared with me that she now has a box of thirty white paperclips that she's found in the weirdest of places. Now her mother understands, "White paperclips is what my daughter is looking for, to acknowledge I'm around her."

Spirit always wants to make us happy. Spirit is always wanting to show us the signs they are around us, to help us with the grief process because they know that on this human plane, we don't understand, and can't comprehend the bigger picture. When you feel your loved ones around you, that is them there; don't discount those feelings. It is Spirit trying to help you cope. Don't think you have to physically feel them beside you in order to validate that it is them. Thank them and ask them to come around more often. They want to let you know their soul continued over to the other side. The consciousness of the soul continues after the body expires. The body is just a vessel, holding our souls within, and our souls are trying to accomplish a mission of learning on this Earth. More often than not, we would prefer learning the lessons here on Earth, rather than having to learn them on the other side.

When loved ones give messages in a reading, such as, "Please make peace with your sister and brother," or "Please extend an olive branch and bring your son back into the fold," they're doing it to confirm they know what's going on in your life and they are trying to help you get your lesson. They want to show they are always around to love you. Love continues, but the grief debilitates us from connecting with our loved ones, because it puts us in a place of fear, feeling we will never get out of that pain. Your loved ones want to show that through love, you will get through your grief. Loving them, even though they are no longer here, and then learning to love those around you, is how you are going to get yourself out of the trench of grief. I'll always be by your side, is their message.

I read for this mother who had lost a little boy, about two years old. He had fallen in the backyard pool and drowned. He showed me having done this once before, and his mother was able to hear the splash and scooped him out of the pool that first time. He confirmed she was not able to be there the second time to save him. He acknowledged in the reading, the little baby boy that was conceived and born right after his passing. He was confirming life after his passing, and his message was "I was supposed to leave this life early; thank you for being my mom, and thank you for continuing to be the amazing mother to my little brother." Through our tremendous grief, there's always an opportunity to let go, forgive, and continue to love. And *that* is why we are here on this Earth, to learn and to love. Isn't that just an absolutely beautiful message for this mother?

Remember, for this speech, I was at a loss trying to figure out what the heck I was going to talk about. I even asked Paul Young, at our lunch break, prior to getting in front of the audience, telling him how nervous I was, asking how he prepares for all the speaking engagements he does all over the world. He said he never does. He just goes up on stage, with trust and an open heart, and allows God to give him the words. All I had in my head was that quote from C.S. Lewis. I took what Paul Young told me, and just got up with an open heart. As I watched myself on that video, I could see that within seconds of standing on that stage, something shifted within me, and these words came pouring out. Now *that* is the power and whispers of Spirit guiding me, as it guides each and every one of us!

Thank you, Spirit, and thank you, Universe, for allowing me the opportunity to do that speech. For pulling me through once again and now for the chance to share it with many more people who could not be in the room at the time! It is truly a wondrous world.

Chapter Nine
SMOOTH SAILING IS NOT LIFE

PRACTICAL STEPS FOR SURVIVING ANOTHER DAY

Time heals nothing. It only brings other issues and tissues and takes what is incurable or unacceptable out of the center of our attention.

—Ana Claudia Antunes
The Tao of Physical and Spiritual

She also said:

*It's all a series of serendipities
with no beginnings and no ends.
Such infinitesimal possibilities
through which love transcends.*

Smooth Sailing Is Not Life

Well, as the title says, in the process of grief there is no smooth sailing! If we can start with that concept alone and stop trying to be normal or act in a certain way, we will already have made progress toward healing. Yes, we've had the breath knocked out of our bodies, are wondering how we are ever going to get out of this pain, are trying to believe in Spirit and the signs our loved ones have sent, but how in God's name am I going to get through the next moment?

That is the key. Each moment, each second is a step, and if you can break them down and start to compartmentalize them, you will help yourself immensely. To start with, you want to arm yourself with knowledge. That first piece of knowledge, of which by now I have hopefully convinced you, is that our loved ones are still with us even though we can't touch them. So let one part of your mind constantly be on the lookout for their signs. As for the heart, the first knowledge that helps is simply having a basic understanding of the traditional steps of grieving.

Elisabeth Kübler-Ross is the first individual to record that there are five common stages for grief and loss. She defined these five groundbreaking stages as; 1. Denial and isolation; 2. Anger; 3. Bargaining; 4. Depression; 5. Acceptance. They can come at different times with different levels of pain. Kübler-Ross's book from 1969 called *On Death and Dying* was revolutionary and is still valid and used today, and there is plenty of material out there on these topics, so I will let the words in the stages speak for themselves. The point is that these stages are just as relevant for the death of a loved one and the grieving process as they are for someone who is grieving an ended relationship or marriage and many other life changes.

Actually, a lot of suggestions in the lists I talk about below can help you no matter what the situation is you are in and struggling with. It doesn't have to only be the death of a loved one. Even signs can come from Spirit or loved ones for a variety of questions. Remember, my story when I asked Spirit for a huge sign to prove that I was supported by them when I took the certification exam through the Forever Family Foundation? A 6-inch feather appeared on the floor in my office, and it is impossible that anyone else had been in the room!

As promised here are some practical tips:

1. **Everyone grieves differently.**

    No two people will experience the same emotions for any circumstance. A dad cries while a mom laughs, perhaps inappropriately, while a stranger feels nothing but rage and a neighbor clams up so much they can't even talk to you. Some grieve in silence and isolation and others huddle together and can never be left alone. It is okay that we are different, and it is even better if you accept just that. *Don't judge yourself and don't judge how others grieve; just let the process unravel.*

2. **Allow yourself time to grieve.**

    Your heart is broken. You can't just skip through and ignore this, or it will come back to bite you in some other way. An accident because you aren't paying attention, an illness because you wore yourself down, an addiction because you swallowed your emotions and wouldn't express yourself. Let yourself let loose and cry as much as you need, throw things—in a safe place, hit something. Let it out. Don't bottle it up. But, *always set a limit.* Why do I say this? Because as humans we tend to let drama enter our lives and we let it last too long. After a certain period of time, the actual release, which is good for you, becomes a burden and actually a detriment to healing.

Therefore, cry, scream, throw inanimate objects safely alone for fifteen minutes, then force yourself to spend the next five minutes calming down and remembering one thing that made you smile about knowing that person or that you learned from this terrible episode in your life. Then, move forward with your day. Of course, you will still feel pain. Of course, your heart is still broken, but each release is a step closer to healing.

3. **Expect the "first" of all firsts to be hardest.**

   The first set of firsts. No matter what date or year the incident or death happened, they are always going to bring up a new set of pains. The first birthday, the first anniversary of the loss, the first wedding, the first high school dance, the first time attending an event alone, the first whatever. You name it, life is a continuous minefield of firsts. Arm yourself. The best way to get through them is to acknowledge you will have funky and mixed emotions, that someone will inevitably say the wrong thing and no matter what, make sure you do one thing to honor that person even if you don't think they are watching. The love from those watching above us is so strong that I assure you they are there with us for every important phase and step. So, instead of feeling like you are doing this on your own, talk to them, play with them, and pretend they are right there with you. Yes, people around you might think you've finally gone off your rocker, but you're the one grieving; do what you need to do! Chances are, if you pay attention, you too will get a sign!

4. **We will never forget.**

   A huge fear that people have as time goes on is that they will forget the loved one's laugh, or personality, or the way they looked or smelled, but that is not true, and we are never asked to let go of a loved one's memories. We are never asked to let go of the individual we love, no matter what stage of grieving we are at. We are asked to move through the pain though and start to remember that not only Spirit but our loved ones want us to remember the good times and not the tragedy of their passing. We are being asked, in due time, to let go of pain, trust, and allow the flow to move from misery or anger or any emotion to connect to the love of the Divine: the love of Spirit and the love of your deceased ones.

5. **You never have to forget, but you do have to find a level of forgiveness.**

In writing this, I want to address that not all deaths are experienced as painful to the survivors. Some people are like, "Finally, goodbye, good riddance. You've caused me enough hell on this Earth; I'm glad you are gone." So, how do you handle that? First, don't let people try to convince you that you don't mean or feel it by saying, "You don't really feel that way you are just grieving." The fact is you might just feel exactly that way! But do yourself a favor, and just like crying, or throwing things safely, you want to eventually bring in a feeling of something about them that helped you grow and without them you would not be the person you are today. In that understanding is where you will start to forgive them for being the person brought into your life to be the catalyst that moved you forward. Without them, no matter the pain, you would not have grown. Thank them for having been in your life and let them and the pain go. Because in the end we have come to Earth to learn and to love, unconditionally.

6. **Treat yourself. Love yourself. Gift yourself.**

   When you are grieving, don't wait for other people to treat you in a certain way because you are hoping that if they love you, they will have read your mind. If you need a spa day, go. If you need a certain plant or flower, get it. If you need to throw out all flowers around you because they bring you to a place of mourning, throw them out, or better yet, drop them off at a hospital or nursing home. Do something that you consider is fun. Take a drive away from everything. Take a train to nowhere. Sit in bed for three days and watch movies and eat ice cream; just do what you feel will make you happy, even if only for a split second, and don't wait for someone else to do this for you. You will most likely be disappointed that they don't react the way you want or need them to. So, do it for the love of yourself!

7. **If you know what you need, just ask someone for it.**

   Just as much as you are grieving, the likelihood is that those around you who care and love you are grieving too. They are most likely feeling completely inadequate regarding what they can do for you. Because of this, it is a wonderful gesture to just tell people, "You can't fix this, but what you can do for me is…" water the plants, send me a caring text message, don't cry in front of me, or in reverse, do cry in front of me and do acknowledge my loss. If you think there is something you need and can muster up the strength, it is easier just to ask for it. However, if you are going to play the "You didn't read my mind, therefore you don't really love me" game, it's better not to say anything at all and simply tend to yourself.

8. **Seek out a therapist or a support group. It is absolutely fine to get professional help.**

   These are the toughest times you are going to ever have to go through, so it is completely fine to get help. If you don't have a network of understanding friends and family, and if you are not being heard, one of the best ways to get through this is with someone who actually understands the process. A therapist trained in death and dying is going to help you way more than one who can't deal with death themselves. You can even find a support group of people who have lost their children or loved ones to suicide or accidents or illness. You will feel best in those groups because they have survived that specific type of loss. Go where you fit the best and know there is good chance that at some point you might outgrow it, but that is just fine as well. And, if you by any chance are feeling even remotely suicidal or feel like you might relapse from an addiction, get help right away. Run, don't walk, to your nearest hospital, or suicide or addiction hotline, and get immediate help. Understanding and trained people are there to serve you. It is their soul's purpose to be there for *you* in *your* time of need. Don't deny yourself or them the chance to do what they were brought to Earth to do.

9. **Accept that you have changed and that is perfectly fine.**

   The fact is, you are not the person you were before. You may no longer enjoy the things that you once adored. Things that were once terribly important to you may now seem abhorrently insignificant. You may now be incapable of experiencing unbridled joy. Some describe living in a sort of parallel universe, existing every day not knowing for what purpose. Some lose their faith. Many are very angry with a God that they were taught to believe was all-protecting. Sometimes, we may need our mourning time for a short period, and then feel like we just want to move on and find some "fun." The truth is that you will never be the same, but look at this as a good thing. You don't want to be a teenager forever—well most of us don't want that, at least! We all want and need to grow, and the more we mature, the more we accept life is wonderful as it is. In each new facet, we start to let go of the things we can't control. So, allow yourself to become that butterfly. Fly!

10. Remove the guilt and blame.

We all have it. We've all done it. You did nothing wrong. If I had gotten to the hospital sooner, or maybe if I had stayed home that day instead of going into work, or perhaps if I hadn't exposed them to this, or we lived nearer to a specialized hospital, or if I had paid more attention to the signs – blah, blah, blah. The ego will play games in our mind as long as we allow. I see this all the time in readings—the "what ifs" that cause us so much pain, on top of the excruciating pain we already feel. Humans are amazing creatures to beat ourselves up! If you can understand that each soul has a contract (lessons) in this world, and each of us has a corresponding contract to play out with each other, you will understand that the soul chose its exit point. We can't play God. We can pretend we can turn back time and see all the things we would have done differently, but we are not in control of death. Our souls already know the lessons we're here to learn, and how we will leave this Earth. As a parent, sibling, or child, we cannot stop the learning of the soul on this Earth, so please be gentle with yourself. And please don't "should" all over yourself.

11. Do not chastise yourself if you feel *relief*.

The weird word, relief. I'm going to address the elephant in the room. Yes, it is okay to feel relief. It can be relief that the long-suffering days are over; it can be relief that you no longer have to deal with that person; it can be relief for many different reasons. I'm giving you permission and saying it is totally fine to feel relief when a loved one (or not-so-loved one) is gone. The question in support groups is sometimes, "How do you go to a service or a memorial or go through the motions when people think you should be on the floor devastated and you have to act like a hypocrite because you are not sad? They are all crying and you are in more understanding and peace mode." Just realize that we all grieve differently and that the people around do not know every step that you have been through. It is not for them to judge and you should not judge yourself. Let your heart feel what it feels and then move on with the other parts of grieving that arise. Whatever you do, do not make yourself feel guilty or think you are a terrible person. You are not. This chapter of your life has ended; if you can move on, more power to you.

12. Make yourself laugh!

Yes, you read that correctly. First, cry, cry, cry, cry out a river if you have to and then find a way to make yourself laugh. It could be a funny movie, stupid or cute pet tricks, a comedy show, whatever it is that gets you going—even getting together with friends to help your mind get off your loss and just enjoy the moment. Spirit is waiting for us to rejoice in life. They are saying, "Continue to move forward, laugh, love, even though I'm not here." Laughter is medicine and you need it! It's good for the soul and it does help heal your broken heart.

13. Keep a calendar/journal.

You may be thinking, *What?* Do keep a calendar, a schedule, a journal, a reminder pad, notes, whatever—but the fact is that you are most likely an emotional mess and need lists right now! You probably are moving from room to room wondering why you came into this room, or you are wandering around aimlessly in the store wondering what you were even supposed to get. The quicker you finish the project and get back to moving forward and the less time you spend in confusion, the more focused you can be to heal. You can even write on that schedule or journal how you are feeling or if you have seen any signs. Is this an absolutely necessary step? No, but you will also be able to look back three to six months later and see that you might actually have made a little progress and realize that perhaps even if you are still in pain that you are somehow functioning a little better now than you were before. And, if you are not? No pressure. Wait another year, and another, until you feel you might have made some healing progress. The best part is that if you pull out your notes years later, I bet you will see signs you never even realized were there!

14. Lower your expectations of others.

I know this is crazy to say, but the unfortunate part of grieving or loss of anyone or anything in our lives is that we carry the heartache, but we want others to be able to understand our hurt, anger, sorrow, and the reality is—they just can't. I have heard many people who have lost children say that they also lost good friends, or at least friends they thought they once had. And now they feel even more alone. Humans do not like sorrow. We bury it inside or run away from it. So when we are in the midst of our pain, those around us don't remember we're hurting, they have their own life going on. Holidays come and go and we get the "Happy Holidays" messages. They don't understand that we're not in a celebrating mood, and our hearts are shattered. As more time goes by, people around us forget even more, and we're left holding the pain—alone. Please understand, they *don't* forget because they don't care about you. They forget because everyone gets too wrapped up in their own lives to remember. And some people just can't handle talking about death, sorrow, hurt, and despair. They may say, "I'm always here for you," and they probably have great intentions when they say that, but when push comes to shove, they just don't have it for the long haul. The pain is our burden and cross to bear. Let go of the expectations you may have of friends and family you know should be there for you. They just don't have it. Find other outlets, like community groups or counselors where your pain is acknowledged and understood.

15. Continue the personal love story to yourself.

Your grief, your transformation, your process—those are your personal love story to yourself, and to the bond of love you have with your loved one in Spirit. Only you in the end can tell and know that story completely. How do you do this? You do your best to try to exercise some, to eat right as best you can, and to drink plenty of healthy water –with plenty of wine and chocolate in between! Ha! You see, *laughter*, as I said above. And then, move into embracing Spirit. When you embrace Spirit, you stop explaining yourself, stop trying to fit in, stop worrying about what others think, and focus on what is important. You learn that people are capable of seeing you and your life only from the level of their own perception, and you can't force them beyond it until their egos, which push them from their unconscious, are ready. Sometimes you even need to say goodbye to certain people who are no longer helping you heal, and if you must, it is okay to simply let them go. In your mind, thank them for the pain or the drama or the level they helped you reach; then let Spirit pick you up and find a new group of loved ones to surround yourself with.

16. Count your blessings.

I know it is really hard right now, but you were blessed by having that person or situation in your life. If you move in a heart of gratitude, you will release the pain more quickly, and you won't ignore all the love you have in front of you and around you. Gratitude is the answer. So, breathe. Breathe in slower and deeper. Breathe in love, compassion. Meditate. Talk to Spirit. Rev up your own intuitive skills, like I will talk about in the next part. And do count those blessings, because if you are willing to look, there are still many around you. How do you start? Remember that journal I mentioned before? Every day, write three things that you are grateful for. It can be something important, like "I'm grateful for my husband, my house, and my children." Or even something simple, such as "I'm grateful for a cup of hot coffee every morning, having several (or many) pairs of shoes to be able to wear," or even grateful that every time you flip the switch, the lights turn on. Be grateful for three different things every day, and don't repeat them. Think about everything you touch each day, and what would life be like if you didn't have that. Then sit in quiet contemplation, think about those three things, and say to the Universe, "Thank you." Breathe in the gratitude. I do this exercise every morning upon waking. I want to start my day being grateful for what I *do* have right now, because in those moments of despair and agony, I need to remember that God is gracing me with so much, and even though my heart is breaking, I am still loved from above.

I hope that as I sum up this chapter you will now realize that grief, as individual as it is to each person, is a necessary process. Yes, it is a dark tunnel for some time, but I promise there is light at the end of it, *if* you choose to keep the light on in you. This deeper grief is a learning lesson, and this is why we are on Earth. It can be the catalyst to even greater and deeper love, although it won't feel like it at the moment of loss. It occurs in its own time.

As I said, if someone were to snip the caterpillar's cocoon to assist in the process, and if they snipped too early, the caterpillar would be nothing more than a liquid entity that had never formed properly. You need to form properly. You want to grieve and then grow. It is not a race. It is a process, and for each one of us, it is different. However, what is not different is that if we choose to listen to Spirit, who is guiding us, pushing us when we can't make it through the tunnel, bringing us to the light of love when we think we just won't make it another day, we then will flow through at a faster and easier pace. My biggest advice is to listen to Spirit and loved ones and start really paying attention.

Again, I reiterate, you are not making these signs and symbols up! Write them down, save them in a special place, and when everyone else looks at you like you have finally lost your wits, hit Looney Tunes land, or finally gone off the deep end, you, Spirit, and your loved one will just smile right back at each other, *knowing* you are having the best connection in the Universe. Remember, ask for specific signs, as I shared earlier—that will save you lots of time trying to figure out who it is!

Smooth Sailing Is Not Life

As you start to move through the pain and see your life evolve, finally accept and realize that there are no coincidences. Each step, each phase was placed in your life for a purpose. The purpose of bringing you to a greater point of deeper love, deeper understanding, and deeper peace. We are asked to flow out of pain and allow the Divine order to run its course. It's a big ask, but that is why we are here.

They say time heals all wounds. Well, I suppose it does, but the saying from Ana Claudia Antunes some days feels more appropriate:

> *Time heals nothing. It only brings other issues and tissues and takes what is incurable or unacceptable out of the center of our attention.*

Ana Claudia Antunes – The Tao of Physical and Spiritual

However, on a good day, a Spirit-filled day, nothing explains life better than this:

> *It's all a series of serendipities*
>
> *with no beginnings and no ends.*
>
> *Such infinitesimal possibilities*
>
> *through which love transcends.*

Part Four

Spirit: The Compass in the Storm

How to Learn, Listen and Allow Your Self (Soul) to be Guided

If you want to awaken all of humanity, then awaken all of yourself, if you want to eliminate the suffering in the world, then eliminate all that is negative on yourself. Truly, the greatest gift you have to give is that of your own self-transformation.

—Laozi

We have come to the final section in this book, and by now I hope that you have learned and started to truly accept that death is never final. Grief is hard; as a matter of fact, at the moment, it feels impossible, but in truth it is yet another passing trip through a dark and unknown tunnel. You will get to the other side, and you will live to smile or laugh again somewhere down the road.

You are also, hopefully, starting to understand that our loved ones on the other side only want us to feel the love, not the heartache. It is now *our* job to awaken to the truth of the experience, that only love begets more love. Only the light of love can clear away the dark corners of pain. Only love can move us forward in our lives in a fulfilling and positive direction.

It is the healthy part of human consciousness that wants this world to be one without pain ruled only by good people and circumstances. We want to live in harmony and in peace and for there not to be any suffering coming to those around us. We say we would rather bear their burden, yet the minute it touches our doorstep, we suddenly don't want to handle it or deal with it anymore. We want it eliminated or to go somewhere else. What can I say? I'm honest. At first I didn't want Anthony to suffer the illness; now I don't want us to suffer his loss. I'm human.

The problem with Earth is that as the humans whom inhabit it, we have universally chosen to learn lessons, and unfortunately, those often come from pain. After all, how many of us learn when life is flowing well? Not many. It is a system set up so that in the struggles of life we learn. If we open our eyes, we may even be able to say, "Aha, that's the lesson." It is our purpose to hopefully learn the lessons and then grow beyond them.

Why we as a race chose this method of education is something you have to take up with your Maker, and I assure you, they have heard from me many, many times! I'm Italian, I verbalize, and I assure you all octaves from my little frame can be heard loud and clear throughout the universe! I'm with you when I say life is very, *very* hard.

What we see in today's politically charged and extremely emotionally confused world is that extremes are rampant. We see poverty for 99 percent of the population and extreme wealth for the 1 percent. The human population is dying younger versus growing older. There are ever-rising levels of illness with increasing, not decreasing, levels of cancer, more diabetes, more people contracting unknown maladies, more suffering, more depression, more pain, more addiction, and more suicide. How in the world can we look at the future and even hope to have a positive outlook?

The world seems to be floating energetically from one extreme to another as we accept and take on more stress and more duties, as we try to do it *all*. We are finding life that is completely overwhelming, some, or even most days. No wonder we are all feeling a little fragmented, a little exhausted, a little divided, and more than just a little burnt out.

How are we supposed to survive in such an upside-down and difficult world?

The *answer* is easier than you think, but you have to believe it. You have to buy into it, and you are better if you don't fight it.

That answer: Spirit.

The ultimate truth is that when knowledge from the incredible forces above—our angels, or Spirit, or the true Source—are on this journey with us, our pain is diminished. The time in suffering, grief, misunderstanding, poverty, illness, or any hardship is lessened, and a feeling of Oneness, *knowingness* of true love takes over and eventually releases the waves of fear and internal tantrums.

That is what I am here to teach in Part Four. I am here to help you understand the fact that we all come to Earth to learn lessons and to fulfill contracts we made *before* we arrived. I know, I *know* how strange this really sounds, but it is the truth.

In this section I teach you the lessons of karma, soul contracts, why we attract the people and problems we do, how to see not only the signs from Spirit I taught in Part Three, but how to read, understand, and build a relationship with Spirit, how to connect to our deeper selves, and how to strengthen the intuitive gifts that are inherent in every human being, if you choose to listen and learn. I'm warning you now though that Spirit does not suffer fools, and because of this, I share the truths about where and what you need to focus on to grow. You can go as slowly or as quickly as you want. That is up to you. But, with what I am sharing now, the quicker you open your mind and your heart to *possibilities*, even if you don't understand them, the quicker you will find your answers sneaking in from Spirit.

Ultimately, each person's lesson is to learn to *trust* the forces around you—the whispers of Spirit that are trying to help you evolve through this experience—while not allowing the circumstance or loss of the moment debilitate you for long. Trusting means *allowing* Spirit to be that compass in the storm, to let it guide you when you can't see in front of you, to allow it to nudge you in a better direction, and finally, to make peace and become One with them and Universe. When you are not separate from One, but *are* One, not only will you never feel alone, but your pain and confusion will not remain as long in your physical and emotional life. Hard lessons will no longer stick to you like sap on a leaf but will glide off of you like water on glass. Lessons will float off of you quickly, and you will move into a healthier space. But *you* have to consciously want to change—*you* have to want to *know* the truth and yell this *desire* from the rooftops. *You* have to want to grow, to change, to become a better person. Spirit will *not* do that for you without your approval. It is a universal law that intervention only comes if we ask. They are required to allow us the continual *free will* to make our own choices—even when we are sabotaging ourselves.

Spirit is a compass—but compasses are guides, and you have to learn how to use them, or they are of no use to you. Do you understand? The power and direction are up to you.

I teach you, like I continue to teach myself, that there is only one way to peace and that is through trusting Spirit. If you can't trust those around you, you must learn the final lesson—the most crucial lesson—you must learn to trust yourself 100% through listening to the messages from Spirit. What better person to teach you than someone who has often had to take the hard road?

I believe in the good in people. I believe that you want to become a future vessel of love for the world. You may not be able to change everything in the world, but you absolutely can manifest things around you, so don't you *want* them better and easier, both for you and every other being on the planet? Don't you want the laws of attraction to work to magnetically pull in good and repel evil? Don't you finally want to grow from being your own worst enemy into manifesting the greatest love emanating to all people you touch, everything you do, and creating nothing but abundance around you? I sure as hell do! When I'm around others, and in the midst of my own pain and despair, missing Anthony and wanting the outcome to have been different, I stop and reflect. I want peace and love in my life, so in that moment, I think about the joy in the little things; I smile, and I open my heart. I don't focus on the pain and agony. I focus on the love, and that helps to heal my heart, piece by piece.

I've shared my heart. I've shared my shortcomings. I'm sharing the intense pain I am in now. Why? Because if just *one* person learns from my hard knocks, from my grief, and from reading the lessons in this book then my mission in life has made a remarkable turn to help others take responsibility toward healing themselves. And, may I say, with one person changed by reading this, Anthony's life and death have meaning. I want to continue to give to those around me and be a vessel for good. My point: I'm happy to be your compass *temporarily*, but even more, I want you to now do the work for yourself, after reading everything, and to make it your life's mission to get Spirit on board!

Chapter Ten
TRUST MEANS OVERCOMING FEAR

Learning to trust is one of life's most difficult lessons. That's because trust is not a verb; it's a noun. Trust is a state of mind and being. If you are serious about learning to trust, you need TNT: Tenacity, Nerve, and Time. But what if the real problem is not that we can't trust other people; it's that we can't trust ourselves?

—Iyanla Vanzant

Isn't it true that learning to trust ourselves is the hardest of all lessons? Why do we always doubt ourselves, second-guess ourselves, hold someone else's opinions higher than our own? It is just all so complicated, isn't it?

All of life in the end comes down to one thing, learning to love yourself unconditionally and then pushing that love back into the Universe. But, how do we get there?

One of the quickest and easiest ways is to first work on releasing fear. Once we start to "let go and let God," as some say, then we can allow all the work Spirit wants to help us with to begin. This can happen only when we acknowledge that Spirit really does exist.

Truthfully, since the beginning of humanity, *one* thing, one *major* thing, has controlled and allowed in fear. *Ego.* Yes, that psychological and complex way of thinking, a mechanism of control. *Ego. Edging God Out*: That thing which prevents us from staying in the flow of *trust*. It's the thing that causes us to question every move or piece of our lives. Like I previously said, as humans, it is in our DNA not to trust, and wanting the answer to every experience becomes the desire. "Tell me who I'm going to marry, and when," "Tell me how long I'm going to live," "Tell me what I am supposed to be doing with my life." We're not focusing on a higher power in those moments and understanding everything is happening for our higher good. Each time we throw out that "tell me" question to know the answer to our future we are saying to the Universal Life – I don't trust the process. I'm afraid I'm always going to be alone, so please give me a ray of sunshine and some answers so I can continue hoping my life will be better than it is. Please tell me what I am supposed to be doing so I can just go out and do it and stop suffering. Please tell me the people to avoid so I don't ever have to get hurt again.

The hard lesson? A Universal Truth. No one can tell you how this works or what it means for *you*, specifically, in the end because you have to find the answers on your own. *Seriously?* Yes, afraid so! But the good news is that now you are going to start to ask for, to *embrace* the messages of Spirit and start to realize, understand, and accept that you are truly never alone. It will get easier.

I really like the quote above and what the inspirational speaker and author Iyanla Vanzant says about trust and it taking tenacity, nerve, and time. I wholeheartedly agree. It really does. It takes lessons and those aha moments and many, many synchronicities that force us to open our eyes and realize there is more to life than what we see. She also makes it clear that our problems are truly not that we can't trust other people, but it is that we can't trust ourselves!

Boy, does that turn things around!

What? We are to blame for our own problems? We sure are, and I talk about that in the next chapter on the Laws of Attraction, but here I want to deal with the concept of fear and how it controls and stops us from having trust. Because if you don't resolve the *fear*, you are going to have a really tough time getting into any form of relationship with your Higher Power.

Starting today, I want your first rule, your Golden Rule, to become Fear Not. As a matter of fact, in many religions and spiritual organizations, are we not told to fear not, the Lord is with us? Monks, swamis, Buddha, Jesus, ascended masters all teach on how to move beyond fear into Universal Love. They have done the hard work. It's time to listen to them. I promise you, it is much easier to integrate and believe the truths I am about to share with you about the spiritual and unseen world when you remove your expectations, open up your mind, and let go of fear. As long as you always ask for the highest and best good in everything you do, you will never open yourself up to negativity, and Spirit will always have your back.

Don't worry, Spirit even has our back when we do stupid and misguided things, but do go back and ask for the highest and best good and you will get turned around very quickly and for the better.

Does this mean releasing your fears in life and letting go promises us a pain-free life? No. But the losses, experiences, and heartaches we have encountered thus far have been our soul's evolution on this Earth. However, because we weren't given and reminded of the contract upon entering planet Earth, we're learning and growing as we go. And, with growth, sometimes the pain here is too much. The pain can immobilize us. We get stuck and we can't take one more step forward. We have to allow ourselves that day or that timeframe and pick up again when Spirit sends us one of those signs or synchronicities that show us that it is time to move again, and that the time is now. Remember: tenacity, nerve, *time*.

The challenge is that fear can be seen everywhere around us, especially with all the fearmongers and media, and it is our responsibility to move beyond it. We cannot succumb to it. But how? Besides being a medium, I am also an Intuitive Development teacher. I want people to learn how to develop their own innate gifts of intuition, perception, and learning to help them understand the higher reason of *why* we are here. Over the past ten years, I have taught courses and, up front, I want you to start to take to heart seven practical steps I have used that have helped others (and myself too) at times to overcome fear and anxiety. Because these were clips of information I have compiled through many years of research and work, I have done my best to share who spawned these thoughts, and if I have missed quoting any original sources, I do apologize in advance, but I thank them for the wisdom!

On October 3, 2008 a magazine article writer from Sweden by the name of Henrik Edberg came up with a series of articles that addressed how to overcome fear and then some others that had great "positivity" articles with tidbits of wisdom through the ages. I have taken my favorite points from him and added more to help you find ways to overcome fear and anxiety and start to actively move into a less fearful world.[10]

Here are some suggestions on how to handle fear that we should all work on and live by:

1. **Face your fear to become stronger.**[11]

   "You gain strength, courage and confidence by every experience in which you really stop to look fear in the face. You are able to say to yourself, 'I have lived through this horror. I can take the next thing that comes along.' You must do the thing you think you cannot do." Eleanor Roosevelt

   In an article on "How to Overcome Your Fear: 7 Tips from the Last 2200 Years" by Henrik Edberg, he came up with this insightful information and shared this after the above quote:

   > Every time you face a fear you gain the 3 important qualities that Eleanor Roosevelt mentions above. And the next thing that comes along will be easier to handle.
   >
   > And if you have to handle a big fear, whatever it may be, and later realise you actually survived it, many things in life you may have feared previously seems to shrink. Those fears become smaller. They might even disappear.
   >
   > You might think to yourself that what you thought was a fear before wasn't that much to be afraid of at all. Everything is relative. And every triumph, problem, fear and experience becomes bigger or smaller depending to what you compare it to.
   >
   > But to gain a wider perspective of human experience

and grow you really have to step up and face your fear.[12]

I have to say that now I am all about standing up and facing my fears. It hasn't always been so easy, though. This does happen to be where age and experience can come in handy. But, to help you with an example, think way back when, to your first or first few job interviews. You may have been frightened out of your mind—heartbeat and anxiety racing for days thinking about it. *What if I blow it? What if they don't like me? What if I don't get the job?* I can relate, because this was a fear that consumed me for days before an interview. Now when I look back, I laugh at myself. Why was I so consumed by that? If they didn't like me, or I didn't get the job—oh well. Not only would that have been a great practice meeting for me, but there will always be another new job down the road.

When you face the fear, face the unknown, you are saying to the Universe: "I trust you. I know I'm not doing this alone; please show me the signs I'm heading in the right direction, and if this situation doesn't turn out the way I'd prefer, I'm willing to be open that you have a higher and brighter outcome for me." How liberating is that to think, feel and say? You see, you will get signs if this is the path you are supposed to take. (I even have a great story I tell later about what turned the thought of this writing this book, which I had been told for years to write, into a reality.) If instead, you are headed down a path that doesn't suit you quite as well, but is comfortable, don't be surprised if something crazy like a "Wrong Direction" sign pops up somewhere on your way to the interview! The Universe can send some crazy messages. Whatever you do, don't set yourself up for fear. Walk yourself through it and allow yourself to look those "demons" in the face. When you do, it almost always ends up positive as a new stepping stone to your next better Self.

2. **Facing your fear can be surprisingly anti-climactic.**[13]

Henrik Edberg stated this after quoting this phrase from Ralph Waldo Emerson on facing your fear. "When a resolute young fellow steps up to the great bully, the world, and takes him boldly by the beard, he is often surprised to find it comes off in his hand, and that it was only tied on to scare away the timid adventurers." He then proceeds with a few more words from his "Timeless Tips" article:

> This is perhaps my favorite quote about fear. *From a distance and in your mind things may seem very difficult and frightening. But when you actually step up and take action I think many of us have been surprised of how the beard of that bully just comes off.* Why is that?
>
> Well, you can't sit around think and waiting for courage and confidence to come knocking on the door. If you do, you may just experience the opposite effect. The more you think, the more fear you build within.
>
> We often build scary monsters in our heads.
>
> Maybe because of things we have learned from the news, the TV or the movies. Or we just think repetitively about something that our minds start to create totally unlikely horror scenarios of what may happen.

As you may have noticed in your own life, 80-90 percent of what we worry about never really comes into reality. Instead things can become anticlimactic when we take action. The beard of the bully comes off surprisingly easily if we just step up and take action.

And many times we get the courage we need after we have done what we feared. Not the other way around.[14]

In the midst of a fearful situation now, I *always* remind myself—what is the *worst thing* that could happen if this fails? I mean, I really let it all out there in my imagination. And surprisingly, whatever has gone wrong, I may not have liked it, but I survived it. Even through Anthony's illness, there was always the possibility he would not make it. That is unfortunately the nature of medicine and disease. And the thought of that would tear me up inside thinking about that possibility, but something inside said, *if* that happens, we will deal with it then. And I let it go. That's all the power I had in that moment: to let it go and trust in something I couldn't understand.

3. **Don't give fear power. Don't worry. "Take action and get busy."[15]**

"Worry gives a small thing a big shadow." Swedish proverb

"Worrying means you suffer twice." Fantastic Beasts

Let me give you a little Psychology 101 advice: The minute you give power to that fear and repeat it in your head, your ego will run with it as far and fast as it can to

Trust Means Overcoming Fear

slow you down or disable you. Let's say, for example, you have a fear of spiders. If you say to yourself each time you see a spider, "I'm deathly afraid of spiders," and freeze with fear or run from the room repeating it, your fear will grow and soon you will start seeing black specs everywhere you go and believe they are spiders. You must "lie" to yourself, play with your mind for a second every time you see one. "Thank goodness I am no longer afraid of spiders." Deep breaths. "Spiders are wonderful creatures for the environment." "Thank you, spider, for helping me grow and learn there is nothing to be afraid of." The bottom line is ego can't hold two thoughts at once for long periods of time, and eventually it is going to believe what you are telling it and move on to something else! That is the beauty of the human mind. You can't let it control you; you must learn to control it. Soon, as I said, you will find that you get over the fear more quickly than you expected, because you didn't give it power, and then it really becomes anti-climactic.

The same goes for worry. Worry is another fascinating, ego-limiting process, and it can make a mountain out of molehill, as the saying goes. You have to do your best to stop yourself from worrying. Ask yourself the same questions: "What is the worst that can happen?" and "Is there anything I can do about it now?" Once you've addressed these two questions, let it go. Why do you think the Bible states in Matthew 6:25-27, "Is not life more than food, and the body more than clothing? Look at the birds of the air: they neither sow nor reap nor gather into barns, and yet your heavenly Father feeds them. Are you not of more value than they? And which of you by being anxious can add a single hour to his span of life?"

Those are beautiful words. Which of us can add a single hour to our life span by *worry*? The truth is, not one of us. This is why we must learn to eliminate it, or at least work around it so that it consumes less and less of our time. We all know that a mind at rest can be our worst enemy if we just sit there thinking and thinking and thinking and allowing our mind to race off into a number of places. If you worry about your fear happening, and it does, then you're going to suffer anyway, right? Worrying about the suffering just makes you suffer twice as much! Worry serves absolutely no purpose. My advice to you is to get rid of worry, take action, and get busy! And, my two cents' worth of wisdom…A busy person with lots of activities just does not have the same *amount* of time to worry. A meditative person will *eliminate* worry.

4. **Fear is often based on unhelpful interpretation.**[16]

> *FEAR: False Evidence Appearing Real.*
>
> -Unknown

At one time I had read an article on building self-confidence that included six essential and timeless tips and this one in particular caught my eye:

> As humans we like to look for patterns. The problem is just that we often find negative and not so helpful patterns in our lives based on just one or two experiences, or by misjudging situations, or through some silly miscommunication.

Trust Means Overcoming Fear

When you get too identified with your thoughts you'll believe anything they tell you. A more helpful practice may be to not take your thoughts too seriously. A lot of the time they and your memory are pretty inaccurate.[17]

Identifying your thoughts and believing anything they tell you can have its polar good sides. Even though I am definitely not for unproductively identifying with your thoughts too much, I am for the productive side of allowing it to open you up to re-examining old beliefs you have. Those older and outdated beliefs can wear you down, throw you off course, and stop you from growing. You need to revisit experiences you may have interpreted in not the most helpful way and see if you can look at them from a different perspective. This opens you up to try again and see what happens this time. Instead of staying stuck in thought, inaction, and fear, you may actually have a positive outcome!

Let's take an example. Someone you know shares with you that someone else has said derogatory or untrue things about you. What's your first reaction? "How dare they! This is false information!" We immediately start to think we have *become* the things that person has said about us, and our minds and thoughts become enraged. We begin to stew over and over again about what was shared. Our minds will believe anything someone tells us, rather than stop, think, and assess—where is this information coming from? Is any of this true, and does it even have merit? *If* your answers to those questions are *no*, then we have to train the brain to look at the situation in another context. What are the feelings that are coming up as we learn about this? Is it lack of importance? Is it lack of self-worth?

Where else in our past did the words or actions of someone else controlling us arise? When did we become easily swayed by others yet know in our hearts it wasn't true?

Remember my childhood? My father always told us we weren't enough, and I believed him. So, of course, throughout my life, if someone said something derogatory toward me, I believed them. Eventually I started to put the pieces together and realized, *Aha*, this is my childhood memories coming to teach me that I *am* enough regardless of what others think or say. Their problem—not mine!

With that, I was able to move on and move forward. Do you know how liberating this is? It feels as though the weight of the world has been lifted from your shoulders! As one of my absolute favorite teachers, Wayne Dyer, said, "How people treat you is their karma; how you react is yours." *Love* that! Don't succumb to *F*alse *E*vidence *A*ppearing *R*eal and be very careful with *how* you are identifying with your thoughts!

5. Don't cling to your illusion of safety.[18]

> *"Security is mostly a superstition. It does not exist in nature.... Life is either a daring adventure or nothing." Helen Keller*

In 2006 Henrik Edberg initially wrote this excerpt and to this day it has value and offers something to think about:

> Why do people sit on their hands? Is it just because they become paralyzed with fear? I'd say no. Another big reason why people don't face their fears is because they think they are safe where they are right now. But the truth is what Keller says; safety is mostly

a superstition. It is created in your mind to make you feel safe. But there is no safety out there really. It is all uncertain and unknown.

You may get laid off. Someone may break up with you and leave. Illness will probably strike. Death will certainly strike in your surroundings and at some point come to visit you too. Who knows what will happen?

This superstition of safety is not just something negative. It's also created by your mind so you can function in life. No point in going all paranoid about what could happen a minute from now day in and day out. But there is also not that much point in clinging to an illusion of safety. You need to find balance where you don't obsess by the uncertainty but also recognize that it is there and live accordingly.

As you stop clinging to your safety, life also becomes a whole lot more exciting and interesting. You are no longer as confined by an illusion and realize that you set your limits for what you can do and to a large extent create your own freedom in the world. You are no longer building walls to keep yourself safe as those walls wouldn't protect you anyway.[19]

I want you to have the strength, the courage, the fortitude to forge ahead. I want you to realize that truly there is not a perfectly safe and secure place and start to accept that that is okay. That is life. But life is meant to be lived. You are not supposed to be stuck in some hidden and fake safety zone that makes you too afraid to venture out. There is love everywhere waiting for you to receive it—you have to be, as the next recommendation says, curious, and then risk venturing out!

6. **Be curious[20], and stay in faith.**

> *"Curiosity will conquer fear even more than bravery will."* James Stephens

Another Henrik Edberg article on "Yoda's Top 3 Words of Wisdom" stated:

> When you are stuck in fear you are closed up. You tend to create division in your world and mind. You create barriers between you and other things/people. When you shift to being curious your perceptions and the world just opens up.
>
> Curiosity is filled with anticipation and enthusiasm. It opens you up. And when you are open and enthusiastic then you have more fun things to think about than focusing on your fear.
>
> How do you become more curious? One way is to remember how life has become more fun in the past thanks to your curiosity and to remember all the cool things it helped you to discover and experience.[21]

I wholeheartedly agree! Curiosity is a wonderful adventure, but I'm going to add another component, and that is to have faith. Not religion, per se, but faith—believing in the unseen. The reason is that a higher consciousness is *always* trying to beat *fear* out to remind us that we will forever be taken care of, even in the midst of our scary experiences. And with this understanding, fog-like fears disappear. When this happens, you feel like a new person, and I assure you that you will be left saying, of that higher protection, "More, please!"

Remember, "The emotions you experience are often as a result of what you focus your mind on."[22] Change what you focus on about something and you can change your emotions about that thing. By focusing on positive thoughts, and especially Acts of Kindness toward others, you change your vibration, and suddenly the energy you were giving to the fear, dissipates and is replaced by feelings of peace, love, and harmony. See what a wonderful world you can create for yourself by changing your thinking and staying in faith?

7. **Remove separation. Remove fear.**[23]

"Who sees all beings in his own self, and his own self in all beings, loses all fear." Isa Upanishad, Hindu Scripture

The ego wants to divide your world. It wants to create barriers and separation, and loves to play the comparison game—the game where people are different compared to you, the game where you are better than someone and worse than someone else. All of that creates fear. Doing the opposite removes fear.

That there is no real separation between beings, that we are one and the same, might sound a bit corny.

But one thought you may want to try for a day is that everyone you meet is your friend.

Another one is to see what parts of yourself you can see in someone you meet, and what parts of yourself you can see in him/her.

There is often an underlying frame of mind in interactions. Either it asks us how we are different from this person, or how we are the same as this person. The first frame is based in how the ego likes to judge people and create separation to strengthen itself (either through feeling better or more like a victim). The second one creates warmth, an openness and curiosity within. There is no place to focus on fear or judgment anymore.

This is of course not easy, especially if you have held the first frame of mind for many years. But you can get insight into this by doing the rest of the things above. As you face your fears the barriers and separation you have built in your mind decreases. You come closer and feel more of a connection to other people.

With action, curiousness and understanding we come closer to each other. We gain a greater understanding of ourselves and others. And so it becomes easier to see them in you. And you in them.[24]

The ego really does wants to divide your world. It wants to create barriers, separation, and loves to play the comparison game. The game where people are different compared to you: The game where you are better than someone or worse than someone else. All of that creates fear. Remember, we are Spiritual beings having a human experience, and we've always learned, from day one, that

TRUST MEANS OVERCOMING FEAR

we are different than everyone around us. Learning to think opposite of what we have been taught and finally know we are all *One* removes fear. When you work on the connectivity of *All*, you begin to see and feel and experience the world a little differently, a little lighter, a lot more loving. Don't build barriers. Work to build bridges of love. The more you do, the easier it becomes. The result? All of a sudden it becomes second nature to see them in you… and you in them.

So embrace others, embrace the world. Know that you are separate yet One and connected. Start realizing that if you can *remove the fear* that you have ultimately battled and won the biggest war: the war of moving from trusting others to trusting yourself. Work daily and diligently at this with TNT: Tenacity, Nerve, and Time, and soon you will find yourself living a much easier and better life! I promise.

Chapter Eleven
H-E-L-L-O Karma

Dreams, Visitations, Soul Contracts, and More!

I Saw That!

—Karma[25]

I have just shared some ideas on to how to face and conquer fear. The bottom line is that with fear out of the way, and with courage and curiosity leading us, we can now be open to how the Universe works and why Spirit is here to guide us. The next step is that you must drop a lot of your previous beliefs that have been hammered into your brain by others and be open to change. Just like I had to stop fearing what my parents said about needing a priest to exorcise those "feelings" and experiences with Spirits, you need to realize that all experiences are there to help you grow. To understand them a little better is to accept them a little easier.

To digress for a moment, I want to bring up something that stumps those who have had religion pushed on them since birth—and I assure you I'm not asking you to dump your religion; rather, think of it as a human tool that still has some flaws in it. God or Spirit or Source or whatever you call them are unconditional love, *not* a religion. Many religions teach *fear*, so it is that part I want you to try to help yourself evolve from. Source is all-loving, all-good. That's it.

I would never ask you to abandon your religious beliefs, and I have struggled with this myself my entire life. Even as a child, going to religious education classes and Mass, I *always felt* there was more to God than what we were being taught. If God is everywhere, then why do I have to sit in front of a priest to have confession? Why must I have to receive communion each week? Why must I abstain from things during Lent, and why, if someone is not baptized, do they not enter heaven? I often wondered, what do the people in other parts of the world that are religiously persecuted and unable to practice their religion do? Does God love them less and not give them a pardon into the Kingdom of Heaven because they didn't follow all the rules? And which rules are the right ones? Christianity? Judaism? Islam? Buddhism? Spirit has shown me over and over again, it's all about love, forgiveness, compassion. That is what you will be judged on when your soul returns to the source in heaven. If you want to honor God, Spirit, and your soul's purpose, then just love yourself and others—especially in those moments when it is the hardest to do so. So, put that as a feather in your cap, and let others be. Your new living motto is Love, Forgiveness, Compassion.

With that said, I want you to participate in healthy religious or non-religious groups for connections and socialization and support. People need uplifting places to be and to go. I'm just asking you to go to places that make you feel good, that truly lift you up and that do not leave you feeling as if you did or said something wrong. I want you to go to places that do not teach anything that leaves you walking out in fear. If you don't walk out feeling light and loved, walk away. That's as blunt as I can get!

Now, after saying goodbye to the tool of human religion, let's say h-e-l-l-o to karma. Honestly, today in 2019 everyone has probably heard or used the word loosely. We can probably even agree that we have a physical body, a mind, and even if people won't say it out loud, most believe we have a spiritual body. Many are even coming to believe that there are no coincidences, but somehow they can't seem to make the leap to the fact that it is not a coincidence that we are on the planet now and it is not a fluke that we were born when we were. Each one of us has a purpose when we arrive at birth, but the problem is that when we arrived, we completely forgot what that purpose was!

So, let's start with the side most people ignore, the spiritual, and jump in with intuitive ability. We *all* have the ability to be intuitive. That is our innate gift—to use that "gut" feeling we each have, to know when something is right or in opposition just feels "off." Do many of us use it? No…because it's not something that is often spoken about as we mature and grow. Do we all have it? Absolutely. Some people's gifts are just stronger. Why? Because it is in their soul contract to come down on Earth, at this time, to use this gift to help others grieve or receive peace. Just as you could shove me behind a piano for seven hours a day practicing, I will never become a concert pianist. Why? Because it's not in my life contract to do so. I offer you steps, and a meditation, to get you grounded and in touch with your innate intuitive ability. The Universe gave this to you as a GPS "Global Positioning System" mechanism when you arrived here for life. But for now, I want to help you envision the world a little different than you were probably taught.

We each have a soul contract and lessons we came onto Earth to learn. I discussed this in Part Three, but I am going to repeat a little bit of the information and then expand on it for those who want to delve a little deeper. As I explained, karma is the aftereffect (the effect of the cause) that we experience in this life. Whether it was a conscious decision or mistake on our part, or something that is done involuntarily and separate from our wishes, we suffer the karma (the cause). The karma is the "lesson" of the event. We talked about the possibilities related to abandonment, loss, letting go, and other possible learning lessons, because that is why we are here. We talked about our soul contracts that we agreed to before incarnating in this realm and the roles we play with other humans in our current relationships.

Now, how do we learn what our soul contract is? Unfortunately, there is no moment of *Aha, I found my soul contract! Here it is, now let me open it up and read the fine print so I can figure out what the heck is going on here.* Our lessons are woven into the fabric of our soul contracts. I now know my father and I had a contract to resolve in this life—no question about that. But did I know it as I was going through the lessons? No. I had to sit, meditate, and do inner work on myself for many decades, to help me understand. And because I didn't learn that lesson of love and forgiveness with him and felt broken, I attracted other relationships and friendships that mirrored that lesson, among others. Do we know exactly what the details of our contract are? No, but if you look at the repeating experiences that keep showing up for you over and over again, you will begin to see a pattern. Do you find yourself never speaking up for yourself over and over again with friends, family? Do you feel like you're always being abandoned by the people you thought would never leave you? Do you always feel like you're giving to others more than they give back to you? Look at your life objectively and see where the patterns keep repeating for you. That is where you will see and understand the *Aha* moment and the lesson behind it.

Can our soul contract change while we are in this body? Our contract is our contract. You agreed to it on the other side, and *if* your free will chooses to learn from it, then other lessons will be given to you as you move along, sort of like an exam with multiple parts. You first have to pass part one before you can be given part two, etc. Just as with school, you have to pass 8th grade before you can get to high school and finish the other levels. As you move along your contract, you are learning and hopefully growing. That is wonderful for the evolution of your soul that is returning to Earth to learn! You can even examine your own life, and looking back, can see the growth you have gone through, and the moments where you could have done better, but acknowledge now that you'd never put yourself in that same space again. That is *growth*!

This makes you ask, "But Gina, what happens if we *ignore* our soul contract and go off the deep end by getting trapped in 'human' life?" I am sad to say that there are many souls here who use their free will and just refuse to grow. That was my dad. You probably even have people in your own life you see just stuck in the experiences and situations in their life. Their fear, stubbornness, ignorance, etc. created a wall around them, where they couldn't grow, expand, or learn from their experiences, and in many situations, refused to learn. Look at siblings who refuse to speak to one another over some stupid fight from ten years ago, or two best friends that never speak because of a money transaction that was never resolved. *Trust* me, there is no earthly situation that cannot be forgiven, *if* the soul wishes to learn from it, they will. And, that is the key—you must *want* the learning.

Do we ever come as soul *groups* to work our contract? And how do we know when we meet those partners, twins, or group members? I touched on this briefly before. We always work in soul groups. Sometimes the groups can be large, like a hundred souls; other times they are smaller, like twenty. And not everyone incarnates all at the same time. Each person you are affiliated with—whether family, friend, coworker, or boss—is in your energy field, because there is some large or tiny lesson you are here to learn from.

My cousin is a somewhat happy-go-lucky guy, but always finds himself in work situations that are toxic, unbalanced, and sometimes degrading. He's been let go several times in his career, maybe because of the way he can get explosive at work when pushed too far, or maybe because the companies just had layoffs. Whatever the case is, he keeps attracting the same scenario over and over again. He's very talented and often gets the ideas to go out on his own, but the fear stops him. Each one of the souls he's encountered here on Earth as co-workers and bosses is in his soul group to help him learn the lesson of valuing himself more, standing up for himself, and taking the risks he needs to. One of his lessons is "Do not be afraid." Will he ever learn? That's up to his free will. But *he* has to understand the pattern, and *he* has to want to change it. No one can change another person and then fulfill the lessons *they* have to complete.

It's fascinating to note that some soul groups decide to come through in masses, to assist the learning and growth of a nation or the world—the Holocaust, Cambodia, Croatia, Bosnia, and our own personal 9/11 just to name a few. These were brave souls that collectively decided to enter and exit together for the soul purpose of changing laws, creating order, and bringing more awareness of needing to create peace to the world. As a world, we rally together with love, support, and compassion during these awful historical moments, only to get caught up again in our individual worlds, creating division and separateness and hatred all over. It's the same law of nations over and over again, but we're just not listening to them or learning.

As a matter of fact, you may even find you are drawn to certain causes and certain people because of a soul group you are a part of but just not realize yet. People ask, "Do we ever *recognize* a soul in our group?" Yes! Sometimes we meet them in school, or as another parent in PTA, or even on the job. Someone catches your eye, and you feel like you've known them forever even though you just met. There is a bond that says—there's something special about you. We all have people in our lives that we feel we have met some other time or place. They are here to assist us, to help us get through this thing we call life.

This leads me to soulmates and who we pull into our lives at what time. The importance of our learning lessons doesn't just happen in this lifetime; the lessons happen over many, many lifetimes. Please open your mind a little more when a religion, even some Christian sects, try to tell you that reincarnation does not exist. It is actually a section that was removed from many of our current Bibles, but early translations did accept this as fact. If we did not reincarnate, there would not be karma. Sorry, it's true. And while we are clearing up misconceptions, our partners, our children, our loves in this life are our soulmates. People think we only marry our soul "mates"—that's just not true.

A soulmate is someone we have incarnated here that has come to help us learn. Good and bad. There are lessons, karma and learning. For the one soul attracted, there is an opposite energy and lesson for the other to learn. It is the perfect storm of life sometimes. And then other times, the soulmate is here to guide us, love us, and support us. We all learn differently. I have many clients that always want to know when their soulmate is going to come into this life. But, how do you know in this life there will even be a soulmate, the way you are thinking of it, that you need to marry? Maybe the soulmates for you are already the people in your life that you are still learning from. We have to stop thinking about Hollywood's "riding into the sunset with a mate in order to be happy" lie. Maybe that person who can't find happiness in a relationship is really here to learn how to find happiness on their own? Now, isn't that interesting!

I don't want you to be one of the poor souls who buys into the lies that are created here on Earth and have it delay your growth. As for clearing up the lies, here goes: There is reincarnation; there is karma; a soulmate is not just that one knight in shining armor you are destined to marry; soulmates can be same or different sexes then we are; and, last but not least, I am going to go out on another limb and say what I said in Part Three, suicide is *not* a sin. Before you go running from the room yelling, "Blasphemer," let me repeat what I've said before. All souls go to heaven.

Heaven is derived of different levels, as I have been explained to in readings. Even souls that committed murder end up at a very low level of heaven, the place some religions call purgatory. Someone like the Dalai Lama enters at a very high level. The rest of us somewhere in the middle. Our job on the other side is to do life reviews and look at the highlights and lowlights of our lives and learn from those experiences. Even a soul that commits suicide is treated with the same learning and care in heaven. In those situations, the soul must see and learn *why* they decided to take a *permanent* solution to whatever *temporary* problem they may have had here on Earth. I want to repeat that: Their free will decided to take a *permanent* solution to whatever *temporary* problem they were experiencing here on Earth. You see, you are here to learn, and the suicide stopped the lesson they should have learned.

In a recent reading, this woman's brother came through, taking responsibility for ending his own life and trying to bring her some comfort. She held herself responsible for her brother's suicide. He was not a chemically balanced man for most of his life. One night, driving intoxicated, and getting into a car accident, he called her frantic. He was being irrational and threatening he had a gun in his apartment. He was showing me the mental fog and instability he was going through. On her way rushing to see him, police had shown up at his place due to the accident. Worried about her brother, she told them he had a gun inside. Taking this seriously, he showed me the police pounding on the door, ramming it open and in that moment of terror, the brother shot himself. This poor woman holds the guilt that if she hadn't said anything to the officers, they would have been able to get him to come out of the apartment unharmed. But what the brother shared in the reading was whether it was that night, or six months later, he would have ended up taking his own life. His soul contract was to leave this life early, as he had done in many lives before, because his free will no longer wanted to deal with the circumstances of his life.

His soul was here to learn the lessons and karma of the past and learn how to forge through whatever difficulty he was going through in this life. He was unable to do that and now the sister holds the guilt of his passing. It has nothing to do with her! And, hopefully, the brother coming through will help heal her wounds and trust her brother is in a much better place with no worries, pain, or mental disease.

I also want to make an additional point, and that is to try not to judge why this happened. There is extreme guilt and shame that comes to people around suicide, so I just want to clear up these few points and make you explore this from a different angle. Perhaps in some way the brother came to Earth this time by choice to leave by suicide just so the sister could learn that this was truly not her karma and not her fault. Unless you do the work to discover all the whys and lessons taught, you are harming yourself and others by placing any *blame* any- where. You see, we don't know where on the Karmic wheel another person is at unless we are trained in looking at our lives and theirs from other dimensions. So, we wonder, with so many possibilities of lessons, which one are we to learn? It all boils down to love and acceptance of others, and love and forgiveness of ourselves. Perhaps that sister was karmically supposed to learn about loving and forgiving herself in this lifetime, and the soul of that brother was the perfect vehicle to teach that.

I wish there was an answer sheet somewhere in the cosmos so we could validate what the lessons *actually are*. Remember in school, you would try to figure out in your workbook what the answer to the question was, and then turn to the back of the book to see—did I get it right? Wouldn't it be glorious if we had a system like that here?

In an odd way, we don't need an answer sheet, though, because there are not a bunch of new answers to all these questions. The answer to all is that Spirit never wants us to suffer here from a loss because when those we love have transcended, it is to a place that is free of all earthly worries and pain. They want to help guide us not to take blame, not to hold on to hurts, not to second-guess ourselves, but to continue loving and forgiving others and ourselves. These facts are the only answer sheets we ever really need in the end.

Now, as for the other big topic I want to shed light on: "Why does a good, all-loving God, all powerful God let bad things happen to good people?" Yes, *that* question, but beyond that, I want to address the emotion, the feelings we invoke against God, or Source, or Spirit as if they are to blame for our misery. I want to once again encourage you to look at this from a different perspective to help you answer this question once and for all. What if I tell you it's not God's decision per se, meaning God is not to blame, because it was a contract you and those around you made (a decision to learn from this scenario and suffering) *before* you even arrived on Earth? If it was your decision, then isn't blaming God just a misplaced emotion? Aren't you actually to blame? And what about the emotion of anger?

Being angry with God means nothing. If you've ever had a child and had to impose a rule or curfew on that child, who was angry and not in agreement with you, you understand. Even as they are storming upstairs calling you "mean" and saying "I hate you," your feelings may be hurt, but you always love that child anyway. All God knows is love, because that is the *only* energy of the universe. It's the *only* language.

When you are in alignment with forgiveness and love, you are in alignment with the universe. Because we are One with all that is. When we are angry, we are putting out that negative energy, which happens to be Law of Attraction—and don't worry; I give you more on that in the next chapter! So, we put out anger, which just rebounds back to us, and what we put out is what we reap: more anger and negativity. Yet the whole time, God, very much like a parent, is looking at us, loving us, and waiting for our temper tantrum to subside so we can reconnect with Him and begin to learn the reason *why*.

We are not being punished. Many people say, "What have I done to be punished this way?" That has nothing to do with the loving God that is always there for us. That is the doctrine of religion that wants us always to be in fear, so we force ourselves to stay under control. But many things happen to us that are completely out of our control. Does that mean God doesn't love us? *No.* There is a verse in the Bible that says, "No weapon formed against you shall prosper." I love when the preacher and author Joel Osteen references that verse. It doesn't mean that bad, horrible things won't ever happen to you. It means that if you believe in a power higher than yourself, that whatever the experience is, it will not pull you down or break you. You may end up bent, but not broken. And, what if beyond that, you have been the actual blessing that helped a soul work through a karmic lesson? All the better for both of you!

Somehow, I still feel a few of you digging your feet in. I know this is rough material and hard to conceptualize if it is all new to you. I hear you saying, "Fine, if I can't be angry at God, how about I get angry at the soul that passed? It's really their fault I am suffering!" It's normal to feel hurt and anger and a variety of other emotions when a loved one has passed. People feel angry sometimes because the person betrayed them by leaving them to deal with crap on Earth and with the heartache. How could this be a loving universal system?

The only use of anger is for learning. It's an emotion just like jealousy, guilt, envy, hurt, sadness, and love. All these human emotions are here to help us learn through the millions of lessons available to our souls. What do you do with the anger you have toward a loved one that has passed? How do you fix that situation now that they are no longer here? It's your job, and now lesson, to learn what you were both here to learn from each other and learn forgiveness toward them, and especially for yourself.

Each lesson is always done with love, and lessons can sometimes hurt and be hard to learn from. Every child has to fall when learning to walk, every heart must feel heartache in order to appreciate love, and every experience brings with it the opportunity for forgiveness and compassion. Anthony has been showing us over and over again the lesson that he wants us all to learn—let it go. Your loved one on the other side no longer holds on to the human emotions of pain and anger. They recognize their part in the lesson and their soul is learning there. God is patient, waiting for us to let go of the anger, as are our loved ones. They now understand the difficulty we have as humans where we overwhelm ourselves with the emotions. Unless we connect to the love and forgiveness behind them, we are missing the entire point. Your loved one is waiting for you to learn this on your end, just as they learned it on theirs.

And, while you are trying to understand all of this, if you happened to be one of those family members who was the victim in an abusive relationship and all you can think is, "What is this karma crap and forgiveness? I never want to see that family member or person again; why do I have to?" For the sexual abuse survivor, the child of an alcoholic or abuser, it would be normal to feel that you are happy that person is gone for good, so why would you want to be part of their group…ever? I understand that it is painful and hard to grasp, but it becomes easier to start to forgive the wrongs perpetrated on us—even as horrible as they are—when we get that we contracted it and that the loved one did it "with" and "for" us. As hard as this is to hear, it is the truth.

Each lesson, whether brief or long-lasting, that is traumatic and horrendous, is for our learning. I understand that no one wants to hear from a loved one that abused them. Fortunately or unfortunately, our souls are always connected to them, because the souls agreed to the lesson on the other side. We may be looking at the experience via the lens of human emotions, but that is not what the souls agreed to. They agreed to the learning and growth that comes out of that experience.

When I began learning about life lessons, soul contracts, soul groups, etc. the lessons behind my childhood made much more sense to me. I always wanted to know how come I couldn't be normal like everyone else and have loving, supportive parents? Was I not worthy enough? My childhood haunted me for decades. But as I began to learn, and did a lot of inner child work, I began to realize the little girl within me was so strong to handle that dysfunction and abuse, and I was not making peace with her or protecting her by being more careful with the experiences I was then later getting myself into as an adult. Once I understood the full circle of things, the forgiveness came—not only for my dad, but also for myself and not taking better care of the little me, and the big me, always.

In sharing all of this, I realize I am asking a lot of you. I am asking you to expand your thinking, to have courage—and even more, to have the courage to think differently. I'm also telling you that it's okay to be *different*! Trust me, I know, and now I even embrace it! But, just like that loving and nudging parent, I'm going to push you even further. Here's where things get really interesting and if this next bit of information is too much, just put it aside for now. Along with the information I am about to share, I do also provide you with some meditative steps and suggestions as to how to proceed, but if this material is way too "out there" for you, I would prefer you put this next topic on the back burner for now and instead start with the lessons I teach in Chapter 13 on how to get Spirit on board. Those won't seem quite as intimidating. But, for those who have moved from worriers to warriors, those who are brave and ripped the Band-Aid of fear off—enjoy the ride of the info below!

When a physician wants to read a physical body to make a diagnosis, it helps to take a look under the microscope at blood work. It is not seen on the outside of the body and visible to the human eye on its own, but it is "readable" if we look harder or have the right instrument. Well, if we tune up our Spiritual instrument, there is actually a place we can go to find out more about ourselves and our many lives. Yes, you read that correctly. Like old records in a doctor's office that we have long forgotten, we have a place that we can go to read our soul journeys and find out our past. They are all recorded in something called the Akashic Records.

The Akashic Records are the energetic records of all souls about their past lives, the present lives, and possible future lives. It refers to a database of every word, thought, or action that is stored energetically and recorded. They contain the information of every soul or Being in the cosmos. The records are continually updated, with each new thought, word, or action that every soul or entity makes. The Akashic Records contain the energetic prints about the journey of every soul through its lifetimes.

Each soul has its own Akashic Record, like a series of books with each book representing one lifetime. The Hall (or Library) of the Akashic Records is where all souls' Akashic Records are stored energetically. In other words, your records for all your lives and the information within is stored in the Akashic Hall.

Anything about the Universe has an energetic record. The records of your soul are located via your full name at birth and birth date of this current lifetime. They are embedded with information about your previous lifetimes, your Soul Origination, current life lessons, and your purpose, as well as future choice points in your life. Understanding this helps you realize that each soul is a unique individual representation of the part of the Divine, each soul has its own gifts and ways of manifesting its human experiences, and that our Soul is the key to unlocking our Spiritual potential.

What the records teach us it that our problems are not happening in a haphazard manner and they are not *meaningless* roadblocks. Your life is working even when you don't think so, and you can move through your life with less resistance when you understand this. This alone helps you look at terrible losses and hardships in a new way (after the initial shock) and allows you to move through life feeling a little less picked-on or targeted. If you can join this truth with the fact that you chose the soul contract, this can even help you start to release anger that you may be holding against the Almighty God that was taught to be benevolent and omnipresent.

On the other hand, when you don't embrace this and don't have the proper reference points, learning from each life event feels like a struggle with no ending in sight. Remembering our purpose through the Akashic Records means helping you see through the fog and veil of what your life experiences are trying to teach you. No more running around trying to solve problems. And we will absolutely address how to handle problems, in the next chapter! Can you even imagine what life will be like when you learn to let unnecessary problems resolve on their own and have fun with the remaining challenges, as you tap into the Akashic Records to see "why" this is happening and that is it for *your* own good?

The question then becomes, "Who do I go see to tap into these Akashic Records?" The beauty is that you can read your own Akashic Records. It takes some practice, but you don't need to be an exceptional guru, and there are many books on the market that will show you step-by-step the process. The real question is: how do you utilize the information? You see, you are allowed access only if you are working toward your highest and best good—yours and tapping into others can never be used for negative purposes. The motivation is even more critical than the skill. If someone attempts to enter the Hall of the Akashic Records with mere curiosity, not to mention malicious intentions, they are rejected (often by getting confused). The curiosity might sound innocent enough, as in, "Let's find out what my boyfriend or girlfriend was like in their past lives." Learning who they were or are won't improve your relationship until you understand who you are. We always want to begin with ourselves. The good news is that reading the Akashic Records that are relevant to you is even easier—you carry a copy of your records, a blueprint so to speak, to use to deepen your understanding of yourself *only*. The records are accessed through being in a deep state of relaxation or meditation, and this is how you can access them yourself. You see, the intention of use is of utmost importance. The power in the fact that anyone can have the same access to the records is like having internet access to the same database of information. It must be used wisely and in total love.

Remember though, the Akashic Records are a great resource, but it's only a resource. It is up to you to utilize it in your life. Accessing the Library of Akashic Records is not difficult. In reality, no special powers or abilities are needed. The same records are accessible by the subconscious mind, other than meditation, through dreams and intuitive exercises. A cluttered mind, ego, little connection with one's Higher Self, and a lack of trust in one's divine power are hindrances that an Akashic Record reader needs to overcome first. It is only when there is complete harmony between the conscious, subconscious or superconscious that truth from the Akashic Records can be determined.

Once you honor and understand how very sacred a process this is, you want to first start accessing it by getting into a meditative state. While the regular intuition can come in a casual way, reading the Akashic Records takes a little more focus. You need to be able to set aside your current thoughts and be open to whatever information you may find. The other prerequisite is the willingness to reveal and accept whatever is recorded about yourself. You might receive disturbing information, such as the way you died in one of your past lives or some serious problems that bothered you for a long time back then—and how you yourself contributed to the problem. If, in your daily life, you tend to avoid problems or neglect challenges, how can you face such information when you read your Akashic Records?

To start the reading session of your Akashic Records, you might want to have a certain ritual. Doing some preparatory meditation is a good idea. Voicing your intention is also a good practice. Say something like, "Let the energy of Love, Light, and Truth prevail on Earth. My Spirit guides, please help me open my Akashic Records so that I may have the wisdom to live this life with more awareness and courage." The "Love, Light, and Truth" part is essential. You are making it clear that you are doing this reading with love, not judgments; with light (spiritual awareness), not confusion; and for truth, rather than hiding in untruth or ignorance. In other words, you are saying that you are open to the truth, whatever it may be, and you are willing to receive it with love and light.

Like any intuitive inquiries, the inquiry for the Akashic Records needs to be clear and direct. Please read the Akashic Records for problem solving. For example, you might want to ask something like, "This [brief description of your issue] is what I've been working on, and I feel there is something more than I know in my present life. If this is true, please provide the information of when and how this problem originated."

You might see a picture or video clip in your energetic eye. You might hear music that symbolizes something. You might feel it, smell it, or taste it. You might just know. Or perhaps it will be the combination of a few of these. Receive the information, ask some additional clarifying questions if you need to, and then close the session with gratitude. You receive just as much information as is helpful for you now.

Now, please do not think you can cram a twenty-minute meditative session in between food shopping and when the kids get off the bus and think you will receive a tremendous amount of insight. Learning to meditate is primary, and you must have a daily meditation practice established. As humans, we're always looking for the quick in and out summary. If that is you, this won't work for you at all. You have to give this time. You have to practice, and you have to be open to *whatever* information comes to you. It might not even make sense to you at first. Write it down. Then, the next time, they may give you another clue. Never negate what is shown to you. This is not a "I'll believe it when I see it" exercise. Your angels and guides will absolutely shut you down if you have an ulterior motive, want it quickly, and have no patience. And please, take your time.

A lot of people who have worked on getting into deep meditative states and have asked for the light and access to the records ask, "How will you know if you have received accurate information?" It will resonate and make sense to you. You might even experience changes. Although this doesn't happen with every access to the records, in some cases situations of pain dissipating or relationships improving, or ending for no apparent reason, can show you that you have accessed a part of your records that make sense for your life. There are also people who temporarily feel down, such as like catching a cold, before they feel better.

Now, let me share with you one of my initial experiences with my own Akashic Records. I had been practicing meditation for many years when I decided to access my records. In that mediation, I asked to be shown some answers as to why my father was as brutal toward me as he was in this life. In that meditation, I was a Roman general or significant soldier and my child had been abducted and killed. My men had found the killer, and I had thrown him into the dungeons, had him chained to the walls and whipped and tortured every day. When I went down to see him, he was barely hanging by each arm with chains, his head bowed, almost lifeless. When I went to pull his head up by his hair, to reveal his face, it was my father's eyes in this lifetime. To this day I can see his eyes, not his face, just the same eyes. I began to cry in the meditation. This made *all* the sense in the world. In that life, he had devastated my heart by killing my child, and I, in return, had him mercilessly tortured. Makes sense to do that back then for such a heinous crime. But now in this lifetime, he tortured my inner child, and I did not take any revenge on him. I ended the karma, hopefully, by letting go of the hurt, and having compassion for him—for the pain we experienced together and for having empathy for others suffering here. That is when my inner healing really began. This is how powerful accessing the Akashic Records can be for a soul's growth. Crazy, right?

Now that I have shared this, is everyone going to run out and start trying to access their Akashic Records? Perhaps not. Actually, I have probably lost some of the readers temporarily because of the material, but what do I ask? Have no fear! Just planting this seed in you may resonate, if not today, soon and it will actually make my next topic seem less weird. So essentially, this has already served its purpose!

If meditating and accessing your Akashic Records is too far out there, and, I realize it is very advanced, then don't worry because we all still have that crazy night life of our own called dreams.

Dreams. Yes, you can't talk about the spiritual world without addressing dreams! Do we all have them? Yes. Do many say they don't dream and have never had any? Yes. Is that true? No! All people dream and if they never got into the deeper dreaming state the body would die. This is now a scientific proof. Extensive research has been done on REM (Rapid Eye Movement) states, delta and theta states, lucid dreaming, and the science of dreaming is evolving. Meanwhile, emotionally and psychologically, you can't talk about a dream without asking what in God's name it means!

Dreams are an amazing and wonderful part of life, and although some appear to us as nightmares and can be scary, *all* are there to help us heal on one level or another. Now, we could spend an entire book on dreams, but the ones I want you to get in touch with are the ones that relate to this book and reveal why deceased loved ones come to us in our dreams, or how to get them to if they do not already.

This is a frequent question from people as they grapple with loss and death, and experiencing dreams of deceased ones can eventually help us grow. So, why do deceased loved one come to us in our dreams? The fact is that it is actually easier for spiritual entities of all kinds (e.g., deceased loved ones, guides, angels) to communicate with us while we are sleeping. Why? Because when sleeping, we are in that "in between place" between our earthly reality and "the other side of the veil" (the spiritual world). It's called the subconscious. During this time, our rational mind, our conscious mind and our ego are not engaged. Things can happen in our dream world that we would normally stop or discount while awake. I want to share with you eight characteristics of visitation dreams so you can start to differentiate them from just a regular dream. Here is the list that I have taught in my classes but written by Anne Reith, Ph.D., a well-known teacher, psychic, and wellness coach:

8 Characteristics of Visitation Dreams:[26]

- **Characteristic #1**: The most important characteristic of a true visitation dream is that it feels "real." It will also be very vivid.
- **Characteristic #2**: If you have to ask whether the visitation dream was really a visitation dream, then it probably was not a visitation dream. They are so real and vivid that you won't have to ask this question. When you do have a visitation dream, you may wonder if it was honestly real; but in your heart or gut, you will "know" it was real.

- **Characteristic #3**: Because they are so real and so vivid, you will remember visitation dreams very clearly for days, months, years…probably for your entire lifetime!
- **Characteristic #4**: The person (or animal) will almost always appear in the dream to be completely healthy and behaving in a loving manner. They will rarely appear sick or injured. They will never be angry, disappointed, depressed, or punishing. They will be "whole, complete, and perfect" because they are now reconnected with God/Source energy.
- **Characteristic #5**: Whether or not they speak to you verbally in the dream, it will feel like a communication, even if they don't speak, but just look at you and smile.
- **Characteristic #6**: When they do communicate (either verbally or non-verbally), it isn't because they want to engage in idle "chit-chat." It isn't easy for deceased loved ones to enter a dream. They come with a purpose, and they will convey the message and then be gone.
- **Characteristic #7**: Most often, their messages fall into the category of "reassurance." They come to let you know that they are fine and that they want you to be happy. They will give you loving support and you will feel reassured by their presence.
- **Characteristic #8**: After a visitation dream, when you wake up, you will often be filled with a sense of peace and love. [27]

I find these characteristics extremely accurate and helpful. A few weeks ago, we visited our first grandson Austin in Pennsylvania. He was conceived when Anthony went to college in PA. Remember, he was supposed to be sterile from chemo? Nope. Austin's mom had remarried, and we were visiting their new home. We speak of Anthony often when together, and her new husband is such a fantastic role model for our little grandson. After visiting, Austin's mom told us the next day, that her husband had a dream of Anthony, who he had met only once many years ago. In that dream, Anthony was dressed in a Steelers cap, and Steelers jacket and walked up to him, gave him a big hug and said "Thank you." No other words. Just a simple smile, hug and thank you. That was Anthony's way of saying he was very honored and proud of the way this young man was stepping up as a father to our little guy. Here we were visiting our grandson, talking about Anthony, and that very night the husband has a dream of him. Spirit always wants us to know they are aware of what's happening in our lives and around us. They are never gone. And, *that* is a visitation dream!

The next big question I get is, "Can you ask for a visitation dream?" Yes, you certainly can! Before going to sleep, spend time thinking about the deceased loved one and ask him or her to come visit you in your dream state. You may also want to ask your guides or other Spiritual helpers to assist this person to come to you clearly. You may want to clear your body energy of any negativity during the day a little before you go to sleep, sort of like cleaning the antenna. Ask your angels to help the chosen Spirit come to you. Open the way for that Spirit to find you. It may take several attempts. There's also the chance the Spirit will not come, not because they don't want to but because they cannot make the journey or they simply don't know how. That's why asking the angels to help guide them to you is important.

Please don't become discouraged if the person doesn't come to you. They want to, but there are many reasons why a deceased loved one may not show up when requested. For example, the soul may be relatively new at entering dreams and may not know how to do it. Or your guides know that you want to know something that your deceased loved one can't tell you because you need to find the answer for yourself. And many times your own personal grief, guilt, and sorrow create a barrier wall around you so that Spirit cannot penetrate your dreams.

That's why it's extremely important that if someone comes to you in a dream that is crossed over, that you share that dream with their loved ones, because they are probably not dreaming of them for themselves. But there's no harm in asking for him or her to come visit with you! And when visitation dreams do occur, be sure to thank your deceased loved one for coming, and send them love and gratitude for taking the time to visit with you.

Now, another fascinating point, if your loved one never visits in dreams, it is sometimes because a Spirit simply cannot make the journey to come to you in your dreams. In that case, ground and center yourself before bed, and ask that you be transported to your loved one. The visitation you are asking for is for you to go to them. This takes patience. Not everything happens immediately, even though our desire is so strong. It is best to stay patient and trust we will see our loved one when the time is right. They may be busy giving you other signs during the day. Remember to always have a note pad by your bed and write your dreams down as soon as you get up. Write whatever you remember, even if it doesn't mean anything to you right then and there. There may be little clues from your loved one that they visited you, once you look at your notes later. The biggest thing I want you to take away is do not be disheartened that you don't see them. But do take notes, create a journal, jot down notes about your dreams, try to find out what the symbols mean—and keep at it. They are making their way, and it just all takes time.

In the end, there are many ways that Spirit tries to whisper communication with us. There are the signs, symbols, numbers we discussed in Part Three; there are dreams and even visitations, there are even soul contracts we can access through the Akashic Records to get a better understanding of why all this is happening in our lives now. But what is the common denominator to all this? Trusting yourself first and believing that Spirit is here to teach you and help you learn the lessons you came here to learn. After all, karma sees all!

With that said, our next barrier or step is to start to understand the Law of Attraction and to see how we can actually be our own worst enemies!

Chapter Twelve
LAW OF ATTRACTION

WE ARE OUR OWN WORST ENEMIES

The law is simple. Every experience is repeated or suffered till you experience it properly and fully the first time.

—Ben Okri, Astonishing the Gods

Karma sees all, Spirit is there for us *always*, our deceased ones send love from above, so why are we still stewing in the dumps? Why are we struggling so much, hurting so much? It is as Eckhart Tolle says in his book *A New Earth: Awakening to Your Life's Purpose*, "Life will give you whatever experience is most helpful for the evolution of your consciousness. How do you know this is the experience you need? Because this is the experience you are having at the moment." Welcome to the Law of Attraction!

One of my absolute favorite topics to talk about is this wild topic of the Law of Attraction. I could talk about this for days and wish I had learned about this law many decades ago. I wonder what would have changed in my life had I learned about it earlier? "The Law of Attraction simply says that you attract into your life whatever you think about. Your dominant thoughts will find a way to manifest." [28] How weird it that? What you think will manifest? Did your heart just skip a few beats as you realized the current topic in your brain was a negative one? Well, you might want to change your way of thinking as you learn more about this concept! And, to be clear, "The law of attraction manifests through your thoughts, by drawing to you thoughts and ideas of a similar kind, people who think like you, and also corresponding situations and circumstances."[29] Take a long, hard, look around you and see what you are manifesting in your friends, your monetary situation and your overall circumstances!

So what does this all mean? Remember, as we discussed earlier in the book, there is a force of energy that is always around us. It's an aura of energy surrounding us and helping us to attract that which we most want or need to create the life we want on Earth. This is a universal law—yes, law—that governs everything around us, from the microscopic atom to every cell in our body, to the energy and balance of all the planets. It is the premise behind "like attracts like." That energy of the universe is bringing to us the exact experiences, situations, and life events that we create through our own thoughts. The law is activated by your thoughts and the feelings behind those thoughts. Whatever is haphazardly running across your mind becomes the emotions and energy behind what you think, feel, and attract to you.

How is this possible? How do my *thoughts* bring to me that which I'm experiencing? Wouldn't everyone's life be awesome if all we had to do was think of something and we could create it? Like rubbing a genie bottle and getting wishes fulfilled! The answer is *Yes*! However, there is a caveat. Our thoughts manifest our reality. How many times have we really wanted something to happen, but deep inside we say to ourselves, "It'll never happen, I'm just not that lucky." We get the feeling of doom and gloom and *boo*m—we are right.

If what you think is "I hate my job," "My marriage is a disaster," "I don't have enough money to pay my bills," "I can't find anyone to love," then by the definition of the Law of Attraction, and "like attracts like," you are radiating negativity and that energy then creates *more* experiences of doom and gloom. Get ready, because disaster is coming your way. You've called it in!

Around our bodies are these beautiful circles of energy called auras. Our aura of energy is like an invisible bubble, circulating around us at all times. We can't see it or feel it, but this bubble helps us detect and connect to the energy around us as well as the energy of other people. We've all been in a situation where we walk into a room, that perhaps two people had an argument in hours earlier, and we can just "sense" the disconnect in the air. There are no words spoken, but our energy (aura) picks up on that situation. That is your energy field working at its best.

As humans, we are a ball of energy picking up signals from our experiences, life events and the people around us all the time. These life experiences shape how we think and feel about ourselves. Because our souls are housed in this earthly body, we forget the connection we have to the divine and assume we are the person, job, relationship or life situation that we're dealing with. We don't remember, as Spirits having a human experience, that we have the potential of the universe at our fingertips. We only know how perhaps we were knocked down and shaped by family members when we were younger, and now we don't feel worthy of anything better. We may want it, but we don't feel worthy.

Our mind is extremely powerful. What you think, you create. There is a saying from Henry Ford, "Whether you think you can, or you think you can't—you are right." And I'm adding—*always* right! What you subconsciously think, your mind takes that energy around you, the one that is always connected to Universal energy, and *pronto*, it brings it to you.

I used to have a friend who would always jokingly say stupid things about herself, degrading herself and when I would bring it to her attention and remind her of what she was putting out there, she would chuckle and say, "Oh geez…God knows, I'm only kidding." No, the Universe doesn't know between what you say and feel, versus what you really think you say and feel. The Universe, God, Holy Spirit is one energy and we are always connected to it. When you say degrading things, you are putting out that negativity. Following it up with "I'm just kidding" doesn't negate the statement you made earlier, or the feelings behind it. It's the feelings that we want to make note of. The feelings behind the thoughts tell the true story about us, what we want to create, and what we can't.

Since the energy of our soul never dies, and moves onward after we've expired from this life, it stands to reason it's being held in our human bodies for just a short amount of time. We came from perfection before incarnating here on Earth. Everything we wanted or needed was at our disposal, because we were always One with everything. Yet once we arrive on Earth, we believe ourselves to be separate from one another, because these different bodies we're in tell us so. We're taught we're not all connected to each other and to Source. But we are, because we always were before we arrived here! Think of a wagon wheel and all the spokes on that wheel that are a part of the whole. Each spoke is connected to the center (Source) and each spoke is connected to the entirety of the wheel (Universe). Each spoke in essence is connected to the other spokes. Each spoke is significant to the wheel working as a whole. That is how we all are as humans as well. We are all connected energetically to each other, but we don't feel it because of our separate bodies. We are taught on Earth that I am me and you are you, and we have nothing to do with each other. If we return to Source after we die, and become One with all that is, then how are we not connected to each other here on Earth? We are. That which I do to you, I do to me.

Our minds create our reality. We've all been told this. But how does that work? When we think of lack in our lives, it creates an energetic connection to the Universe, through our feelings, and we attract to us events and experiences that show us more of that same lack in our lives. When we focus on love, and gratitude for what we already do have, we put out an energetic connection to the Universe, through our feelings, and the Universe responds with more love and things to be grateful for in our lives. Source/Universe is impartial. It is designed to give you that which you truly *feel* about yourself, deep down. Not what you think about yourself, but those quiet moments when you don't *feel* like you're enough or are worthy of having it all.

The Universe, by law, is required to give you back that which you think and ultimately feel about who you are. It's all about the feelings behind the thoughts. There are many ways to smile. Someone could smile at you, and you can feel the warmth emanating from their soul. Others can smile at you, and you can feel the ugly or wicked energy behind that smile. That is the connective energy we all have with each other as we pick up the energy around us. They are either emanating love through their smile, or sarcasm and hate. We are able to communicate via feelings, and the energy of our auras, with each other.

Ultimately, all of this comes down to *gratitude*. Wait, what? I'm supposed to be grateful for the crappy situation I'm currently in? I have no job, but you want me to be happy about that? I can't find anyone to love me and I'll be alone all my life, but I'm supposed to be grateful that I'm alone? No, no, no. When we sit in negativity and cannot feel the joy already present in our lives, and focus on what's not working, we pull more of that negativity into our lives. When we switch the situation to being in thankfulness for what already exists in our world, the focus is placed on the love, gratitude, and blessings. And by law, you attract what you are putting out—more joy, love and positive experiences. Just as metal is pulled to a magnet because of the energetic properties of both ends, your gratitude becomes the magnet pulling you toward positive experiences. The more gratitude you can see in your life, the more positive energy you have flowing through you, and the more abundance you attract toward yourself. Law of Attraction. It really *is* that simple.

How in the world do we do this? That is also very simple. Don't focus on what's not going right in your life, because that which you focus on grows. Let me repeat that. That which you place your focus on, whether positive or negative—grows. If that's the case, focus on the good that is already present in your life, not the negative. "Well," you may say, "maybe I don't have anything good in my life." I say that's impossible. If at first you're having a tough time figuring out what is good in your life, think about the small things. I have a toothbrush that I can brush my teeth with every day. Wow, there are millions of people in this world who do not have that luxury. What would life feel like for me if I didn't have that? Or, whenever I need light, I just go and flick the switch on. Wow, again millions of people in the world don't have that luxury—I really am blessed to have light at my disposal. Or, I can go to my closet and have more than one option for shoes to wear that day. Wow, how many people go barefoot in the world that have no shoes, and here I have choices in my own closet. "Well," you could respond, "if I compare myself to every person in this world, then of course there will be those who are better off than me, and those I am better off than." Yes! But we are not here to compare ourselves to others; we are here to see that within our own challenging lives, where we want to create more positive change, we are already blessed and should focus on the gratitude of these tiny things. When we focus on the tiny appreciation and gratitude, we find more things to be grateful for, and we start to realize we are *already* blessed. When we put focus on that blessing and really feel the joy behind this gratitude, the Law of Attraction brings us more things to feel grateful for.

So, to help you out with this, please start a gratitude journal. Or get out a few pieces of paper. On it, each morning, when you wake up, write down five things you are grateful for. Number them 1-5 and list five separate things. Yes, in the beginning we say things like, "I'm grateful for my children, for my house, for food in the fridge, etc." And that's good. Now look at your list, and really *feel* the emotions behind that. What would it feel like without my children here? What would it feel like to not have a home to keep me sheltered? What would it feel like, if I opened my fridge and it was empty and bare? Then for each gratitude, feel the gratefulness behind already having these blessings. Smile at each one, and after you focus on the blessing of having it, say thank you to the Universe with a smile. Each morning, you will be listing five things you are grateful for. You will realize, *hmmm*, what would life be like if I didn't already have this? Then feel the emotion of gratitude for having it, smiling and saying thank you. You will start out every day saying thank you five times, and all day long feeling grateful for those five things. You will begin to start out each of your days, already saying thank you for what you have. You will be putting out into the universe your gratitude for what is here. And by law, the Universe will feel your emotions emanating outward and bring you more experiences for you to be grateful for.

Now, here is the kicker to this. Every day, write five things you are grateful for, and never repeat them on that list. Never repeat on your list that which you already wrote down on another day. What? Impossible you say! I'll run out of things to list in a few weeks! No, you won't. Because as you list your gratitude and begin to shift your energy to positivity, you will find more things to be grateful for. Do you like to put your key in the ignition and have your car turn on without hassle? Yes. Do you like turning on the heat on a cold day and being warmed? Yup. Do you like deciding if you'll have pasta or chicken for dinner tonight? You betcha! Everything you touch throughout a day, becomes something for you to be grateful for. Every conversation you have with someone that is kind, you show gratitude. Think about what life would be like if you stayed in gratitude for everything you touched, smelled, saw, spoke of. You would change your entire outlook on life, which then shifts the energy within you. You would start transmitting some serious positive energy out to the Universe and in return, you will be attracting to you more positive things to be grateful for. It's the Law. It works the same way every time, just like the Law of Gravity works the same way each time. Drop a pencil, a cup, or an apple. They are all going in the same direction—down. This law never fails, and we all understand it, right? Well, the Law of Attraction is another Law of the Universe. So if one law works, so do the others. This is why I said I wish I had learned this in my earlier life and years. The things I could have manifested—wow!

Do I use this law every day? I try to! Am I human and forget sometimes? Definitely. I was reminded of this law a few months ago. It was a very cold January here in New York, and with everything going on after Anthony's passing, I was not monitoring the oil to heat our home. One morning, I woke up and the furnace wouldn't turn on. Great—freezing weather outside, no oil, and I knew the oil company probably would not come out that day, because they were also dealing with other customers like me. I called and was told they would be there around 1:00 p.m. Since the furnace had shut down overnight, the house was freezing. I had clients to do, and no heat. Had to cancel them for the day. I waited hour after hour. Had to put a coat on, then scarf and hat, then gloves. I huddled under a blanket, all the while waiting for them, freezing and calling them every few hours, annoyed I had to wait. Yes, I said that right…annoyed. Around dinner time, they finally showed up and filled the tank. But earlier in the day, I actually had to check myself. *I am just waiting for oil. It's on its way. Thank God we have money to purchase the oil to heat our home so we can be comfortable in the winter. What would life be like if I had to wear a coat, scarf and gloves every day of my life?* When I went to a place of gratitude, immediately I started to laugh at myself. I suffered for what—eleven hours? *So what? Gina, get over yourself and get back to gratitude.* And that's exactly what I did. I sat and wrote the many things I was grateful for, and it changed my energy immediately.

A girlfriend of mine started this process a few years ago, and she was doing great. A doctor's bill came in the mail for $500 she wasn't expecting. She started to get scared (negative energy) that she just couldn't pay this off, but immediately put herself back in gratitude (positive energy) for what she already had in her life. She went to 7-11 to get coffee the next morning, as she always does each day before work, and purchased a scratch-off ticket. Well, she won $500! Can that happen to you too? Yes! Because this law is for everyone.

Turn your negativity around. If I have the power to attract to me either positive or negative experiences, then why would I waste any time focusing on the negative? Start out each day just saying thank you and appreciating the small things. Within a short while, you will see more positive experiences multiplying for you. Like attracts like—get on it today and see how differently you will start to feel about your life! When you take the focus off of what isn't working, the Universe begins to straighten those experiences out all on their own. It's not for you to fix. You just get into alignment with the flow of energy, stay on the positive side of gratitude and gratefulness, and the Universe will straighten out the rest. Just try it! Give it a good thirty days before you stop, and watch what happens!

I hope you are starting to learn that you have the choice, *free will*, to make your life as hard or easy as possible! The Universe is set up with laws, and we are here to learn. Wouldn't you rather zip through those painful moments and get on with enjoying life rather than spend your life in pain just waiting for a second of relief? It's your choice. Where do you think the idea of us being our own worst enemy came from? It came from the fact that we attract our own pain.

Have you heard about people who create "dream boards" or "vision boards"? They are pictures we place on an oak tag or cardboard or picture frame, which represent what we want to physically manifest in our lives. We focus on those pictures, and call in the feelings behind them, and in essence say thank you to the Universe because we know and trust they are on their way to us. People create them because they are calling on the Universe to attract the information and the positive desires they would like to manifest in their life. This is a wonderful process and even in writing books, Wayne Dyer would come up with a title, create a mock-up book cover, which he would look at while writing his book. The words would just flow through him, as he focused on that cover. Okay, maybe it isn't *quite* that easy, because if I could tell you the number of title changes I went through on this book, that would be another story, but I can tell you that most of it just flowed and developed and each piece somehow fell together and all in the midst of the deepest and most painful mourning of my life. Spirit (and Anthony) have my back. I had been told for years by Spirit to write a book, and now the time has arrived, and the people fell right into place to have this dream manifest. I am so very, very grateful!

Here's a wonderful example of Spirit having my back—hundreds of these types of experiences have occurred in my life. For years I would hear in meditations from Spirit, "Write the book," "Write the book." My answer was always the same. I don't know what to write about, who would buy it, and I have *no* clue about how to go about the process. One day, I was drying my hair, right before a client reading, and I heard again in my head, "Write the book." Now, I got annoyed. I said to Spirit, "Stop saying this. I have no idea how to start this process, and have zero connections. If this is important, show me the next step." That next client proceeded to tell me that she had written a book, according to the last reading she had had with me, and confirmed the people I had told her she would meet to accomplish this task. Immediately, I could hear Spirit smirking like "Told ya." Okay, I asked her if she could possibly share her contacts, and she was all too willing to help. And, *voilà*, enters into my life, my heaven-sent book guru. My *bella angela della scrittura* (my beautiful writing angel). And the rest of the history, you're now holding in your hands. That's how Spirit works. I had been thinking of this book for years, could see myself writing it, and I could feel people reading it and learning from it. I just didn't know how to manifest it, but I kept thinking about it and wanting it to happen. Spirit provided the right people at the right time to make it all happen. Law of Attraction at its finest!

So, will you do me a very big favor and stop being your own worst enemy? That can be your gift to the Universe. I have been very, very clear on how. Along with the lesson of trusting yourself first, with Spirit on board, as I discuss in the next chapter, becoming your own

BFF (Best Friend Forever) and dropping the enemy routine will net the greatest love and life you could ever imagine. It will bring the success you deserve and have worked hard for and it will bring really loving and quality people your way leaving those negative Nellies and naysayers for someone else to deal with. The world can be a magnificent place if you let it, even amidst some very real heartaches. Trust the law. Learn your lesson once, *the first time*, and move on to bigger and better manifestations of love. You deserve it! And, the Universe deserves the loving, wonderful, you.

Chapter Thirteen
Spirit on Board

Steering Your Life with Spirit in Charge

Often we don't even realize who we're meant to be because we're so busy trying to live out someone else's ideas. But other people and their opinions hold no power in defining our destiny.

—Oprah

I'm calling this Chapter *Spirit on Board* because you know those signs on the back of vehicles with the pictures that show who is in the car and tell how many people are in the family? Well, they originated in the '80s when the "Baby on Board" sign was created to alert emergency services so that if there was an accident to make sure to look for a baby on board. Well, I want you to start thinking of every day of your life as preparation for a new adventure and inviting in positivity and praying you learn your lessons the first time. I want you to start paying attention to the signs and quite frankly, driving around with Spirit on board—hey, maybe I should start a sticker of my own!

This chapter takes a look at ways that you can deepen your commitment to growth and really listen to the tides of change in your life. You don't want to just be knocked around and go wherever the wind blows you anymore. You want direction and positive change, and for this you need to really, really start to pay attention to what you are manifesting and who or what you are calling in.

Speaking of winds, there is an interesting practice among sailors for commandeering their vessels. The sailboat physically gets bumped around, *but* the sailor knows that the wind is what you have to pay attention to. Without it, you may not move anywhere at all. If you are an aware and knowledgeable sailor, you look around and search out clues. For example, it's been said, "When sailors see a wind line approaching, they know to prepare for the increased force on the sails and boat. They may have to shift weight to the windward side of the vessel to compensate or they may have to let the sails out a little to prevent being overpowered by the gust. If they've prepared well, the boat will accelerate when the gust hits the sails."[30]

Isn't this what happens to us? If we prepare and are armed with knowledge, we can start to prepare ourselves against being overwhelmed, or being caught in the storm. But first, we must come to the point that we will allow ourselves to let go of fear; that we will pay attention; that we will "listen" or "watch" for signs from Spirit. And once we choose to acknowledge the fact that we *can* overcome and let go of fear, negativity, and pain even in the midst of the wildest storms, by *using* versus *fighting* the winds, it is then, through Spirit, and our acceptance of this Higher Love, that everything can change for the better. We as humans can finally accelerate as the gusts hits our sails!

What a wonderful life it would be if we could soar and sail with understanding the winds and feeling Spirit within us. What a wonderful, beautiful peace we would create around us if we allowed life to be smooth sailing—even in the midst of the storms.

Universally, we really don't want to be the unsuspecting, naïve sailor who hops in a boat and has no idea of what they are doing in the middle of the waters. And boy, do I know! I've been sailing and canoeing several times myself. I remember there was *a lot* of work, moving and positioning, especially with sails, to get in the right spot, in order to catch the winds or go in the direction you are hoping. What a mess if you didn't know what you were doing! It was all about anticipation, planning, positioning, and timing. Then when the winds caught; smooth sailing. Then, the winds would change again, and if you weren't paying attention, you had to reassess and reposition quickly. Back to planning, positioning we'd go. When the position of the sails or the timing was off—*bang!* The little sailboat capsized!

One time, on our honeymoon, my first husband and I were in a small two-person sailboat. We had no clue what we were doing. I swung the sail around without advising my husband I was doing that, and it hit him square in the head. I reacted and did not communicate. The other party involved got hit really hard. Then, because we didn't know what we were doing, we capsized a few times. And once I was immersed in the ocean, my fear of deep, dark water kicked in, and I was flailing around, terrified, and desperate to turn the boat back up so I could climb back in. So, you can see that sailing, to me, means hard work, planning, and the outcome sometimes still failing. But, to be honest, the same can be said of what happens in life. Just because you plan, that doesn't mean you are guaranteed a result. But if you do learn and do attain knowledge and do prepare yourself by watching the signs of the winds, listening to the whispers of Spirit, that will make the journey much less scary. Perhaps, if I had prepared for a sailboat trip, by learning to allay my fear of deep water or if I had taken a few sailing lessons, my experiences would be completely different. But, like many of you, I tend to *dive* right in! We just wanted to get out on that water and have some fun! I'm sure you have all done this at some points in your life.

The funny thing is that I do swim! I became a junior lifeguard at fourteen, but then, of course, I saw the movie *Jaws* at that age, and refused to get back into the water—*any* water—deep ocean, or even a deep pool. The fear of the unknown underneath me, what I can't see, even in a crystal-clear pool, still to this day scares me to death. This just goes to prove how highly triggered we can get by movies, advertisements, and media, especially when it comes to bringing out our deepest fears. And it shows us the power of our minds. Imagine being afraid of being in a deep pool, when I can easily swim and tread water. It makes no sense! But my mind puts me in a state of terror, not logic, and I am completely paralyzed. We've discussed how to work on your fears, and as I've said in this book, I'm human and I'm still working on some of mine!

The point is that we have had and do continue to have a *compass*. It has been here the entire time. It is Spirit. The question is: Will you pay attention, and will you follow the signs? Will you finally be brave and curious and venture out and dip your toes in the water toward a new and wonderful life? Will you leave the safety of the shore? As I said in the introduction to this book, in reality our body is a vessel, like a ship, that is placed in numerous crazy storms. We are knocked and rocked and shaken and shocked until some days we don't even know if we can take another moment. As we age, we seem to lose more and more parts of ourselves, and some days we don't even remember why we are here. Well, it's time to learn and accept why we are here. Heck, it's time to do more than that! It's time to *embrace* our purpose!

So, will you embrace Spirit and stop explaining yourself, stop trying to fit in, stop worrying about what others think and focus on what is important? Will you let the issues or problems of others be their ego and not yours and focus only on what the lesson is for you to learn with them? Will you let their karma serve its intended purpose and not try to take it on as your own? Will you say thank you for the pain and drama and then let the situation or people go? It's all up to you.

Remember I said in Chapter Eleven I was going to address problems and how to handle them? You'll never believe how simple it really is. John F. Kennedy said, "The Chinese use two brush strokes to write the word 'crisis.' One brush stroke stands for danger; the other for opportunity. In a crisis, be aware of the danger – but recognize the opportunity." That is just beautifully said. It is true that we need to see that obstacles and crises are opportunities waiting to happen. These obstacles, or problems are not just annoyances with no value; they actually exist to serve a purpose in your life. Wouldn't it be glorious if the next time something happens to you, that after your initial reaction (which is the human response), you immediately think, "Aha, there is learning here; what is the lesson I'm supposed to learn about myself?" (This is the spiritual response). The absolute beauty of understanding the rules, principles, and laws to life is that you then can learn and begin to understand that there are only three *approaches* to problems and once you understand, you can start to work through them. Here are your choices:

1. You ignore them. Or try to ignore them. But what you don't know *can* hurt you; and, funny thing, you actually *know* your problems despite your effort to ignore them. Let's say you have an issue with your sister-in-law and just don't appreciate how she acts, speaks, or the lack of respect she shows you. Some of us may be inclined to say "I'll just let it go, don't want to start

World War III," but each time she acts up, it festers inside you, and you begin to resent it. Before you know it, you're complaining to anyone that will listen as to what a "*b*-ruja" w-*itch* (sorry, someone had to say it) she is. As it festers, the resentment grows, and each time you see her, there is an anticipation of how she'll behave, and *voilà*, she never disappoints. Each time an experience happens with her, you sweep it under the rug instead of addressing it, and your resentment grows. The problem becomes that eventually that rug gets so high that *you* end up tripping over the one thing you wish to ignore.

All ignoring a problem does is make the problem that much bigger down the road. Being oblivious to that fact or hoping that it will miraculously change on its own won't change a thing.

2. You try to solve them. If you are in this camp, you probably have read books (many books!) on self-help and personal development. You may even have attended seminars and workshops. You know what to do. But then, why do you still have problems? An example would be that of a close friend who takes advantage of you and your friendship. You're always there for that person; they either always need a ride from you, or need to borrow money, or you do special favors for them. Because you're a good person, you want to help this friend out, but they do not reciprocate for you. It becomes a one-way street, and you feel taken advantage of. All the self-help books you read teach that you should love yourself and speak up in a loving, gentle way, owning your truth and expressing that lovingly, whether the person understands it or not. So why is this *still* an issue for you? You may feel deep down inside that if you speak up, this person will no longer want to be your friend. You may feel

uncomfortable with them having an issue with you speaking your mind, and perhaps you're afraid they will be angry with you and no longer wish to be your friend. You know what to do, but you may not be strong enough and not have the trust in speaking up for yourself. You keep enabling the friendship, even though this isn't really a friendship at all, just a one-way street.

You've read the books, you just have trouble putting the tools in action; hence the problem(s) will always persist.

3. The third approach is looking for the *lessons* behind the experience. This is an approach few know and have had much less practice with. You understand the fundamental nature of life's problems and come to accept them, not fight them. I don't mean accept the problem and be okay with having it, but acknowledge this is a chance for you to learn from *what* is happening. This transforms problems into opportunities. This is what I've taught you in this book. In *knowing* you can access the tools within you, you can change what is happening around you. This approach may sound crazy and absurd, but it really isn't. Most people spend many, many years trying the first and second approaches before they finally figure out personal development can only go so far and in the end, this approach is the answer. When we get to option #3, you are looking at *What is this experience trying to help me learn about myself?* In option #1 with the sister-in-law, maybe your lesson is to stand up for yourself, and not be afraid of confrontation. Well, where in your upbringing were you taught it's not about you, and we don't make waves, and to just suck it up? In option #2 with the friend, maybe your lesson is to not be taken advantage of, and you have a right to say *no*. Again, where in your past did people

try to hurt you and take advantage of you over and over again, where you didn't have the power or strength to know you had every right to draw the line in the sand and say *no*. Our lessons keep repeating themselves over and over again, until we realize the *aha* moment of "Yes, I haven't dealt with this from my past. I'd better deal with it now." It is co-creating with Spirit and getting Spirit on board and working every day to increase, strengthen and deepen the bond until you operate on automatic pilot!

The third approach to resolving problems is something you need to commit to wholeheartedly, and no matter how deep and dark the uncharted waters you are in this moment, you can start to meditate and create the opportunity to let Spirit be your compass. It doesn't matter if you are in the dark tunnel or completely off the tracks—Spirit will come to help, but only if you ask!

To help you create that connection, here are some lessons that I have helped others explore and ones that I feel confident will help you increase receptivity to Spirit, whether it is for yourself in day-to-day life, or if you have aspirations of improving your intuition:

1. **Claim Your Desire**

    That being said, whether you are already intuitive and want to improve your gifts, or are just starting out and trying to find the compass in the storm, you need to determine, "Why am I doing this?" Sit quietly and contemplate the *why*, which is you conveying your desire to the Universe, to Source, or to God. What is it that you want to create for yourself? Is it a better understanding of who you are? Is it to sharpen your intuitive skills? Is it to create a sense of balance and peace in your life?

Examine carefully the reasons why you want to improve your intuition for yourself, or even become a medium, if that is truly your calling. If you are doing this with thoughts of impressing others, or for showing off, you will not get very far. One of my mentors along my path of studying was fond of saying, "If you put yourself on a pedestal, Spirit will knock you right off." Spirit, the Universe, Source, is not impressed by your abilities. Intuition is an innate gift that was given to each of us and should be treated with respect and gratitude. You already have this gift of intuition with you. It is up to you whether you want to fine-tune it, so you can make navigating this world a bit easier on yourself. Who doesn't want a compass in the storm, or a map when we're lost? Why make life harder on ourselves when we've been given the tools to help us along the way?

And for those of you reading this book who very much want to be a medium, check yourself for the reasons "why." The most important purpose of being a medium is communication with Spirits who have crossed over, showing evidential information that even though we experience death, our energy is always with our loved ones. It is about bringing comfort and peace to those suffering and in grief. It is not about impressing people in a store that you have a special gift. I will always remind my students learning mediumship that this is not about having a TV show, or taking someone's money. This gift, and those that pursue it as a profession need to give it the respect and honor it deserves. I have a medium friend that was doing a restaurant event in her local town. Someone she knew had called up to reserve a seat for the event, and because this person was intuitive, she started to read the manager of the restaurant over the phone. The manager didn't ask for this; the other woman just wanted to show how gifted she was. For what purpose? For the manager to say, "Oh wow, you are amazing!" Spirit does not tolerate self-serving efforts and at some point, those that continue to do this will get knocked down. No question. You must be humble and have a desire to serve. It takes a lot of commitment and hard work to become a successful medium…and time. It isn't something that will be handed to you, or that you can rush. The comfort and peace you bring to those who have lost loved ones, by communicating with them on the other side, is immeasurable, and it is a true gift that goes both ways.

Express a heartfelt desire to develop your intuition for your higher good, or the higher good of those you will serve. Ask assistance from your Spirit Guides and angels, even though you may not distinctly know who they are yet. Your Guides will begin working with you on fine- tuning your skills. It takes commitment and hard work to sharpen these skills, so do not be disheartened if it takes you some time. Some people develop more quickly than others or seem to grasp the concepts easier than others. Do not be deterred. Intuition is there for all of us. Work at your own pace, be patient, and do have fun!

2. Raise Your Energy and Vibration

What is vibration? It is the energy within you, and the energy you emanate outwardly. All energy vibrates, and all matter vibrates, whether it's a single atom, a plant, or a human body. As we discussed before, positive pulls in positive and negative pulls in negative; therefore, be very clear with your intentions. If you just want to work on improving your own intuition skills, it's important to clear away the negativity around you, and change the energy within you to positive. All physical matter vibrates at a much slower rate than spiritual energy. Our bodies, as humans, vibrate at a much slower speed than Spirit. Since your loved ones no longer inhabit a physical body, they are vibrating at a much higher level than we are. In improving your intuition, or even connecting with your own loved ones, we need to raise our vibrations, while Spirit slightly lowers theirs. But they cannot lower their vibrational level too much. The higher we raise our own vibrations, the more easily we will be able to communicate with our Guides, angels, and Loved Ones in Spirit. Then, how do we improve our energy and vibration? We must practice meditation. The more you practice this, the stronger your connection to Spirit becomes and the easier it will be to hear and connect with your intuition, and, if you're studying mediumship, easier to transmit messages from Spirit.

During your meditation, clear your mind and envision yourself surrounded by the healing and powerful white light of the Universe/God. Affirmations are extremely powerful phrases that we vocalize in order to raise our vibrations. Saying these affirmations, before beginning a meditation (our voice vibrates itself), sets your intention and actually causes a change in the energy around us, and sets things into motion. Some sample affirmations you can say are:

"I am beauty and love and light."

"I am surrounded and infused with the healing light of God."

"I am filled with love for my fellow human beings."

"The love and light of God flows to me and from me."

Or you create your own affirmations. Anything is fine, as long as it's of a positive nature. It is important to say these affirmations several times a day, and to say them out loud. Just thinking them is not the same thing and will not be nearly as effective. Meditating and saying affirmations should become a permanent part of your everyday life, as these practices help you connect to the Oneness of where you came from, and which you are still a part of.

The most important affirmation you should be saying while thinking about the feelings of peace and love you want to create in your life is saying, "I want this...therefore I will it to be." Say this aloud, while sending a heartfelt wish out to the Universe, as often as possible. And then, *thank* the Universe for what is to come. *Believe* that your intuition is developing and you are connecting to the force of the Universe. You are becoming One with all that is, and your energy will shift and change, and so will everything surrounding you.

3. Like Attracts Like – Positive or Negative

Not only should you start by meditating and saying affirmations, you should focus on making your entire life more positive and affirming. Think positively, and avoid pessimistic thoughts and words. These detract from our vibratory level. Instead, smile, laugh, make others laugh, and focus on exuding love to all you encounter. Whenever I am feeling down and not particularly happy with someone, I put a smile on my face as I am speaking. I am not happy, but the smile shifts my focus to happiness, and the words I say have a power behind them. How can you fight and have cutting words when you're smiling inside? You can't. Even when I am exhausted and have phone readings to do, because I can't see the person, I feel just a bit more disconnected. I have found that immediately putting a smile on my face when saying hello, shifts my energy immediately and suddenly I am plugged into their energy faster than if I had not done that. Same for you. Notice as you speak to people around you with a smile within, that they even react to you differently. Not only will this raise your vibration, it will improve the quality of your life.

4. Control Your Mind

Does this mean I can control others with my thoughts? No! This is about the control of your own mind. Our minds are extremely powerful, and yet we don't even realize when our thoughts are sucking us down. It's important to catch your thoughts immediately. We must train our minds and create discipline. Now, this is not easy, because for most of our lives, we've succumbed to whatever the mind was thinking. Noise, noise, and more noise! When sitting down to meditate, your mind must be focused and centered. In order to connect to your intuition or hear the next step you must follow for whatever you're going through or if you want to enhance your gift to hear Spirit correctly, you must be focused. This can be a very uncomfortable process at first, but it's crucial. Throughout our days, we have a tremendous amount of "mind static"—thoughts swirling around in our heads. You are driving down the road, but your mind is on the last conversation you had with your spouse, and then immediately it switches to what errands you need to get done that day, then off your thoughts go to what you still need to do at work. Is it any wonder we are a species of constant stress and anxiety? How can our brains handle all this noise? We must develop the mind discipline necessary to reduce and eliminate this static. The most effective way to do this is to spend time in meditation and prayer, every day. Start with increments of five minutes, then begin to increase the time as you get better at it. In the beginning, as you quiet your mind, you may get a million thoughts flooding in all at once. Don't be disheartened. Just acknowledge that thought, let it float away from you, and bring your focus back to the meditation, or just concentrate on breathing in and out through your nose. You may have to do this many times over. Remember, you are *teaching* your mind how to be quiet. This takes time and focus!

If you are having trouble focusing or trying to clear your mind in order to meditate, you can certainly achieve the same results by holding one thought or picture in your mind that brings you a sense of happiness and peace, for five minutes at a time, without distraction. It may not be easy for you in the beginning to keep your mind completely blank for five minutes, because remember, your mind always wants to go, go, go! It isn't easy at first, but with practice, it will get easier. Start off with guided mediation tapes from your local library, or YouTube, where you follow a gentle voice as it gives you visual cues to focus on. Get comfortable with that first. Then over time, when your mind is more under control, you can just put on soft music in the background. Eventually when you get really good at meditation, all you'll need is to just center yourself, close your eyes, and you are connecting. This is not about being hard on yourself. Many of my students who weren't used to having mind discipline struggled with this for quite some time. Please don't have any expectations. This is a journey and a process, and it takes time to learn this new skill. Be gentle with yourself!

5. Protect Your Energy

Just as with static you hear on a radio, we need to keep our channels clear—or better, if we are in a negative mood, change the channel! Remember, we are all made up of energy swirling within us and around us. Things like stopping smoking, eating a balanced diet, drinking plenty of water, getting the rest your body needs and daily exercise are very important factors in improving your connection and intuition, especially for mediumship development. Think of your body as a pipe, and the connection you are trying to make to your intuition is the water flowing through that pipe. If you let the inside of the pipe get all gunked up with negativity, poor diet, not taking your health seriously, it all affects the quality and purity of the energy flowing through you. You must keep the pipe clean and uncluttered from debris. On a daily basis, you can picture yourself standing under a shower fall of light from the Universe above. And as this light washes over you, allow it to take away all that negativity, worry, and fear you are holding. See it in your mind's eye as it washes away from you and into the ground below, where it is transmuted into clear energy by the Earth. This is a wonderful exercise to do every day, but also amazing to do before walking into any kind of negative or hostile environment.

6. Practice Makes Perfect!

Just as you can't ride a bike without practicing first, anything we want done well in life must be learned over and over again. I remember when I was first married and decided to make fajitas. My mom never really had us cook, because she was the homemaker, and we always had school and work. So the first time I tried cooking, I got it all wrong. Who knew meat and veggies don't cook at the same time? In one night, I made that dish three times, and still didn't get it right. One of the most difficult aspects of intuitive development, and closing down the static mind, is the ability to distinguish between "Am I really connecting, or is this my own imagination?" Contrary to what is shown in movies, when we're connecting, Spirit usually doesn't come through to us with the noise level and force of a marching band. The messages we receive are quiet, still, and subtle. They are *whispers.* They are very easy to miss if we're not paying attention. This can create a tremendous amount of doubt in our hearts. The best way to eliminate any doubt in your mind is to test your progress. When the phone rings, or text pings, ask your Spirit Guides in your mind if the caller is male or female. Make a note of the answer you feel you receive and see if it's correct or not. Ask your Guides how many pieces of mail you will receive that day in your mailbox. Ask how many cars will be in the parking lot of your destination when you arrive there. (Obviously you should only do this with small parking lots, otherwise you'll be out there all day counting cars.) Or, ask your Guides what color top so-and-so will be wearing that day at work. The aim is to ask your Guides questions that are easily verifiable and keep a record of when you receive the correct answers, and when your own imagination takes over. Eventually you will be able to tell the difference.

I teach my students to play this awesome card game. Take out a deck of cards, shuffle them really well, and have them in your hands, face down. You will be flipping them over into a pile in front of you, and milliseconds before you turn them over one by one, you will call out what you think the color of the card will be…red or black. When my students do this in class, those that think too much before turning over the card do not get as many right. Those that just go with the flow, don't think much, but just connect with what they feel the color of the card is. So amazing! They are even surprised how many are right. What are we doing with this exercise? We are learning to trust our intuition. And as you practice these examples, you will begin to notice a change within you that feels one way, and the answer comes out right, versus when your head (imagination) is getting in the way giving you the wrong answers. Try these exercises; you might just shock yourself!

Now, if you do want to work on accessing your intuitive ability and learn how to use this as a tool to help deepen your connection to Spirit, I have included a meditation for you. It is a guideline to show you how to connect to Universal energy, while grounding and protecting yourself. In this meditation, you will bring to your mind all the beautiful things you wish to create for your life and bring forth your loved ones on the other side, to listen to their advice, feel or hear their love and constant guidance. You have the power to manifest and to intuitively grow stronger. The longer you work at it, the more you will create your own program and process, but for now remember that all energies, thoughts, and actions are connected and you are pulling up your highest and best asking for Spirit on board to prepare you for a better future with more insight and awareness.

Meditation

At the beginning of every meditation, it's important always to ground and protect yourself, before moving into any type of meditative state. Slowing down your breath, calming your body and mind, are essential in creating the proper space around and within yourself, so you receive the maximum benefit from the meditation. The beginning of every meditation is what I call "bringing in the Light." And whether I am preparing for client readings, or am just doing my own daily meditation work, I always do this visualization and breathing exercise first. Once you develop this technique by practicing it every day, it will be a very useful tool that you will always have with you. Use it whenever anything upsetting happens in your life. Use it whenever you are aware of internal tension. Use it to set aside time to communicate with loved ones, by quieting our minds, and letting go of the chatter that allows us to better "hear" or "sense" our loved ones. It's so easy to do. It can be done lying down or sitting up; it's totally up to you. You can even be sitting in your car parked somewhere, or use a mediation to help you fall asleep. I highly recommend everyone start their meditation by grounding in the Light.

Once you have created a meditation like the one below, write it out and make it your own. The best way to follow this meditation at first is to record yourself reading it, using a cassette recorder, digital device, or even an app on a smartphone. Then play it back whenever you wish to connect to the Divine! Eventually you will be able to do this process and pull in Spirit in less time, without needing the full meditation, because you will be programmed to focus quickly and deeply and move into Source and Spirit with more ease. However, on the days that you are more agitated or less able to stay in the moment, always pull the full meditation back in. There are times we all need to get back on track.

Breathing in the Light Meditation

Take a moment and get into a comfortable position. Whether lying down, with your hands by your side, or sitting in a chair, with your feet firmly on the floor, hands in your lap. Begin by closing your eyes. We're going to begin a slow breathing exercise to relax your physical body and your mind. With your eyes closed, start taking slow, deep breaths in through the nose and out through your mouth. Each inhale filling your lungs to the count of 4, and as you get to the top, hold your breath to the count of 4 and then slowly exhale to the count of 4. Very controlled breathing, slowing everything down, and feeling your body beginning to relax.

Take another deep breath in, slow and controlled, to the count of 4, feeling your body fill up with energy, and again, as you get to the top of your inhale, hold for 4, and slowly exhale to the count of 4. With each inhale, visualize calming, soothing energy entering your body. With each exhale, visualize yourself releasing any tension you're currently holding in the physical or emotional body and release that energy back into the universe.

As you breathe deeply, filling your lungs with air, notice how your belly begins to rise and fall, as each breath is filling your entire chest cavity and abdomen with nourishment. Each breath, slow and controlled. Allow yourself to feel tranquil and at peace, as you continue to breathe in a very self-controlled manner. Visualize exhaling everything that's on your mind—you can come back to your worries later—but for now, let your mind become clear and empty.

Take one last deep breath in, holding it for 4 seconds and exhaling slowly to the count of 4. Feel your body relaxing even more.

Now that you have taken a few deep, controlled breaths, allow your breathing to become more comfortable and at your own natural state of rhythm. Bring your attention to your breath, to the sensation of breathing. Just notice it. Focus on either the small rise and fall of your chest, or the sensation of the air coming in and out of the nose. Just feel your breathing. Feel the rhythm of your breathing. Notice the contraction and expansion of your diaphragm and your chest. Stay with that sensation, placing your awareness on the breath, the chest, or focusing on the air gently flowing through your nose. Whatever you prefer to focus on, just sit with this sensation. Don't force the breath or bear down too heavily with your focus. Let the breath flow naturally, and simply keep track of how it feels. Stay in the moment, allowing you to connect with your body. Savor it, as if it were a beautiful sensation you wanted to prolong. If your mind wanders off, simply bring it back to focus on your breathing. Don't get discouraged. If it wanders, just bring it back, and eventually it will feel easier with each practice.

Allow yourself to become very relaxed; as you do so, allow yourself to let go of the day's struggles, and drop your shoulders if you're holding tension there.

Now imagine a beam of white light coming from above you and hitting the top of your head. That light warms the top of your scalp, and imagine the light slowly moving down your face. Allow all the muscles in your face to relax. See the light cover your ears to help you hear, slowly moving down over your throat to help you communicate, and allow the relaxation all the way down over your neck and shoulders. Allow this beautiful white light to flow down over your chest, over your heart to help you feel love. Imagine the light continuing to move down over your belly, covering your mid-section which will help you sense intuitively. See the warming light move down over your hips, bringing light to the part of your body that carries you each day. Slowly move down over your leg muscles, down over your knees, all the way down to your calf and shin muscles, into your ankles and feet. As you imagine this light moving from up above your head, all the way through your body, and then out through the bottoms of your feet, you are helping to clear and balance yourself with each breath. At this point, you should notice that your breathing has become more regular and your visualization is no longer on the breath, but on the light of healing you are bringing to your entire body.

As you visualize this light leaving the bottoms of your feet, imagine it spreads out like roots of a tree. Allow those roots of light to spread as far, wide, and deep as you can possibly imagine, anchoring you to the Earth that stabilizes us. The light from above brings with it healing light and energy, clearing out our body and mind of the concerns of this Earth, and washing them back into the ground where they are transformed and washed away. You are now connected to the Divine above and grounded to the solid energy of the Earth below. Allow yourself to enjoy this for a few minutes of peace, connecting to the Divine, grounding yourself for whatever meditation work you wish to do next.

As you sit so peaceful and quiet, enjoying the sense of Oneness with all that is around you, I want you to start imagining all the beautiful things you would like to create in your life, all the magical moments you want to attract into your energy. Envision each one carefully, in detail and full color, and imagine what your life would feel like if you already had those things as part of your world. Use your vivid imagination, see these things occurring in your life, and feel how different your life would be if they already existed. Allow yourself to dream, let go, and trust that they are already on their way. Give yourself some time to sit, imagine, and focus on what you wish to call into your life. Do not rush this process.

Now that you have given yourself enough time to imagine your life of love, laughter, ease, and family, think of someone you would like to connect to on the other side. See this loved one approaching you, and both of you sitting down on a bench right beside you. You give that loved one a hug, see them as happy, healthy, and loving as can be. They are visiting you from Heaven, and they are in their original perfect form. See your loved one smile at you and allow yourself some time to just sit and talk with that soul. You are allowing yourself to spend this quiet time connecting to them after all this time. Allow them to speak to you. What would you ask them, and what would be their response back to you? Allow time to connect, bond, and have a beautiful conversation with them. What does your loved one want you to know from the other side? What is their message?

After you have given yourself enough time, allow both of you to get up from that bench, and give your loved one a big hug. This isn't goodbye. The next time you do this meditation, you will see them again and be able to talk more. Trust that you made a visitation connection with that loved one today, and trust the conversation was held between both of you. When you are ready, open your eyes, smile, and say "Thank you."

Creating a connection with Spirit is ultimately the most important thing you can do while on Earth, because it extends through this lifetime and beyond. It is part of what you came here to do especially since you are reading this book! Universe really does have your back, and the more you work with meditation, controlling and focusing your mind, and paying attention, the more you will see this!

I have mentioned to you that the whispers of love and winds of Spirit energy are always seeing things from a much higher perspective, yet as humans, we are always seeing things from the horse-blind perspective. It's time to take off the blinders and embrace Spirit as your guide. It's time to live a life full of pure and compassionate intentions and stop being petty and making excuses or playing the "he said, she said" game. It is time to take the driver's wheel but know that a higher power is actually steering.

Spirit on Board

Please understand, my heart wants you to sprout and grow and become a blessing to the world. I want you to think of the wind and everything you feel from the motion of it, even when you can't see it. I want you to smile at Spirit and say, "Thank you, Spirit; you are love and I love you!" I want you to finally make peace with the storms in your life and let the whispers of the love around you, the impetus of Spirit, guide you. I want you to finally let Spirit be your compass and get rid of the other ego crutches you have been using your whole life and to finally learn the lessons of the Law of Attraction and that unconditional love awaits you everywhere, if you let it. I want you to accept that you are more than just a body and that Spirit is there to guide you and even help you change direction when you didn't think you needed it, send you warning signs like "Do Not Cross," and accept that the only thing you can really control in this life is your attitude. Make that attitude one of gratitude—every single solitary day, no matter what has just been dumped in front of you. Feel the wind, feel the peace, feel Spirit and let it whisper its love songs in your ears. Pay attention to those wind lines as sailors do. Adjust your sails accordingly!

I told you, this is not a sprint—it is a marathon, and we need to take our time and enjoy every moment we can. We need to realize we are not alone, and we need to let those who are around love and embrace us, because tomorrow they may be gone, physically.

Another word of advice—don't neglect your vessel. You have only one for this lifetime! Do your best to honor it every day and give it sustenance of real and healthy things and then go explore, dream, have fun, but stay on course! No matter how rocky it gets, you can come through this too and see the glorious daylight and sunshine the next phase will bring.

And, whatever you do, stop being so busy listening to others that you stop listening to yourself. *You* define your life. *You* define your destiny. *You* determine what whispers you will heed and what compass you will follow. Please, listen to me when I say the only compass you want on board is Spirit. Hone your skills and your own intuitive gifts, and stop driving like a maniac letting everything hit you along the way. Ignore the competitive streak of others, and as I remind myself as well, "stay in your lane," because that is the one being guided by Spirit, and that's the one that keeps you serving in the Light. In the end, I promise, a life on "automatic" with Spirit on board is much better than grinding the gears and messing with the engine and stalling out halfway through your life. Trust me, I've been there! Take a little love from some of these teachings; I won't lie to you!

Spirit is now your new *compass* steering you through the storms. I release them to you! And, welcome to the new, enlightened *you*.

Conclusion

Whispers of Love

Walk with the dreamers, the believers, the courageous, the cheerful, the planners, the doers, the successful people with their heads in the clouds and their feet on the ground. Let their spirit ignite a fire within you to leave this world better than when you found it.

—Wilferd Peterson

What a ride! I shared with you from the beginning that my life has been a roller-coaster and now you have read, felt, and almost touched a part of me, including the most recent death of our son. This book would not have been possible if I had not felt Anthony's strength through me, with Spirit's force, to get this written.

On a positive note, my family and I have just come off an incredible weekend of events where we finished up all the fundraisers of the past week (to say nothing about the numerous ones over the last six months since Anthony's death) and have raised $25,000 dollars in this short amount of time for local charities such as The American Cancer Society, Unsung Siblings Foundation, and the Leukemia/Lymphoma Society in memory of Anthony. And, we are looking forward to assisting with Ronald McDonald House in the fall. It has been an added whirlwind, but as exhausted as we all are, we feel so deeply grateful and rewarded knowing that we are part of helping others to find a cure. There are no words for such moments as these.

And in case you don't think Anthony was there or that I haven't given you enough signs, he threw us a huge one of approval on the way home that last night of the leukemia fundraiser. My husband had left to return home a few minutes earlier than I did. On my way home from the event, talking to Anthony in the car, I was asking him to please send me a sign that he was aware of all the events in his honor. Within minutes, turning down a road because I was parched and wanted to get some water, I suddenly saw a car in front of me and on the license plate, the first three letters were HUG. Yes! He was smiling down on us. When I returned home, my husband was sitting waiting for me, and I told him about the magical sign. He immediately shared that on his way home from the event, he was having the same exact conversation with our son, asking him if he was aware of everything done in his honor, and when asked for a sign, the song "Happier" by Marshmello came on, as well as the song "Without Me" by Halsey. Both are songs he has sent us on the radio and in restaurants since the day he passed. What amazing validations! There is no doubt he was there and seeing it all.

As exhilarated as I am to be writing this final chapter, the conclusion of this book, it always comes with the mixed emotions of knowing

CONCLUSION

that now I must step out into those next unknown, uncharted waters that I write about in order to get this book into your hands and to continue to share the messages of Spirit.

I have taken you through the steps; taught you about pain and grief; shared some of the language of love from above; and taught you that through using Spirit as compass and watching the signs all around us, your time in the storms can be lessened and perhaps, sometimes, even avoided. I've shared crazy things and sad things; painful things and funny things; big ideas and little hints; and here we are at the end of this journey together. But for you, now armed with knowledge and tools, my heart knows that there was something special and unique in here to share with the world, and for those souls ready to hear, to vibrate at a higher level and to heal! You see, I did in the end have something new and different to say!

I feel strongly and do have faith that you will start your life as a new beginning, a new day, with a new outlook and a new way to embrace the world around you. You can now actively start to become infiltrated by the incredible love that whispers to us from above at all times. The harmonies of the universe are here to create and make our own mix, our own elixir that becomes our lives living with Spirit as a guide while experiencing a human life. We are a necessary, needed, and loved part of the universe, and I have so much more to share with you on this journey.

Now that I have proven that love never, ever dies, that it simply morphs, and also convinced you how truly blessed, guided, watched, and loved from above you are, I want you to truly open your eyes to pay attention and see the signs. Please open your ears to hear the whispers and sometimes even words that Spirit and loved ones are sending you. Start to honor the clairs I talked about, and acknowledge that you, too, inherently have some of these gifts and can refine and tune them.

You have the power to rise above your grief and current pain to live a guided and gifted life.

Yes, the storms and struggles of life will pop up all around you. It is how you respond to them that will change, and it will even get to the point that if you do allow Spirit to guide you, as that compass we discussed, then you will not be knocked around as hard, feel as though you have been thrown upside down as *long*. And, *yes*, you will move through the changes and lessons of learning that you were brought here to experience, and finally let go and "go with the flow."

On the point of hard knocks, I know the "fairness" meter doesn't register *easy* in your life or you would not be reading this book, but I also know that since your "fairness" meter has registered *hard* to *impossible*, it means that you are already growing or have grown in such ways that most humans will never get to experience. Your contracted lessons prior to arriving on Earth are being handled and exceeded by your commitment, your love and your willingness to learn and to move *through* the struggles, storms and pains of life.

We carry our loved ones with us everywhere we go—we see signs every step of the way—we feel love in every moment *if* we allow ourselves to. Let go of what others think, of their expectations of what you believe a normal life is supposed to be and dare, *I dare you*, to embrace the beauty of being "different." That being different, the term I once hated, is now the reason for my existence. It has forced me to learn to love myself enough to be there as a guide and a gift to others. It is the essence of everything that I am and I do. And, if I can get through this, I promise, so can you.

Choose to see another day—but do it with hearing the *whispers* of love. It's time. It's your time. Time for the pain to leave. Time for the sun to rise. Time to embrace the benevolent universe out there that the

CONCLUSION

naked eye can't see, but the heart can most definitely feel. It's time to see the signs, hear the whispers; in everything you do, with everyone you touch.

May peace, light, and love embrace you every moment of your new day and may you embrace the new knowledge that is going to start tapping at your door—okay, knocking loudly—because now that you've opened your mind, I welcome *you* to the other side of the storms! Pull out that tissue box and shed some sad and happy tears; find those pieces of your heart that are shattered and scattered all over the place, start to assemble them with the tools I've shared, and get through that dark tunnel as quickly as you can. There is a universally loving world that stands in the light ready to embrace you, warm, cuddle, and move you to an even more wondrous place.

I want you to do as the quote says and "Walk with the dreamers, the believers, the courageous, the cheerful, the planners, the doers, the successful people with their heads in the clouds and their feet on the ground. Let their Spirit ignite a fire within you to leave this world better than when you found it." You are not supposed to just take up space on this loving Earth or get consumed by the hurt, negativity and suffering here—you are chosen to rise above or you would not have been through the pain and transitions that you just have. No matter if it is a bad break up, an illness, a death or some other loss; you are meant for so much greater and the door is now wide open for you to step in and live it!

While nearing the end of writing this book, my daughter sent a beautiful saying to me that goes like this:

> *"I had to make you uncomfortable, otherwise you never would have moved."*
>
> —Universe.

I couldn't have summed this book up any better. That growth from pain, that learning, that lesson of unconditional love for yourself and others is in the end *why* we are all here. So, get Spirit on board, raise your hands and head high. Give yourself a big hug, and then give a huge shout-out to Anthony and all your loved ones who are watching and whispering to all of us from above. Then, *oh boy*, fasten your seat belt and get ready for your *ride*!

And stay tuned, because I already have the next books lined up to write, ranging from how to allow the winds of change to become the pathway to peace, to the Gina's Stay in Your Lane Lessons, Messages of Love from Above, and so much more to share. I honor my gift every moment as I continue to share the messages piling in from Spirit and loved ones to teach you how to move through your storms.

I thank my readers, my clients, family, friends, the mass audiences, my fund-raising events, Universe, Spirit, and Anthony. Once again, *thank you* for sticking with me on this crazy roller-coaster. That little wounded girl within me finally grew into her voice! Miracles do happen, and there is a silver lining to every cloud. Anthony, your passing suddenly does have meaning. Thank you for showing me the larger picture to the pain.

I can't wait to meet my readers along this next path to hear all the new ways them *Whispers of Love* have touched you now that you are open to acknowledging them. I love you all!

In Love & Light,
Gina

Bibliography

Aiken, Lewis R. *Dying, Death, and Bereavement*. 4th ed. Mahwah, NJ: Lawrence Erlbaum Associates, 2001.

Alexander, Eben, MD, and Karen Newell. *Living in a Mindful Universe: A Neurosurgeon's Journey into the Heart of Consciousness*. PA: Rodale, 2017.

Alexander, Eben, MD. *Proof of Heaven: A Neurosurgeon's Journey into the Afterlife*. New York, NY: Simon & Schuster Paperbacks, 2012.

Alexander, Eben, MD. *The Map of Heaven: How Science, Religion, and Ordinary People Are Proving the Afterlife*. New York, NY: Simon & Schuster, 2014.

Allison, Bobbi. http://www.bobbiallison.com.

Alvarado, Carlos S. "Mediumship, Psychical Research, Dissociation, and the Powers of the Subconscious Mind." *The Journal of Parapsychology* 78, no. 1 (2014): 98+.

Armstrong, Stephen. "Generation X-Files: The Psychic Schools Have Never Been So Busy, and It's Not the Doris Stokes Brigade Who Want to Learn, but the Young, the Prosperous and the Educated. Stephen Armstrong Uncovers a Paranormal Boom." *New Statesman (1996)*, August 7, 2006, 22+.

Attig, Thomas. *The Heart of Grief: Death and the Search for Lasting Love*. New York: Oxford University Press, 2000.

Bauer-Maglin, Nan, and Donna Perry, eds. *Final Acts: Death, Dying, and the Choices We Make*. New Brunswick, NJ: Rutgers University Press, 2010.

Becker, Carl. *Time for Healing: Integrating Traditional Therapies with Scientific Medical Practice*. St. Paul, MN: Paragon House, 2002.

Boss, Pauline. *Ambiguous Loss: Learning to Live with Unresolved Grief*. Cambridge, MA: Harvard University Press, 2000.

Byrne, Rhonda. *The Secret*. New York: Atria Books, 2006.

Byrne, Rhonda. *The Magic*. New York: Atria Books, 2012.

Browne, Sylvia. https://www.sylviabrowne.com/books.

"Can We ALL Learn to Be Psychic? Top Medium Gordon Smith Says So but Can He Convince a Very Sceptical MARIANNE POWER." *Daily Mail (London)*, May 28, 2012.

Calderwood, Kimberly A. "Adapting the Transtheoretical Model of Change to the Bereavement Process." Social Work 56, no. 2 (2011): 107+.

Caputo, Theresa, and Kristina Grish. *Good Grief: Heal Your Soul, Honor Your Loved Ones, and Learn to Live Again.* New York, NY: Atria Books, 2017.

Carter, Chris. *Science and Psychic Phenomenon: The Fall of the House of Skeptics.* Rochester, VT: Inner Traditions, Bear & Company, 2012.

Cerulo, Karen A. *Never Saw It Coming: Cultural Challenges to Envisioning the Worst.* Chicago: University of Chicago Press, 2006.

Chopra, Deepak. https://www.deepakchopra.com.

Conversations Beyond Proof of Heaven. Directed by David Hinshaw. Performed by Eben Alexander, MD, and Raymond Moody, M.D., Ph.D. MudPuppy Productions, 2013. DVD.

Devotion: Holy Spirit and Wind Analogy; Living by the Spirit. Accessed May 18, 2019. https://www.-free.org/Devotions/devotion_Spirit_wind.htm.

Dyer, Wayne W. *Your Erroneous Zones: Step-by-step Advice for Escaping the Trap of Negative Thinking and Taking Control of Your Life.* New York, NY: HarperPerennial, 1991.

Dyer, Wayne W. *Change Your Thoughts, Change Your Life: Living the Wisdom of the Tao.* Carlsbad, CA: Hay House, 2009.

Dyer, Wayne W. *The Essential Wayne Dyer Collection: Includes the All-time International Bestsellers: The Power of Intention; Inspiration and Excuses Begone!* Carlsbad, CA: Hay House, 2013.

Edberg, Henrik. "7 of My Favorite Timeless Tips from the Last 2500 Years." The Positivity Blog – Practical Happiness Tips. May 25, 2010. Accessed April 30, 2019. https://www.positivityblog.com/7-of-my-favorite-timeless-tips-from-the-last-2500-years/comment-page-1/.

Edberg, Henrik. "How to Overcome Your Fear: 7 Tips from the Last 2200 Years." The Positivity Blog – Practical Happiness Tips. July 24, 2017. Accessed April 30, 2019. https://www.positivityblog.com/how-to-overcome-your-fear-7-tips-from-the-last-2200-years.

Edberg, Henrik. "Helen Keller's Guide to Courageously Looking the World Straight in the Eye." The Positivity Blog – Practical Happiness Tips. August 29, 2017. Accessed May 18, 2019. https://www.positivityblog.com/helen-keller.

Edberg, Henrik. "Yoda's Top 3 Words of Wisdom." The Positivity Blog – Practical Happiness Tips. July 03, 2009. Accessed May 7, 2019. https://www.positivity-blog.com/yodas-top-3-words-of-wisdom.

Evans, Abigail Rian. *Is God Still at the Bedside?: The Medical, Ethical, and Pastoral Issues of Death and Dying.* Grand Rapids, MI: William B. Eerdmans, 2011.

Bibliography

Forever Family Foundation. https://www.foreverfamilyfoundation.org.

Gallup, Inc. "Three in Four Americans Believe in Paranormal." Gallup.com. June 16, 2005. Accessed March 26, 2019. https://news.gallup.com/poll/16915/three-four-americans-believe-paranormal.aspx.

Goop: A Modern Lifestyle Brand. Accessed February 09, 2019. https://goop.com.

Gregory, Richard L., and O. L. Zangwill, eds. *The Oxford Companion to the Mind.* Oxford: Oxford University Press, 1998.

Heinz, Donald. The Last Passage: Recovering a Death of Our Own. New York: Oxford University Press, 1999.

Henry, Jane, ed. *Parapsychology: Research on Exceptional Experiences.* London: Routledge, 2005.

"How to Build Self Confidence." Accessed April 30, 2019. http://shemin.co.il/magazine/how-to-build-self-confidence-6-essential-and-timeless-tips.

Hyslop, James H. *Contact with the Other World: The Latest Evidence as to Communication with the Dead.* London: T. Werner Laurie, 1919.

"Is FEAR - Holding U Back." Accessed May 18, 2019. https://www.sparkpeople.com/mypage_public_journal_individual.asp?blog_id=5223065.

Jackson, Laura Lynne. *The Light Between Us: Stories from Heaven. Lessons for the Living.* New York, NY: Spiegel & Grau, 2015.

Jakobsen, Merete Demant. *Shamanism: Traditional and Contemporary Approaches to the Mastery of Spirits and Healing.* New York: Berghahn Books, 1999.

Jelly, Awesome. "8 Signs That You Have Been Visited By A Deceased Love One In Your Dreams • AwesomeJelly.com." AwesomeJelly.com. February 28, 2017. Accessed May 8, 2019. https://awesomejelly.com/8-signs-that-you-have-been-visited-by-a-deceased-love-one-in-your-dreams.

Katie, Byron, and Stephen Mitchell. *Loving What Is.* Harmony Books, 2002.

Kelly, Lynne. *The Skeptic's Guide to the Paranormal.* Crows Nest, N.S.W.: Allen & Unwin, 2004.

Krippner, Stanley, and Harris L. Friedman, eds. *Mysterious Minds: The Neurobiology of Psychics, Mediums, and Other Extraordinary People.* Santa Barbara, CA: Praeger, 2010.

Kurtz, Paul, ed. *A Skeptic's Handbook of Parapsychology.* Buffalo, NY: Prometheus Books, 1985.

Lukoff, David. "Exploring Frontiers of the Mind-Body Relationship." *Journal of Transpersonal Psychology* 46, no. 1 (2014): 129+.

McClenon, James. *Wondrous Events: Foundations of Religious Belief.* Philadelphia: University of Pennsylvania Press, 1994.

Marks, David, and Richard Kammann. *The Psychology of the Psychic*. Amherst, NY: Prometheus Books, 1980.

Moses, Omri. *Out of Character: Modernism, Vitalism, Psychic Life*. Stanford, CA: Stanford University Press, 2014.

Mqreman, Christopher M., ed. *Teaching Death and Dying*. New York: Oxford University Press, 2008.

Murchison, Carl, ed. *The Case for and against Psychical Belief*. Worcester, MA: Clark University, 1927.

Osis, Karlis, and Erlendur Haraldsson. *What They Saw ... At the Hour of Death*. 3rd ed. Norwalk, CT: Hastings House, 1997.

Parkes, Colin Murray, and Holly G. Prigerson. *Bereavement: Studies of Grief in Adult Life*. 4th ed. New York: Routledge, 2009.

Qualls, Sara Honn, and Julia E. Kasl-Godley, eds. *End-of-Life Issues, Grief, and Bereavement: What Clinicians Need to Know*. Hoboken, NJ: Wiley, 2011.

Radford, Benjamin. "Here to Hereafter: Can Psychics Really Talk to the Dead?" LiveScience. October 20, 2010. Accessed March 26, 2019. https://www.livescience.com/10164-psychics-talk-dead.html.

Rasmussen Poll. "Most Americans Believe in the Afterlife." Rasmussen Reports. Accessed March 26, 2019. http://www.rasmussenreports.com/public_content/lifestyle/june_2017/most_americans_believe_in_the_afterlife.

Riches, Gordon, and Pam Dawson. *An Intimate Loneliness: Supporting Bereaved Parents and Siblings*. Philadelphia: Open University Press, 2000.

Rosen, Rebecca, and Samantha Rose. *Spirited: Connect to the Guides All around You*. New York, NY: Harper, 2010.

Rosen, Steven J., ed. *Ultimate Journey: Death and Dying in the World's Major Religions*. Westport, CT: Praeger, 2008.

Russo, Kim. *The Happy Medium: Life Lessons from the Other Side*. New York: HarperElixir, 2017.

"Spiritism." *The Columbia Encyclopedia*. 6th ed. Columbia University Press, 2018.

Smith, Gary Scott. *Heaven in the American Imagination*. New York: Oxford University Press, 2011.

Stenger, Victor J. *Physics and Psychics: The Search for a World beyond the Senses*. Buffalo, NY: Prometheus Books, 1990.

Sumegi, Angela. *Understanding Death: An Introduction to Ideas of Self and the Afterlife in World Religions*. Chichester, England: Wiley-Blackwell, 2014.

Sutcliffe, Steven J. *Children of the New Age: A History of Spiritual Practices*. London:

Bibliography

Routledge, 2002.

"The Law of Attraction." Steve Pavlina. August 18, 2006. Accessed May 18, 2019. http://www.stevepavlina.com/blog/2006/08/the-law-of-attraction.

"The Law of Attraction - Meaning and Definitions." SuccessConsciousness.com. Accessed May 18, 2019. https://www.successconsciousness.com/law-of-attraction-definitions.htm.

The Shack. Directed by Stuart Hazeldine. Performed by Sam Worthington, Octavia Spencer, and Tim McGraw. 2017. DVD.

Vanzant, Iyanla. https://iyanla.co/trust.

Winfrey, Oprah. *What I Know for Sure*. New York, NY: Hearst Communications, 2014.

Winfrey, Oprah. *The Wisdom of Sundays: Life-Changing Insights from Super Soul Conversations*. New York, NY: Flatiron Books, 2017.

Williams, Lisa. https://www.lisawilliams.com.

Williamson, Marianne. *A Woman's Worth*. London: Rider, 1994.

Windbridge Research Center. http://www.windbridge.org.

Young, William P. *The Shack*. Newbury Park, CA: Windblown Media, 2007.

Zukav, Gary, Oprah Winfrey, and Maya Angelou. *The Seat of the Soul*. New York: Simon and Schuster, 1989.

Zukav, Gary, and Linda Francis. *The Heart of the Soul: Emotional Awareness*. New York: Free Press, 2007.

Zukav, Gary. *Soul to Soul Meditations: Daily Reflections for Spiritual Growth*. London: Free Press, 2008.

Notes

1. Spirit is collective and multi-dimensional. It is not just one being. It is the One. Part Two explains this in further detail to help the reader understand why the plural of 'they' versus 'it' is used, along with its significance.
2. http://www.rasmussenreports.com/public_content/lifestyle/general_lifestyle/june_2017/most_americans_believe_in_the_afterlife. Accessed March 26, 2019.
3. https://www.livescience.com/10164-psychics-talk-dead.html. Accessed March 26, 2019.
4. https://news.gallup.com/poll/16915/three-four-americans-believe-paranormal.aspx. Accessed March 26, 2019.
5. https://www.amazon.com/Science-Psychic-Phenomena-House-Skeptics/dp/159477451X. Accessed March 26, 2019.
6. Ibid.
7. https://www.foreverfamilyfoundation.org/site/after_life_science. Accessed April 5, 2019.
8. Ibid.
9. https://www.positivityblog.com/how-to-overcome-your-fear-7-tips-from-the-last-2200-years. Accessed April 30, 2019.
10. Ibid.
11. Ibid.
12. https://www.positivityblog.com/7-of-my-favorite-timeless-tips-from-the-last-2500-years/comment-page-1/. Accessed April 30, 2019.
13. https://www.positivityblog.com/7-of-my-favorite-timeless-tips-from-the-last-2500-years/comment-page-1. Accessed April 30, 2019.
14. https://www.positivityblog.com/how-to-overcome-your-fear-7-tips-from-the-last-2200-years. Accessed April 30, 2019.
15. http://shemin.co.il/magazine/how-to-build-self-confidence-6-essential-and-timeless-tips. Accessed April 30, 2019.
16. Ibid.
17. https://www.positivityblog.com/helen-keller. Accessed April 30, 2019.
18. Ibid.

Notes

19. https://www.positivityblog.com/yodas-top-3-words-of-wisdom. Accessed May 7, 2019.
20. Ibid.
21. https://www.sparkpeople.com/mypage_public_journal_individual.asp?blog_id=5223065 Is FEAR - Holding U Back. Accessed May 18, 2019.
22. https://www.positivityblog.com/how-to-overcome-your-fear-7-tips-from-the-last-2200-years. Accessed April 30, 2019.
23. https://www.positivityblog.com/how-to-overcome-your-fear-7-tips-from-the-last-2200-years. Accessed April 30, 2019.
24. https://www.pinterest.com/mariquita7768/i-saw-thatkarma. Accessed May 5, 2019.
25. https://awesomejelly.com/8-signs-that-you-have-been-visited-by-a-deceased-love-one-in-your-dreams. Accessed May 8, 2019.
26. Ibid.
27. www.stevepavlina.com/blog/2006/08/the-law-of-attraction. Accessed May 18, 2019.
28. https://www.successconsciousness.com/law-of-attraction-definitions.htm. Accessed May 18, 2019.
29. https://www.-free.org/Devotions/devotion_Spirit_wind.htm. Accessed May 18, 2019.

www.ingramcontent.com/pod-product-compliance
Lightning Source LLC
Chambersburg PA
CBHW021511200325
23810CB00008B/159